This book is due for return on or before the last date shown above: it may, subject to the book not being reserved by another reader, be renewed by personal application, post, or telephone, quoting this date and details of the book.

HAMPSHIRE COUNTY COUNCIL
County Library

100% recycled paper

Anyone for England?

Anyone
for England?

A Search for British Identity

CLIVE ASLET

LITTLE, BROWN AND COMPANY

For William

A *Little, Brown* Book

First published in Great Britain in 1997
by Little, Brown and Company

Typeset in Garamond by
Palimpsest Book Production Limited,
Polmont, Stirlingshire
Printed and bound in Great Britain by
Clays Ltd, St Ives plc

Little, Brown and Company (UK)
Brettenham House
Lancaster Place
London WC2E 7EN

Contents

Foreword

I was born in southern England, in what I have always felt to be the epicentre of the middle class. This book, on the theme of British national identity, is written from that personal viewpoint. I think of myself as being both English and British, but it would be too much to hope that all English, let alone all British, people share my instincts.

Still, what seemed to be the certainties of my upbringing were widely held. I detect a sense of nostalgia for the loss of those certainties – not just because they are lost, but because they have not been replaced by others. My vantage point is not eccentric: much of the population lives in southern England and is middle class. At a time when five million Scots seem likely to impose their agenda of constitutional reform upon the forty-nine million of us who live in England, it is perhaps the English constituent of the United Kingdom whose culture most needs to be nursed.

There is already the stirring of a debate about who the British feel that they are, and how they wish to represent themselves. This book is intended to stimulate it. We hear a lot about Great Britain plc, with the implication that everything can be measured by the bottom line. We hear less about what a genuine public company would call its core values. I want to identify some of these core values for Britain, and ask what state they are in as we move towards the millennium.

Another personal perspective is given by my being the editor of *Country Life*, a magazine that is itself a kind of national icon. I am grateful to my colleagues on it for their views, sometimes gathered in our weekly editorial conferences, and in particular to Michael Hall, who read the manuscript. I must also thank Nicholas Foulkes, my editor Alan Samson and my wife Naomi for their support.

1

Car-boot Britain

'Who in the world's England, unless I am?'
Lord Theign in Henry James, *The Outcry*, 1911

*The Englishman who visits Mount Etna will carry
his tea-kettle to the top.*
Ralph Waldo Emerson, *English Traits*, 1856

*What can the England of 1940 have in common with
the England of 1840? But then, what have you in
common with the child of five whose photograph
your mother keeps on the mantelpiece? Nothing,
except that you happen to be the same person.*
George Orwell, *The Lion and the Unicorn*, 1941

When I was very young, in the early 1960s, my father always
bought an English car. The first I can remember was, I think,
an Austin A40. It had a rounded silhouette, rather as though the
whole vehicle had gently inflated along with the tyres. It cannot
have gone at much more than a stately pace, or perhaps no car
did then. So the run from Surrey, where we lived, to Wales,
where we would go on holiday, was an epic journey, requiring
an overnight stop somewhere near Oxford. Whenever we went
up a hill, I would torment myself by looking out of the little

back window, imagining that, as we laboured ever more slowly towards the summit, the gradient would prove too much for the car, and we would roll helter-skelter backwards to the bottom. Painted black, like many cars of that time, its styling could best be described as conservative. Altogether it emanated an air of sedate dignity, somewhat in the manner of a good butler.

Before long, we had graduated to a Wolsey 1560: a larger, altogether boxier vehicle, which was light blue. Like the Austin, it had leather upholstery, as did the Rover 100 which superseded it. Eventually we scaled the heights of a Rover 3.5, the back of which seemed to be the size of a small drawing room. Leather upholstery was not the only thing these vehicles had in common. My father would refer, affectionately, to each car of the moment as 'the bus' or 'the tank'; as we trundled through the countryside it conveyed a sense of impregnability, engendering the notion that any other vehicle would be bound to crumple if it was foolish enough to collide with us. It was the solidity of the British marques which appealed to my father, who was himself a rather solid sort of person. Foreign models might be faster, more technically advanced, better value; but the British machine had weight of steel on its side. In this it seemed typical of most of the other products of native manufacturing that surrounded me. It was an axiom of the household – probably of the country as a whole – that British goods were made to last. They did not, at that date, quite have the Empire behind them, but certainly the remnants of the imperial tradition.

It must have been about 1970 when I made a fearful discovery: my father's next car was to be German. It seemed scarcely conceivable. Today, when so much of industry is multinational, it would be more difficult to make a sensible buying decision guided by chauvinism, even if that is what British people wanted to do. A quarter of a century ago, the map looked simpler. My father, more even than others of his generation, had an instinctive commitment to the national endeavour. I am sure that he paid more in tax than he really had to. Further, like most people whose normal lives had been interrupted by the Second World War, he had no special love for Germany, German products or German culture. Later, he took badly to the early stirring of my

2

undergraduate passion for Wagner. So the choice of a BMW over a Jaguar seemed shattering. What on earth had changed in my father's view of the world to make him do it? The answer was nothing; his tastes and preferences remained the same. But he had been forced to recognise that the qualities he most valued were now best expressed in a foreign product.

The arrival of the BMW caused some portion of my mental landscape to be rearranged. This was not simply because I did not much like it, though I didn't. It was not as commodious as the last of those Rovers – the 3.5 being an enormous brute – and I found the cloth upholstery to have a mean air after all that leather. It felt hard, and did not subside with a satisfying escape of air when one threw oneself on to it. Presumably it was more reliable. However, while actually being more expensive, it managed to be less ostentatious. That was another characteristic that, until that time, had seemed peculiarly British, albeit not calculated to impress a teenager. But my father admired the car so much that it hardly ever came out of the garage; he generally preferred to take my mother's small runabout, a Wolsey 1100. Altogether it was an unsettling episode.

I recall it now because that personal sense of confusion has, it seems to me, come to settle at a more profound level on the nation as a whole. When I was growing up, I knew very clearly what it meant to be British. It would probably be better to say English, but at that distant time English people were not so acutely aware as today that their instincts were not shared by the Scottish, Irish and Welsh. One knew – or thought one knew – where one was with British people and British things. One knew how they would feel and act, and what kinds of things were important to them. The Englishman was still 'a tight fit in his place', as J. B. Priestley put it. To look around and notice the changes that have overtaken me in what is still a relatively short adult life has something of the effect of the arrival of a ticket collector during a soporific train journey. It wakes me up with a jolt.

The purpose of this book is to discover what ideas my one-year-old son will form about his national identity. Compared with our European neighbours, we have often been less rigorous

3

in cherishing it. Perhaps over the last thirty years we have had to accommodate ourselves to greater changes in perception and way of life than them, as a result of the uncomfortable process of adapting ourselves to the European ideal. This is nothing new. 'The English character is gradually losing the insularity that has long been the moral heritage of our geographical situation, and is divesting itself of the tastes, prejudices, and habits which have been regarded as inseparable from the race,' observed T. H. S. Escot during the Edwardian era of the *entente cordiale* with France. But over the last twenty years the process of *rapprochement* has accelerated. This is not only an instinctive process, arising naturally out of greater contact between peoples, but an artificial one, imposed from the chambers of the European Commission.

The Commission's drive for 'harmonisation' within Europe, in the interests of 'social and economic cohesion', aims to steamroller flat national excrescences in the attempt to form a level playing-field. It is understandable that the half-crown and sixpenny piece should have been sacrificed to decimalisation in 1971, but the replacement of the old dark-blue British passport – splendidly embossed with the lion and unicorn of the royal coat-of-arms – with a smaller red one, in European style, looked like a gratuitous assault on a familiar icon. The reduction in the size of the passport, which went from stiff board to bendy cover, seemed to symbolise a national shrinkage. The use of miles as the unit of measurement on Britain's roads has been protected for the time being, but the officials who secured that exemption failed to remember that distances are also measured at sea: knots must go. Sooner or later, no doubt, motorists will be compelled to drive on the right-hand side of the road. Individually these things may not seem to matter very much, but taken together they erase many of the eccentricities to which the British have clung with affection. They are what marketing people would regard as Britain's unique brand properties, like the curvy shape of the Coca-Cola bottle and Toblerone's triangular profile; they are rare, hard to achieve and beyond price. They may only be details, but as the architect Mies van der Rohe said, 'God is in the details.' That observation seems particularly relevant to the present decade, with its emphasis on the individual. Constantly we find we are having an outdated agenda, reeking of the corporatism fashionable in the 1970s, forced upon us.

Outsiders tend to regard the English as arrogant, and it would be difficult to think otherwise if one were to look only at a turn-of-the-century imperialist such as Lord Curzon, Viceroy of India, who dedicated a volume entitled *Problems of the Far East* 'to those who believe that the British Empire is, under Providence, the greatest instrument for good that the world has ever seen ...'. But even contemporaries found Curzon too much. It would be just as true to say that the English are the reverse of arrogant; we are the nation which eternally hovers at doorways, inviting the other person through first. Perhaps the habit of self-effacement stemmed from a kind of arrogance: we believed we could afford it. Traditionally we never felt the need to trumpet our strengths because they seemed to us quite obvious. We were not triumphalist about triumphs. 'It is the custom, and a very bad one,' wrote Horatio Nelson, 'for the English never to tell their own story.' Now we seem to be taking our own self-deprecation at face value. The mental landscape, like the physical landscape, is changing. These are not just changes of detail, equivalent to the occasional uprooting of a hedgerow: whole mountains of attitude and perception have been moved, apparently without our noticing. We need a map of the new scene.

I have begun with an anecdote about my father's cars because ideas of national identity do not sit comfortably with the English habit of mind. The English do not like theorising; they prefer to experience life empirically. It might be said that a book about the English identity is itself a very un-English sort of a thing, and I am inclined to agree. The fact that I find myself writing one only illustrates the pass to which we have come.

In previous ages, the Briton's distrust of intellectualism did not inhibit him from developing a powerful sense of British-ness. To the American poet and philosopher Ralph Waldo Emerson, writing *English Traits* in 1856, the English actually seemed to have a greater cohesiveness than other nations. As he put it:

The intellectual organization of the English admits a communicableness of knowledge and ideas among them all. An electric touch by any of their national ideas, melts them into one family, and brings the hoards of power which their individuality is always hiving, into use and play for all. Is it the smallness of the country, or is it the pride and affection of race, – they have solidarity, or responsibleness, and trust in each other.'

The belief that the English could be identified as strangely, singularly and sometimes remarkably themselves would have been shared by twentieth-century writers such as J. B. Priestley and George Orwell. 'When you come back to England from any foreign country, you have immediately the sensation of breathing a different air,' wrote Orwell in *The Lion and the Unicorn.* 'However much you hate it or laugh at it, you will never be happy away from it for any length of time. The suet puddings and the red pillar-boxes have entered into your soul.' Yet the other day the editor of a national newspaper remarked to me, in a tone of despair, that 'Britishness no longer exists'. He overstated the case, but his comment illustrates how far the process of erosion has gone. It leaves the fifty-eight million people who make up the British nation in a state of spiritual uncertainty.

Identity expresses belonging, and it appears almost to be a universal human need. People usually want to know where they come from. Adopted children frequently seek to discover the facts about their natural parents and possibly meet them. Families who can trace their history back through several generations take pride in it, and national and local record offices are thronged with amateur genealogists seeking information about their family origins. Thirty years ago most of them would have come from the United States or Australia. The American conservationist David Lowethal, in his book *The Heritage Crusade and the Spoils of History*, recalls how amazed he was to discover that, in the early 1960s, few of his English academic colleagues could trace their great-grandparents:

Told that Americans made a point of knowing (or inventing)

6

all their forebears back to New World arrivals, they retorted, 'Well, we don't need those family details; we have a secure *national* identity.'

It is notable that the fashion for family history has now become almost as widespread among the British as it is among Americans and Australians.

The inhabitants of a nation also like to feel a relationship between their present and the past, though sometimes that past is remote. Italians are proud that their country produced not only the Renaissance, but also the Roman Empire. This is as true of ways of thinking and feeling as of historical events. William Wilberforce, Edward Lear and W. G. Grace – to take three historical figures at random – all seem a world away from our own, yet the emotion which inspired their labours still strikes us as being somehow typically English. 'Do such things as "national cultures" really exist?' was a question with which George Orwell grappled in *The English People*. He concluded that:

This is one of those questions, like the freedom of the will or the identity of the individual, in which all the arguments are on one side and instinctive knowledge is on the other. It is not easy to discover the connecting thread that runs through English life from the sixteenth century onwards, but all English people who bother about such subjects feel that it exist ... D. H. Lawrence is felt to be 'very English', but so is Blake. Dr Johnson and G. K. Chesterton are somehow the same kind of person. The belief that we resemble our ancestors – that Shakespeare, say, is more like a modern Englishman than a modern Frenchman or German – may be unreasonable, but by existing it influences conduct. Myths which are believed in tend to become true, because they set up a type, or 'persona', which the average person will do his best to resemble.

The imagined continuity is pleasing. The force of that continuity can be felt as much by minorities, who have only arrived in this country recently, as by families who have lived here for centuries.

One of the strengths of English culture is its ability to assimilate newcomers. I remember from schooldays that I was unique among my friends in having four English grandparents (even so, my mother's maiden name was Humphreys, presumably indicating that the family came from Wales at some point). Yet we all thought of ourselves as being English. Besides, powers of identification are partly powers of imagination. Watching a film, we have all found ourselves imaginatively involved with, say, the fate of a 'Little Mermaid', even though we know her to have been created from a cunningly drawn two-dimensional image. It is ridiculous to suppose that a Sikh or Afro-Caribbean child could not identify with the Duke of Wellington at Waterloo, or to a lesser extent with traditional tastes and preferences. The greatest living dandy, maintaining a tradition that goes back to Beau Brummel, might well be the boxer Chris Eubank. In his autobiography, Nelson Mandela describes a childhood in which he was brought up to accept English laws, customs and ways of behaviour as more or less perfect. Growing up in Alexandria, the young Mohammed Al-Fayed, now owner of Harrods, thought that the officers in their white ducks on board English ships going through the Suez Canal personified rectitude and probity, in contrast to the prevailing regime in his country; that was what motivated him to pursue a business career in Britain. Subsequently Mr Al-Fayed has done as much as anyone to demonstrate that some aspects of the system do not live up to the imagined ideal; he admits to suborning the system by giving MPs money to ask questions for him in the House of Commons. However, that all lay in the murky future as the young Mr Al-Fayed gazed at those lustrous ships. The point here is that if children such as those mentioned could identify with English values in their own lands, minorities can hardly feel themselves excluded from doing so when they live here.

Among teachers, a different attitude prevails. It is widely assumed that the best way to respect the components of a multicultural society is by emphasising and promoting the values of minority faiths and traditions within the whole. There is something to be said for this. Children, of whatever background, should grow up to understand something of different cultures from around the world, particularly when representatives of those cultures may be their neighbours. They should be aware of spirituality, the importance of faith in some people's lives and the various forms that faith takes. But it must also be right that an emphasis is placed on the Christian religion, if only because without knowledge of the Bible half the Western tradition in art and thought becomes meaningless. Not to have some familiarity with classical mythology puts the other half beyond reach. Yet children now grow up in ignorance of these two value systems, upon which the culture not just of their own country but of Europe as a whole, as well as the Americas, is based. To say that young people should be encouraged to appreciate the traditional culture of Britain is not to assert that it is better than other cultures, merely that it is the special birthright of British children and has its own worth. It should provide the *terra firma* from which their voyages of discovery, across unknown seas of culture, faith and thought, are launched. There is a danger that this firm ground will be replaced by quicksand.

Introducing a conference on Arts in the Curriculum, held in February 1997, Dr Nicholas Tate, chief executive of the School Curriculum and Assessment Authority, referred to a recent report on the sources of racism published by the University of London Institute of Education and the London Borough of Greenwich:

I was struck by the way in which some of the white children interviewed experienced themselves 'as having an invisible culture, even of being cultureless'. 'For some white English pupils,' the report adds, 'the celebration of cultural variety actually seems to include all cultures that are not their own. White pupils, to some extent, seem like cultural ghosts, haunting as mere absences the richly decorated corridors of multicultural society.'

Dr Tate continued: 'The challenge therefore is to use the arts in schools so that they help in the creation of a society that is proud of and transmits its cultural traditions, both those of majority and minority cultures,' in the hope that young people will respond both to the rootedness of this society and feel committed to its future existence.

Those educators who are inclined to see British majority culture as hostile to multiculturalism fail to recognize its most striking historical characteristic: namely, plurality. The British tradition is not xenophobic, inward-looking and insular; it has, on the contrary, always looked outwards and sought to incorporate within itself the best that it could find elsewhere. The cathedrals of the Middle Ages bear witness to a period of architectural internationalism. Henry VIII brought the sculptor Pietro Torrigiano from Italy and sought to emulate the Renaissance that he knew to be happening in that country. James I employed Rubens to decorate the ceiling of the Banqueting House, while his son, Charles I, persuaded Sir Anthony Van Dyck to join his court. He assembled one of the greatest art collections that the world has ever seen, largely with masterpieces from Italy. At the end of the seventeenth century, the British decorative arts were immeasurably enriched by the arrival of Huguenots fleeing France after the Revocation of the Edict of Nantes. In the eighteenth century, the best plasterers decorating British country houses were Italians. Sir Joshua Reynolds and his friends established a Royal Academy after the French model. The tradition of the Grand Tour expressed the awe felt by the British educated class for the classical world. Composers such as Handel, Haydn and Mendelssohn received a warm welcome in London. The downfall of Victorian visual taste was its very openness to foreign influence. Nineteenth-century Britain had a sponge-like capacity to absorb foreign habits and flavours, reflected lexicographically in the number of words of Indian origin that are still in more or less common use: chutney, chintz, pukka, kedgeree, thug, juggernaut, numnah (a saddle-blanket), jodhpurs and so on. Even adherents of the Arts and Crafts movement, intended as a bastion against the homogenising tendencies of industrialism, were proud to maintain their contacts with the Continent and the United States. A culture as eclectic as the British can hardly be regarded as threatening to minorities: if anything, its avidity to embrace exotic influences might be said to have caused the mainstream to lose definition.

No one could expect a country's sense of itself to remain constant for ever. Naturally, it evolves with history. Nevertheless, it must share some common values or it will fall apart. In the past, the inclusion of most people into the common whole meant the exclusion of others. Blacks, women, homosexuals and Jews have all at different times been excluded. Today's challenge is to support ideals to which as many of the population as possible can subscribe. But the danger may not be that the British are too excluding of those who display divergent tastes and attitudes, but too inclusive. One aspect of national identity must be the assumption of shared standards. Those standards have become elusive, in an age in which it seems that virtually no manifestation of individuality, or even perversion, is too extreme to find general censure.

National stereotypes never precisely fit the individual's perception of his country. Still, they are necessary counters in the game of self-definition. What form these counters take is a matter of some concern, since people naturally live up (or down) to the image that is projected. If, as used to be the case, we believe ourselves to be remarkable for phlegm, intrepidity, considerate manners, robust common sense and a liking for tea, people will seek to assert their difference by playing up those characteristics. If we regard ourselves as brutal, drunken, loutish, hating foreigners, anarchic and concerned solely with the gratification of the individual at the expense of society, these coarse and unmannerly instincts will be reinforced. So it is worth asking how our self-image has evolved.

It was the unspoken assumption, by many British people, that Britain was the nation which did things well. Our role on the world stage might have shrunk from that of leading man to character actor, but at least we could produce The Beatles, win a World Cup and show our high level of humanity by running a free, incomparable National Health Service. 'You may not know it, 007, but Major Boothroyd's the greatest small-arms

11

expert in the world,' M. tells James Bond in *Dr No*. Of course, one thought when reading such things, he would be. It did not seem so unreasonable that Ian Fleming should invariably portray Britain as having the edge over other countries. When the Defence Secretary Michael Portillo tried to revive this spirit, by declaring that no other nation possessed a crack regiment as tough as the SAS, his remarks did not seem to inspire pride but ridicule. Not so long ago, British people going to France would be cautioned to drink only bottled water. Nowadays it causes some readjusting of national spectacles to discover that the European Union finds our drinking water rather worse than that in some partner countries. James Bond's taste in cars now coincides, somewhat improbably, with my father's: BMW is favoured over Aston Martin.

The BSE crisis has challenged us in that part of our political anatomy in which formerly we had felt particular confidence and pride: our bureaucracy. In the summer of 1996 the Belgian agriculture minister attacked the notion that the British system could be trusted to administer a cull of cattle competently, without oversight from partner nations. This from Belgium! The British, if they think about Belgium at all, tend to regard it as a shambles of a country, its inhabitants distinguished for their appalling car driving, unspeakable taste in leather coats and propensity to smoke pipes even in the fatted luxury of Brussels restaurants. It is a country ankle-deep in corruption – in fact hardly a country at all, given its recent origin and simmering feud between Flemish and French speakers. Now even Belgium questions Britain's capacity to run its own show.

The French are able to improve their railway lines to accommodate the high-speed trains heading for the Channel Tunnel, but not the British. Equally, no underground link was provided to Docklands during its boom-town development in the 1980s. There are no parks or avenues or other civic amenities there. Consequently, the 1990s saw the value of property there tumble, and in the next century it could become a slum.

It was another cherished belief that Britain's superior education system produced the best scientists in the world; sadly, they were let down by the failure of British industry to fund the development of inventions such as the hovercraft and jet engine – but then brainwork was a more noble activity than trade. To some extent this gratifying superiority has been sustained. It is sometimes said that Trinity College, Cambridge, has more Nobel Prize-winners among its fellows than the whole of France. This is a marginal exaggeration. Nevertheless, it is an incontrovertible fact that Britain rejoices in sixty-one Nobel laureates to Japan's four. The lesson may be that Nobel Prize-winning does not alone ensure economic prosperity. Doubtless something could be done to exploit this genius for academic research; in the meantime, one wonders how long Britain can maintain the tradition. Higher education is in disarray. Even the British boffin has been transmuted into a more worldly individual, now that much of his research must be funded by industry, and professors have become administrators. The intellectual culture of the nation has been further eroded by the practice of charging admission to museums and art galleries, to which even the British Museum is expected to succumb. It used to be a proud tradition that entry to such institutions was free to all, thus symbolising the value that successive governments placed on excellence. Its decay is a caries of the British soul. It is emblematic that the Victoria and Albert Museum should now have magnificent Indian, Chinese and Korean galleries, reflecting the sponsorship it has obtained from foreign firms, while the primary British galleries remain half-closed and shabby. How have we allowed this to happen?

We used to be the nation of fair play; the tolerant nation. 'Then I saw floating above the stern the Union Jack – the flag under which so many refugees, Russian, Italian, French, Hungarian and of all nations have found an asylum,' remembered Prince Kropotkin, fleeing from the Tsarist police. 'I greeted that flag from the depth of my heart.' Since then, the refugee crisis has gone the way of tourism: it was all very well when the people after asylum were a few Russian princes and the like, but another matter now that asylum-seeking has become a mass industry. It is now impossible to maintain the noble tradition from which Kropotkin benefited, and we may mourn its passing as an inevitable consequence of living on a disturbed and overpopulated planet. What also seem to be dissolving are the attitudes of tolerance towards foreigners and their ways that went with it. Take the Euro 96 football championship. When Britain played Germany in the semi-final, headlines such as 'Let's Blitz Fritz' might charitably have been interpreted as an example of misplaced humour; but the gloating shown at the prospect of English supporters drowning out the chants of their German equivalents, whom they outnumbered by 70,000 to 4,000, revealed a brutal, bullying attitude that most people would not until recently have recognised as British. Of course it could have been worse; on the night, the players on the pitch behaved courteously, and the violence erupted only in Trafalgar Square. We have got into the habit of being grateful for sometimes very small mercies. Friends who were at Wembley tell me that the atmosphere of the crowd was far more hostile towards the Germans than the television relay suggested; that it was not just a handful who booed and whistled during the German national anthem. Behaviour off the pitch – though, happily, on this occasion, not on it – showed how far assumptions about sportsmanship have been abandoned. Even to mention them seems quaint.

Yet one does not have to be very old to remember when the sporting code was universally respected in Britain, when to have transgressed against it would have been regarded as a matter of national disgrace. But then, concepts of disgrace and shame have evaporated in the face of the collapse of shared values. Otherwise, few of the English squad could have taken part in the competition, following their trashing of a Club class compartment on the aeroplane back from Hong Kong. James Hewitt, a former officer in the Life Guards, would not have been able to show his face – nor would the newspapers have shown it, smirking, on their diary pages – after his revelations, aired by Anna Pasternak in her book *Princess in Love*, about his supposed romantic adventures with the Princess of Wales.

Euro 96 was exceptional as a moment when almost all the nation – an estimated seventeen million of us – were doing the same thing at once: following the match. There used to be many rituals and traditions that fulfilled a similar function.

One was called 'Watching the Nine O'Clock News' – a point in the evening when the nation gathered around that domestic idol, the television set, to receive knowledge of the day's events from the BBC. Now the multiplicity of choice in television channels reflects the tendency of everything that once looked immemorial to fragment. Monolithic corporations have downsized. Job security is not the certainty for the middle classes that it used to be; nor is the adequacy of pensions or the infallibility of the National Health Service.

Against the predictions of some future-gazers, 'the office' has not died; people like going to the office, chatting to colleagues in the corridor, more than anyone had imagined. But gradually the inevitable decentralisation caused by information technology has begun to take place. This is not just a matter of more people working from home. Technology encourages an extreme individualism, symbolised by the Internet, which frees users of the constraints of place; they do not need to communicate with the people with whom they happen to share the accident of geography, nor to conform to the values of those around them. They can communicate instead with other individuals, perhaps far-flung, who share the same specialist interests or obsessions.

One of Mrs Thatcher's most memorably misquoted sayings was that society does not exist. What she meant, of course, was that the natural unit of human organisation is the family, not the state. Perhaps the reason why her remark was so avidly seized upon – and quoted out of context – was that society, for reasons that did not all have to do with Mrs Thatcher, seemed to be disintegrating. Mrs Thatcher herself is an example of a belonger; she was of the belonging generation. She belonged to the Oxford Union, to the English Bar, to her constituency party, to the parliamentary party, to various political cabals and Cabinets, to the Church of England. Now it has become notoriously difficult to persuade young people to belong even to that loosest outer circle of identity – the democratic system – by registering their vote. Nor do they have much belief in other forms of shared value, such as morals. Moral choices are held to be a matter of individual preference, much as buying a pair of trainers or selecting a television programme might be.

15

Collective ideals have lost currency. The inevitable consequence of television, video and the other components of the home entertainment revolution has been that people do not need to assemble so often in one place. According to the Football Association, attendances at football matches have recovered to 22 million per season since the nadir of the mid-1980s – but that is still a long way from the 40 million who went in the years after the Second World War. There are almost more soldiers than spectators at the Trooping of the Colour. Generally, people prefer to be cocooned in the capsule of their living room rather than bumping up against their fellow humans at public events – a distaste for coming together which is not confined to children, glued to their video games. One of the rituals of the English countryside used to be the village fête, which might almost have been an image of England itself. It may not have been terribly exciting, on some occasions it caused almost more rancour than it was worth, but the cakes, jam and jumble were all sold in aid of some community endeavour, usually the church. Fêtes have fast been outrun by car-boot sales, at which each individual sells his old junk for himself. This is the social equivalent of privatisation, a perfect expression of the 'Great Car Economy' beloved of Thatcherism. No doubt 'car-boot Britain' has advantages: not everyone liked putting on a flowery dress or Panama hat for the British fête. But we are not comfortable with it yet; it has no grace.

We were famously the nation of stiff upper lips. We did not complain; we saw things through. With camaraderie and black humour, the residents of the East End toughed out the Blitz; and so did the King and Queen, in Buckingham Palace. In later years it became almost a point of national honour that our trains would not run on time, so that the stoicism of the railway travelling public could be displayed at its best. During the very hot summers of the mid-1970s, whole villages were reduced to collecting water from standpipes. People blamed the exceptional weather, and got on with it. In 1995, the drought did not cause anything like such deprivation. This time, however, such shortages as occurred were not accepted in long-suffering silence: the public blamed not the weather but the government and the directors of the newly privatised water companies. It was as though they regarded the spraying of their lawns and roses with unlimited quantities of water as a fundamental right. It took a Somali, speaking on the radio, to observe that, from the perspective of her country, to use the word drought at all in this context seemed little short of obscene.

We kept ourselves in check. In the words of Noël Coward:

> *We British are a peculiar breed*
> *Undemonstrative on the whole.*
> *It takes a very big shock indeed*
> *To dent our maddening self-control.*

How is it then that rage has become tagged to almost every activity of life? Road rage, trolley rage, even cinema rage – these expressions have all been coined to denote the uncontrollable outbursts of fury, sometimes violent, that occasionally accompany such minor inconveniences as someone queue-jumping at a supermarket check-out. I have not heard that this rage fever – could it be called rage rage? – has afflicted the Continent. One would not expect it to; it was always there. Traditionally the French and Italians have waved their arms, shouted and sometimes hit each other at times which the buttoned-up English found comically inappropriate, while the Germans were thought to behave unpredictably under pressure. Now it is the famously self-repressed English who have had their lid screwed down too tight, for too long. We are ready to erupt at any moment.

This is odd, because we used to think of ourselves as a nation of old-fashioned courtesy and respect. As the parental Rover rolled around the countryside, passing AA men saluted; it was a subject of concern that they should do this, even when cornering their motorcycles sharply. In one respect, courtesy survives almost to an alarming extent. When drivers are not attacking each other, or pedestrians, because one or other of them is thought to have occasioned a few seconds' delay, they follow rituals of etiquette unknown in other countries. I suspect that more accidents are perpetrated by drivers who have temporarily taken their eyes

17

off the road to wave in acknowledgement to some *gentillesse* by other road-users than result from an afflatus of road rage. Nevertheless, it is impossible to imagine that a modern German visitor would agree with the pre-war opinion of the German, Kurt von Stutterheim, writing *Those English* in 1937, that the British are more polite than the people of other countries.

Rather, they have become loud-mouthed and offensive, the strongest elbowing their way to the front of crowds or seats on public transport, and asserting their presumed right to create as much noise and unpleasantness for neighbours as they like by filthily abusing, threatening and sometimes attacking anyone who is rash enough to ask them to stop. On City dealing floors nowadays, traders have to be disciplined for foul language, disgusting behaviour towards female colleagues, and general aggression. Survivors from the *Herald of Free Enterprise* ferry disaster off Zeebrugge, in which a hundred and ninety-three people drowned, describe how men pushed women off staircases in their effort to reach the decks. To suggest that there is any value higher than self-preservation would today seem ludicrous. Once, though, actions would have been judged against an ideal of self-restraint, even if it was one which few people managed to achieve.

We used equally to be a nation whose citizens received a rather warmer welcome when they travelled abroad, thanks to their quiet manners and perhaps their hosts' memories of the Second World War. To many of my parents' generation, a chief pleasure in going abroad was the opportunity it gave to lament the failings of other countries, particularly if they were Mediterranean, with their backward economies, rubbish by the side of the road and inability to make tea with properly boiling water. The thing was, they were not organised. We, on the other hand, were – which was why we had better drains beneath our streets and no beggars above them. Begging would have been anathema to a people as independent and honourable as the British. In the City and elsewhere, the Englishman's word, whatever the Englishman's competence, was still his bond.

In terms of our self-image, the certainties of yesterday have become the anxieties of today. Our sense of difference from other

18

countries has been eroded, and this is disorienting. Business and marketing have become international, with the result that the kinds of goods on sale in Paris and Bonn are scarcely different from those in London. The big supermarkets in Britain offer food products from all over the world. Modern communications, such as the Internet and satellite broadcasting, defy national regulation. Money has become electronic, being flashed from one side of the globe to the other within seconds.

Our discomfort at the narrowing of the gap between ourselves and other countries is made worse by the realisation that, while we may be prepared to become more like our neighbours, our neighbours often have little desire to be like us. They were long irritated by the smugness of a country whose memory of Empire gave it a sense of self-importance belied by its real place in the world. There may well have been a measure of jealousy in their attitude: we had bluffed our way to the top table. Now Hollywood has joined others who are taking their revenge. It used to be that the importance of the English market for American films ensured that the cosy, swashbuckling, tea-on-the-lawn view of England to which directors instinctively responded was good box office. Now, in a different economic climate, Hollywood is less careful about offending English sensibilities: in fact, it seems rather to enjoy doing so. It is easy to portray the English as imperialist and therefore the new 'men in black hats': hence *Braveheart*, glorifying the Scottish struggle of William Wallace, and other films sympathising with the IRA. Directors have also begun to make their villains speak with British accents, even when using American actors.

Until the Second World War, the British knew who they were; afterwards began the descent into anxiety. If this bold statement is true, it is not just because winning the war failed to regenerate Britain in the way that losing it ultimately did Germany; nor that the withdrawal from Empire and the Suez crisis forced the British to accept that they could not fill the clothes of their world-dominating grandparents. It is also that in the 1950s Britain embraced modernism as a social creed. In the 1930s, it had been a fashion for an élite; a few sophisticates had their London flats done up with chrome fittings, but elsewhere a solid conservatism prevented the acceptance of a foreign dogma. After the Second World War, Britain embraced the international orthodoxy, building motorways on the model of those in Germany and redeveloping old cities in the hated glass-and-concrete style of Le Corbusier. Modernism hated tradition and nationalism in equal measure. Britain arrived late at the modernist party, but it stayed rather longer than most. Only in the last decade has it decided to leave, and it is not quite sure where to go next.

Modernism preyed upon insecurities that the British have always felt about culture, having tended to feel that culture necessarily came from somewhere else. For most of its history, Britain has believed itself to be a cultural limb, in the extremities of which blood from the Graeco-Roman heart of civilisation pulsed only feebly. The view has been challenged quite correctly by cultural patriots, and they are particularly right to challenge it now: in the 1990s Britain's artistic stock throughout the world is high. London swings again. But perhaps because of the eclecticism of the Grand Tour that filled the grandest of British houses with masterpieces from overseas, perhaps as a legacy of Empire, which opened some minds to the riches of foreign cultures, there remains a feeling that Englishness in the arts is provincial. It is typical of this sentiment that the 1996 Proms season should have opened with a performance of Haydn's *Creation*, sung in German despite the composer's clear intention that he had wanted it to be performed in England and there sung in English.

These days, arrogance is not a quality that one hears foreigners speak of so much in relation to the British. Our cultural insecurity and self-doubt are evident and, in this weakened state of morale, we have been particularly vulnerable to the homogenising tendency of Europe. In other countries, regional identities have been made stronger by Europe; the identity of England has weakened. Those decades of superiority towards the countries in which we travelled have taken their toll. Perhaps they could not make a decent cup of tea? It has turned out that they could make politics in a way that defeats many exponents of that art in Britain. One of the saddest sights of the European Commission is that of a newly appointed British minister fumbling to put on headphones for the first time. It would be impossible for, say, a French politician to rise to prominence without first knowing how to play the European game.

The difference between the British and the Continental approach only underlines the extent to which the European game is not our game. We still prefer skittles at Westminster to boules in Brussel, we relish the knock-'em-down style of our adversarial tradition. There is a particular intimacy and clubbishness in the Houses of Parliament, whose merits are that they encourage a belief in unspoken assumptions about behaviour and the national interest. They are not merits that naturally shine through the medium of television; in fact television has been cruel in exposing an absurd rigmarole – which could be tolerated and even relished when members played that curious game among themselves – to public glare. And Parliament has been televised since 1989.

We used to be proud that our system was unique. Now membership of the European Union has forced us to recognise that, as well as unique, it is also extraordinary, sometimes bizarre. That we have been led to question our own judgement of this institution has caused a generalised and unfocused acceptance, in some quarters, that reform would be a good thing. Tony Blair, for example, asserts that the House of Lords should be reformed by abolishing the voting rights of the hereditary peers. That would, at least for the time being, leave us with an upper house composed entirely of placemen appointed by the Prime Minister. Ultimately, according to Mr Blair's scheme of things, a system of election would be introduced; but who knows how long it would take for agreement on the method for electing the new Senate, and its rights *vis-à-vis* the House of Commons, to be achieved? It could be decades. Moreover, by itself, reform would hardly accomplish the objectives expected of it, since the butt of public criticism over the conduct of Parliament has been the Commons, not the Lords. The assumption that salvation must lie in reform, even when the goals of reform are unclear, is another symptom of the nation's lack of ease with itself: its uncertainties about being British.

It is obligatory in this context to refer to the Euro-nonsense that appears to flow in an unstemmable tide from Brussels. Examples of the genre are legion. A fruit merchant in Hull was forced to give away £3,000-worth of nectarines because they were too small to sell. Equally, the Henry Doubleday Research Association, which has launched its 'Adopt-a-Veg' appeal to help save what it calls, graphically, Britain's 'threatened vegetable heritage', is prevented from selling examples of the seven hundred rare seeds in its Heritage Seed Library in shops, because they have not been registered in accordance with European requirements. These are just two instances that have crossed my desk recently, selected at random. Day and night the ogres of Brussels can be heard stamping about the corridors of the European Union, as their cry of 'Fee, fie, fo, fum, I smell the traditional habits, tastes and foodstuffs of an Englishman' reverberates across the Channel. The symbol of our subjection to the forces of control will be the European construct (though not necessarily forced upon this country by the EU), the identity card. An identity card scheme was within an ace of being launched in 1996, before apparently being quashed by the Prime Minister as too electorally unpopular.

Waste of nectarines and the frustrations of specialist seed producers are bad. What is really worrying about Euro-nonsense is that much of it does not emanate from Europe at all. We generate it ourselves. The majority of the legislation that has been used to close down fish-smokeries in Scotland and craftsmen in the West Country has originated from Westminster, and has then been stringently over-interpreted by local officials. Altogether it is remarkable, given the free-market obsessions of Thatcherism; these wretched officials have done as much as they can to shackle the market wherever possible. Our new propensity for red tape makes a mockery of the old idea of Britain as a country famous for its liberty. Everywhere we seem to be tied up in it, like Gulliver in Lilliput. Daily life has become more regulated by bureaucracy than it ever was under the Hapsburg Empire. The British themselves have been largely responsible, and that is an alarming reflection of our new sense of national identity.

Our feelings of unease with ourselves would have baffled

earlier generations, brought up on a potent myth of England which every school-child drank in with the free school milk. England was the country that did things differently, and very often first. King Alfred unified it, at a time when most Continental countries were still a flux of warring tribes. The Norman invasion had the merit of being the last and the new lords, after a lapse of time, had the good taste to absorb much of the culture of the old Saxon earls. English became the unifying language in the fourteenth century, when Chaucer used it for his poetry. The nation's notorious lack of prowess at speaking Continental languages probably dates from Henry VIII's decision to break with the Church of Rome, for which the lingua franca was Latin. Throughout the world the lingua franca is now English. That is as much an accident of the economic power of the United States as it is a legacy of Empire; but for whatever reason, we benefit from it. 'There are only two languages in the world,' a Member of Parliament told me recently, 'English and money.' That is a sentiment which Henry VIII would have understood.

The Reformation, providing England with a monarch who was also head of the established church, created a powerful symbol of national cohesion. Later came the Civil War, which for a time melted the glue that bound the different forces within the country together. But it could be presented as an abberation – an object lesson in bad nation management. The thing about revolutions is that, as George VI commented to President Truman in 1945, 'We don't have those here.' The Civil War caused the balance of power to readjust itself, without overturning the already immemorial institutions by which England was governed. By the standard of the French Revolution, a century and a half later, it was not even particularly bloody.

The Glorious Revolution of 1688 allowed for the expulsion of an unpopular monarch and the installation of a more satisfactory one with, outside Ireland, the minimum of disruption; it had hardly been a revolution at all. The continuity of our history makes the sense of experiment about so many aspects of the present age, from the genetic engineering of plants to European monetary union, particularly unsettling. This more than anything seems un-British.

The Glorious Revolution set the scene for the onrush of firsts that used to be the pride of British history teachers. In 1707 we were the first country to be unified within our natural frontiers, preceding Italy, Germany and Belgium by more than a century. The Union with Scotland could only be swallowed with a gulp. Within Great Britain, England and Scotland were equal partners, with their own separate identities, never satisfactorily subsumed into the greater whole. England's relationship with Wales and Ireland, however, had always been as the dominant cultural force, which sought to overpower and exterminate the minority way of life. The solidity of the British system provided the secure floor upon which the pioneers of the Industrial Revolution could toddle their first steps; more firsts came with the development of spinning-machines, other industrial processes and scientific agriculture. The wars against the French, culminating in Waterloo, had the effect, like other wars, of forging a common sense of ourselves – producing heroes such as Horatio Nelson in whom the whole nation could rejoice, while recognising traits that seemed inescapably English. Nelson personified indomitable courage, of course: but also loyalty, duty, a nearly religious sense of mission, a distaste for politics and a country background. Even the relegation of sexual passion to the level of light comedy identified him as a classic English male.

In the nineteenth century, it was the longevity of the English tradition which the nation's image-builders most wished to commemorate. This is expressed in that supremely evocative emblem of nationhood, the Palace of Westminster. Not only did Whigs salute the Middle Ages as the origin of Common Law and Parliament, but so did the Tory Prime Minister Benjamin Disraeli, with his romantic ideal of the 'One Nation'. That prefigured the consensus politics that prevailed between the First and Second World Wars, and persisted for some decades thereafter. The image that embodied the vision of a united but disparate country, adumbrated by the Tory Prime Minister Stanley Baldwin and shared by successors of other parties, is that of the village. Everyone from the squire (or King) to the labourer (the Labour Party) had his place, though there was nothing to stop the labourer, in the shape of Labour Party leaders such as Ramsay MacDonald, swapping clothes with the gentry. As David Starkey wrote recently in *The Times*: 'The result was that peculiar British version of the two-party system in which Labour and Conservative alternated power with all the decorum of cricket teams on the village green.' The King presided over this political game as the umpire, while the Queen became patroness of voluntary charities. 'While the trappings and traditions of monarchy, many of them rather recently invented, became the festivals and folklore, the BBC became the schoolmaster and the Church of England the rector of the Great British village.'

But something happened to the village. Like Ambridge in the radio soap opera *The Archers*, life there became more and more fractious and strife-torn, as the old guard struggled to maintain the ideal of community in the face of mounting social pressures and an unending series of misfortunes. The cosiness of the village had little appeal for Mrs Thatcher, whose tastes were altogether more stringent. She grew up in a small town in Lincolnshire, and wanted to move on. She thought that everybody did: that they should. It might have been expected that her successor John Major, with his south London childhood, would have had even less feeling for the village ideal than herself. Not so. Memorably, Mr Major articulated his vision of Englishness in a speech about the Maastricht treaty in 1993:

> Fifty years from now Britain will still be the country of long shadows on county grounds, warm beer, invincible green suburbs, dog-lovers and pools-fillers and – as George Orwell said – 'old maids bicycling to holy communion through the morning mist' and – if we get our way – Shakespeare still read even in school.

The intelligentsia widely ridicule this ideal, which is not without elements of cliché, but I suspect that the wider public shared the Prime Minister's instincts.

Mr Major was again pilloried by media sophisticates for fighting the 1992 election from the vantage point of a soap-box; on that occasion, the electorate expressed their preference for

Mr Major's homely, makeshift and unmistakably English style of presentation over the show-business techniques then used by the Labour leadership, by re-electing him, in defiance of the opinion polls. Tony Blair, now his 'New Labour' opponent, has never shared so specific a vision of national identity with an audience. But given that a talisman of his speeches is 'community', it might be that he would find the nation-as-village idea congenial. When he summons up a picture of England – as it might be, from a hammock in Tuscany – it is the country aspect, typified by walking across Scottish moors, that rises in his mind. 'The countryside of County Durham is where I grew up, where I spent my childhood and I adore it,' he told me in an interview in 1996 – surprisingly for someone widely portrayed as the beau ideal of Islington Man.

Mr Blair might have referred to the 'clatter of clogs in the Lancashire mill towns', an element of the original George Orwell passage, from *The Lion and the Unicorn*, upon which Mr Major neglected to draw. Orwell went on to evoke 'the to-and-fro of the lorries on the Great North Road, the queues outside the Labour Exchanges, the rattle of pin-tables in the Soho pubs'. 'Old maids biking to Holy Communion through the mists of the autumn mornings' were only part of it; but it is significant that it was only on this villagey aspect that Mr Major chose to draw. For both the Prime Minister and the Leader of the Opposition, the essence of Britishness lies in the countryside.

What is absent from Mr Major's thinking, and probably Mr Blair's, is the village fête. As yet, Mr Blair has had no opportunity to demonstrate his ability to engender feelings of togetherness, but it is clear that Mr Major has no instinct for the great communal occasions or endeavours that cheer everyone up. He is the victim of his predecessor's rhetoric. Mrs Thatcher made it a virtue to be penny-pinching, and often she was. But it meant that even when she was spending royally she had to present herself as being mean. I suspect that few people realise that, in real terms, the spending of every government department, except the Foreign Office, has increased since 1979, generally by more than a third. Projects that were liberally funded to enhance national prestige – such as the redecoration of 10 Downing Street and the Foreign Office, and the construction of a princely new building for the DHSS in Whitehall – were kept virtually secret from the public. Mr Major has raised taxes without persuading the electorate that the government is spending more money. The village fête is off again this year. Even the great celebration planned for the millennium has caused nothing but rancour, and the result already exudes the dreariness of a bring-a-bottle party.

Something of this change can be seen reflected in British films. Fifty years ago, the flag for the British film industry was carried by Ealing Studios. Hidden behind their lawn in a suburban street, even the structures that formed the physical embodiment of the Studios seemed typically British: so different from the megalomaniac style of Hollywood. Even more striking is the extent to which Ealing films consistently represented the contemporary British values of the day, which seems almost to have amounted to a conscious policy. When the BBC bought the Studios in the mid-1950s, a plaque was erected to commemorate the quarter-century during which 'many films were made projecting Britain and the British character'. In his autobiography, the supremo at Ealing, Sir Michael Balcon, wrote of the 'sense of national pride' that the films inspired. This pride did not rest on the stiff-upper-lip heroism of the patriotic films made during and, later, about the Second World War: rather, it translated the values of such films into the humdrum circumstances of daily life. As George Perry has commented in his history of the Ealing Studios, *Ealing Forever*, many of the Ealing films, such as *Whisky Galore!*, *Passport to Pimlico* and *The Titfield Thunderbolt*, 'adopted the theme of the small group pitted against and eventually triumphing over the superior odds of a more powerful opponent. The quality shown to win is dogged team spirit, the idiosyncrasies of character blended and harnessed for the good of the group.' Most people agree that *Kind Hearts and Coronets*, in which Alec Guinness played eight members of the D'Ascoyne family – at one point, seven in one shot – distilled the essence of Ealing: Guinness's 'demure, understated genius, brimful of subtle ironies, was a faithful reflection of the studio itself', wrote Peter Ustinov in the introduction to Perry's book. Typically, Ealing flourished in adversity.

These days there is no shortage of adversity for the British film industry and, if it does not exactly flourish, at least it manages to get by. But its contribution to Britain's self-image is not the same. The social realism of the 1960s was followed by a tide of nostalgia, washing out from *Chariots of Fire* and the television adaptation of *Brideshead Revisited*. This tide has never ebbed. So nowadays, while films of various genres are made in Britain, it is striking that nearly all the most memorable of such works are retrospective. These costume dramas can be well acted, but as likely as not they will be adaptations of novels written at the turn of the century or before. They can also be very beautiful, but often their beauty is achieved through the nostalgic re-creation of that aspect of British life which has changed more than any other over the past century: the upper-class world of the country house. Watching a film by Merchant Ivory is, for some of the audience, rather like sitting an exam in architectural history: those with an interest in such things delight in identifying the different locations. The English countryside becomes the equivalent of an essential fashion accessory. Even some films that are not based on the novels of Jane Austen, Henry James or E. M. Forster, such as *The Remains of the Day*, still evoke the pre-Second World War country house, with the hierarchy and snobbishness which have now more or less vanished from what survives of that existence. There is nothing wrong with it – yet one pines for Ealing's ability to anatomise contemporary Britain.

Naturally there have been exceptions, from *Four Weddings and a Funeral*, a comedy of upper middle-class manners, at one end of the scale to *Trainspotting*, a gritty portrayal of drug-abusing teenage no-hopers, at the other. It is not a criticism of the quality of these films to say that they do not radiate a consistent message about the British character; such an objective would seem ludicrous to most film aficionados. Still, one cannot but note that they do not. Nor, in this respect, does television throw the British public a lifeline. The vein of comedy repre-sented by *Dad's Army* – very Ealing, in depiction of a band of unlikely individuals combining together against a common threat – survived in the hugely popular series *Only Fools and Horses* (rather fatuously criticised by educationalists as offering a poor role model to Britain's young people). But even comedy has become less affable. The humour of *Fawlty Towers* turned on the manic behaviour of the bitter and frustrated Basil Fawlty, creating a sense of harshness developed by Jennifer Saunders in *Absolutely Fabulous*. The Rabelaisian satire of *Spitting Image* and the biting asperity of Chris Morris's *Brass Eye* are anything but genial, reflecting the cynicism that has become a distinguishing characteristic of the 1990s.

It is easy to diagnose some of the causes of this crisis in British identity. At the time of writing, the Conservative party has been in power for eighteen years – by British standards, a very long run. Whatever benefits it may have brought, it has made politics tedious. There have been few great national projects to rally the populace, to make them feel that life is about more than the daily grind. Or rather, there have, through the Lottery. But the media has become so mired in cynicism that even that great money fountain, whose golden rain should fall with such refreshment on our parched and wilting cultural garden, has been more the subject of controversy than acclaim. The government can do nothing right. Perhaps politicians can do nothing right. The Labour Party has added to our confusion by transforming itself into a professedly centrist movement, shedding much of its traditional ideology along the way. When a deputy leader such as John Prescott announces himself to be middle class, one knows something is up. In marketing terms, the party has sacrificed 'brand heritage'. In power, though, it is far from certain that they would be capable of regenerating faith in the system of which they are part.

On the mantelpiece of his constituency office in Trimdon, County Durham, Tony Blair has a bust of Oliver Cromwell. I asked him if this reflected the Cromwellian sympathies of other party leaders – Margaret Thatcher having been an admirer and John Major representing Cromwell's constituency of Huntingdon – but he would not be drawn. Nevertheless, there is something ominously Cromwellian in what *The Times* columnist Matthew Parris has called the 'routine recourse the Labour leader has to extravagant imputations of personal wickedness in his opponents'. Mr Blair is at the head of his own New Model Army, or perhaps New Moral Army. The tone of the 1997 election campaign was very different from that of Labour's 'New Umpire' poster for the 1929 election, showing Ramsay MacDonald bowling out Stanley Baldwin on the village green. However, New Labour may find that their attacks on supposed Tory sleaze redound against them; the public has lost faith not just in Conservative politicians, but in politicians.

Indeed, they have lost faith in leaders generally. We feel this more acutely because, formerly, we tended to accord them too much respect. The end of the deference culture was overdue; but when it came, the wave of reaction swept most figures who would normally be at the head of society off their plinths. Most obviously this can be seen in the relentless abasement of the royal family. But society's refusal to be led by its supposed leaders extends into most quarters of the establishment: the police, the church, most of the professions. Doctors may be the only group to be exempt. Oddly, they may have retained public respect precisely because, with the reorganisation of the Health Service, a vocal number of them have disassociated themselves from the Establishment, through open criticism of government policy. Still, even doctors no longer personify the securities that they used to, in a more certain world. We have no cure for Aids, we understand next to nothing about Creutzfeld-Jakob Disease; old plagues, such as tuberculosis – that we thought had been vanquished – have reappeared in drug-resistant form. From Dr Lydgate in *Middlemarch* to Dr Kildare on television, it seemed that doctors were both the new priesthood and social heroes; now they seem to be rather closer to the sawbones and apothecaries of a previous era than we had thought.

Nationally, we have acquired the habit of looking on the gloomy side of life, particularly in reference to ourselves. Surely Britain is the only country in which a steady increase in the success children achieve in their A-levels would be greeted with lamentation? It is assumed to reflect skulduggery by the examination boards in setting easier papers. In fact, there are some obvious explanations of why standards in examinations might be rising. Anyone of my age admits that they now work much harder than they used to do: if anything, they tend to take school work too seriously sometimes. In addition, girls' education has improved to the level of boys'; girls are now highly motivated to pursue their own academic and later careers. There are other countries – Germany and France for example – where exam results have got better, and there it is regarded as a cause for celebration. It is Britain alone which suffers from the depressive condition in which even triumphs are felt as calamities.

This national propensity to mope struck the *Financial Times* writer Michael Prowse, when he recently returned from six years in the United States. As he wrote on 15 March 1997:

> Reading the British newspapers in Washington last year I mentally prepared myself for a difficult transition on my return to the UK. Mr John Major's government was apparently one of the most unpopular in modern political history. That, surely, had to mean the UK was doing extremely badly. How, I wondered, would I adapt to this dismal country after six years in the dynamic, entrepreneurial United States?
>
> A few months later I must report surprise and bafflement. If you have never left the UK – or not visited it recently – you are probably unaware that things have got better, not worse ... The infrastructure – despite predictable complaints about lack of funding – is in better shape than in the late 1980s ... Even public agencies seem more efficient and customer-oriented. After complaining recently about misdirected mail, I got a letter from a local Post Office manager, followed by a telephone call to explain what action had been taken and an invitation to ring back if there were any further difficulties. Years ago I doubt that a letter of complaint would even have been answered.

Affluence is reflected in the 77 per cent increase in total household expenditure, allowing for inflation, which took place between 1971 and 1995, according to *Social Trends*. Yet the

British refuse to acknowledge the bounty that Fortune some-times bestows on them. Our lack of confidence in our shared nationhood causes us to shun national symbols, which is true of the British generally. Arriving at Miami airport recently, I was struck by the number of times I saw the Stars and Stripes for sale. Quite ordinary vans carried stickers bearing the legend 'God Bless America'. Patriotism of this spontaneous kind hardly exists in Britain, where the only opportunity most people (outside Ulster) have to buy the Union flag is imprinted on a pair of boxer shorts. Recently the flag enjoyed a vogue as a fashion motif, with Liam Gallagher and Patsy Kensit pictured on the cover of *Vanity Fair* in bed beneath it, and Geri of the Spice Girls adapting it as a microdress when performing at the Brit Awards. In this post-modern age, in which every piece of symbolism self-consciously echoes some previous usage, the adoption of the flag as pop motif is an attempt at 1960s revivalism. But in the 1960s, the flag really meant something: it was a focus of deeply held convictions. So acts against it carried a frisson no longer felt in the Britain of the 1990s. We have not followed the American example in nurturing the myth of the flag. There is no ceremony of saluting the flag each morning in British schools; perhaps we would not want there to be. It is a mark of civilisation that suburban gardens do not sprout flagpoles, flying the Union Jack. Still, anyone who wished to fly the flag outside a house in London would probably be prevented from doing so by planning regulations. The lack of any place for the flag in daily life has made it possible for this most powerful of all symbols to be abrogated as the emblem not just of Britpop but of fascist thugs.

There was a time when people routinely stood to attention during the national anthem, wherever it was heard and whatever they were otherwise doing. By the 1960s, it had become the signal for filmgoers to start trooping out of the cinema when it was played at the end of the programme. Now, children are not taught its words. Again, this is all very different from America, where families regularly – and with apparent pride – join together in singing the American anthem at the close of football and baseball matches. What is true for Britain as a whole is doubly so of England. A sense of persecution gives zest to the self-expression of the other countries in the United Kingdom. The Welsh proudly wear leeks on St David's Day; the Scots celebrate St Andrew's Day and drink themselves patriotically stupid on Burns Night; the Irish variously sport shamrocks on St Patrick's Day or relive the Battle of the Boyne on 1 July. But nobody in England wears a red rose on St George's Day; many people do not even know when St George's Day is. Red nose day has a greater currency than red rose day. We have no equivalent of the American Thanksgiving Day, a feast celebrated by everyone whatever their ethnic background or religious persuasion.

I suspect, too, that the figure of John Bull has lost some of its former vividness; certainly he lacks the ubiquity of Uncle Sam, his American equivalent. It seems agonisingly appropriate that the bulldog, another national symbol, should in real life have become a wheezing caricature of its former self: overbred, prone to buckling of the legs and devoid of the old athleticism, tenacity and aggression of the sporting dog, for which it was valued by our forefathers. A degree of spurious consternation was manufactured when, in the summer of 1996, a survey discovered that the British were not longer predominantly a nation of dog-lovers, but preferred cats.

The urge to purchase British goods, not simply out of piety but because they were believed to be better, was felt keenly by my parents' generation, but has now lost its potency. In many areas people want to buy French toothbrushes, Italian shoes and American leisure clothes for the specific reason that they are not British; their foreignness evokes a certain glamour. But for the most part we do not question the origin of products. It seems astonishing that Britain can import so much food from other countries in Northern Europe when it is perfectly capable of producing the same food itself. The bill for Danish bacon alone runs to £1 billion.

Nor does England set much store on the little symbols of daily life which signal our sense of individuality. Old-fashioned telephone boxes, black taxis, policemen's tall helmets are apt to seem faintly ridiculous in British eyes, even though they are the details which foreigners most associate with our cities. Consequently, the public accepts their disappearance with a sigh. How different Paris is from London. The French may adore science and technology, but it would not occur to them to do away with the immemorial grilles and kiosks that typify the Parisian streetscape: indeed, in some cases they are exporting them to us – one of their lavatories has appeared in Sloane Square.

Individually, the disappearance of the commonplaces of life may not seem more than trivial; but we need to step back and take stock of the sum total of what we have lost. Take the colour red – the royal colour, the colour of guardsmen's tunics. It used not only to be worn by many more of His Majesty's forces – such as my wife's grandfather, who joined the Indian Army before the uniform changed during the Boer War – but is also, by extension, the national colour. It was once seen everywhere: on buses, tube trains, fire-engines, telephone boxes and everything to do with the Post Office. Fire-engines and post-boxes still wear the livery, but precious little else does. British Telecom abandoned red in favour of yellow, believing red would be associated with a fuddy-duddy image of a public utility, not a fast-moving communications business for the twenty-first century. The Post Office has not yet dared paint pillar-boxes another colour, but it has started to replace red with an unattractive shade of sage green around post offices – no doubt with its eyes to privatisation.

Some would say that modernisation is inevitable and desirable: for example, British Telecom's aesthetic failings may be outweighed by the incalculable improvement in the operation of the telephone service, including the payphones formerly housed in old-fashioned red telephone boxes. Nevertheless, there is no reason why new telephone equipment cannot be placed in old boxes, to preserve continuity and keep alive a symbol of Britain. It is a failure of the British imagination that modernising should necessarily mean ditching national identity. But the powers that rule over our telecoms industry share the same relativism of values as many other sections of the community, such as teachers. Living in a society that hesitates to make absolute judgements about anything, they believe that one aesthetic option is just as good as any other, and that the public will get used to whatever it is given. It will get used to it, but it will have suffered loss.

The irony is that British Telecom themselves have come to realise the potency of the old red boxes, since they have adapted their latest boxes to incorporate domed tops and scarlet panels in a crude parody of the Scott design. Presumably they have been advised by their marketing consultants of the value that resides in the 'heritage of the brand'. If so, it comes too late for the streets of Britain's cities, where British Telecom's example has set the standard for its competitors, such as Mercury, who are now erecting their own booths which are every bit as gincrack.

Recent studies suggest that the English language, our greatest cultural inheritance, is in a more vital condition than one might have supposed. According to the Oxford University Press's *Atlas of English Dialects*, spoken English is barely more uniform in its accent and vocabulary than at the end of the last century. In different parts of the country, 'clammed', 'leer', 'leery' and 'thirl' are all regularly used as alternatives to standard English's 'hungry'. Studying the geography of dialects may seem a silly occupation – or it may seem daft (across a swathe of England), soft (in a pocket in the middle of it), barmy (through a long sliver running south of the Thames) or fond (up in the North-East). One might have expected the steamroller of the modern world to have flattened the way we speak into a featureless tarmac of sameness, but in fact, diversity bounces back (unless it stots, daps, glances or tamps). To the authors of the *Atlas*, Clive Upton and J. D. A. Widdowson, the explanation for this regional vigour lies in the long history of the language. British English, as they call it, has been spoken for some 1,500 years; in North America, where English has been used for only 400 years, there is nothing like the same variety of dialect. History permeates the language at every point, though it is sometimes as hidden as a fossil microbe in a meteorite. For example, that Cornish word for hungry, 'thirl', is not really so outré as it seems: in Old English it meant 'hole', and it survives as the second half of nostril (nose hole).

The survival of dialect in such rich variety, demonstrating the relish that is widely taken in non-standard English, gives the lie to reformers who have sought to abolish the Book of Common Prayer on grounds of its supposed difficulty. Unusual words and ways of saying things give pleasure.

The survival of so much variety of dialect, against the odds, also suggests that people are more successful in establishing local allegiances than one might have supposed. We live in an increasingly mobile society. In many villages, the number of inhabitants to have been born in the area is small; so if dialect is surviving, that must partly be because newcomers and their children are adopting the traditions of the locality, proud to define themselves by geography. It shows how unnecessary have been the BBC's efforts to bring more regional accents on to television and radio. Fifty years of standard English in broadcasting have not dented the robust regionality of speech. It is appropriate that a great national institution, such as the BBC, should continue its old policy of promoting what might be termed classical English – it expresses the unity of the nation.

This book is not intended to be a diatribe against change, nor a nostalgic lament for a lost world of fogeyism. As some landmarks of the national psyche disappear, others rise up, and I do not contend that all the lush pastures of British identity have become desert. Still, the new landscape is, to many people, as yet unfamiliar territory in which they feel lost. Often it seems so different from the homely, reassuring landscape in which they were brought up that they also feel worried. They do not know *where* they are, because they do not know *who* they are. The fertile lands have suffered erosion, and this erosion of national character can be associated with the collapse of moral character. People tend to respect the things they know and feel part of; in such an atmosphere they are less likely to act destructively, committing crimes, than in a world to which they owe no allegiance, to which they do not feel that they belong, and in which they feel no pride.

One of the most noticeable aspects of the last decade has been the emergence of apparently new types of crime, such as indiscriminate massacres by armed men, frenzied murder of men by women, young children killing toddlers, and muggings by girl gangs. These phenomena are new, and their advent surely reflects the loosening of the bonds that formerly restrained the people who might have committed such excesses. There were many such bonds, imposed by family, church and community as well as nation, but a sense of what was acceptable behaviour in a Briton played its part, reinforcing the others. Since the 1960s, the concept of self-restraint has been out of fashion, replaced by the idea that it is healthy for the individual to project his or her inner feelings on to the outside world. This is not always good news for the outside world, which may have preferred the days when the dark side of humanity was repressed. With the weakening of family ties, religious faith and a sense of community, it becomes even more desirable that shared feelings of what it means to be British should be reinforced. The British culture – unlike, for example, the Sicilian – has always been one in which people rubbed along pretty well. It may have been short on tempestuous passion, but it was correspondingly long on moderation and self-control – which, for most people, made life rather safer than in the lands of vendetta and *crimes passionnels*.

What this book will do is draw attention to the extent to which our culture has changed without, perhaps, our noticing it. I shall lift some of the stones from which our special sense of ourselves has been constructed – our love of landscape, our romance with the sea, what we eat, what we wear, and so on – and see what lies underneath. Naturally these things change with time, but it is worth asking whether the changes I shall highlight are part of an evolutionary process, or whether they constitute a rupture with the past which should cause us to think again about what it means to be British. There is a point to this question, because our ideas about who we are do not emerge spontaneously but are cultivated, instilled and developed; we accept some, we reject others. In order to take control of the process, we must at least know what is going on. The worst thing we could do is continue to pay lip service to ideals which have lost contact with modern life; that can only cause disillusionment.

There is plenty of evidence to show that British people want to celebrate their common identity. After the Falklands War in 1982, the nation was swept by a surge of confidence, not through any great mood of jingoism but because the public relished seeing something immensely difficult being done, before all the world, apparently supremely well. The commemoration of VE and VJ Days confounded cynics by the warmth of emotion that united so much of the country. The campaign to reintroduce two minutes' silence on 11 November, as well as the nearest Sunday, received wide backing. In the 1980s, the royal weddings caused the nation to bury its collective nose in a Kleenex of pride and sentiment; the sad outcome of those marriages could not then be predicted. It remains to be seen whether the celebration of the Queen's wedding anniversary in 1997 – to be marked by the largest ever pageant of the horse – will prove similarly moving. Horses are not for everyone, and it may be that the media will feel obliged to smother the baby in its cradle. For most of the media, only bad news is news, but I suspect that these journalistic values may not be those of the public. The majority of the people want to feel part of the same national enterprise. As religion and family life decay, a sense of belonging to the nation is all the more to be valued, as one of the last bulwarks against the anarchy of unfettered individualism.

So the British remain willing to play the game; but sometimes they find that it is not the game they were brought up with. Nowhere is that more true of that world from which metaphors of Britishness, as here, are most naturally drawn: sport.

2

England's Big Task

Sports are being made too much of, and men who follow them have allowed themselves to be taught that ordinary success in them is not worth having. All this comes from excess of enthusiasm on the matter; – from a desire to follow too well a pursuit which, to be pleasurable, should be a pleasure and not a business. This is the rock against which our sports may possibly be made shipwreck. Should it ever become unreasonable in its expenditure, arrogant in its demands, immoral and selfish in its tendencies, or, worse of all, unclean and dishonest in its traffic, there will arise against it a public opinion against which it will be unable to hold its own.

Anthony Trollope,
British Sports and Pastimes, 1868

If one were writing of France, of Germany, of Italy, of Russia, of Spain, no one would notice the omission of a chapter on sport ... It is very different in England. The first thing to attract my attention on my latest visit to England was the announcement on all the newspaper bulletins: England's Big Task. *I happened to know that the Prime Minister was seriously ill, that there was fierce debating in the House of Commons upon the estimates for the navy, and upon the new licensing bill just brought*

in by Mr Asquith, and that there was fighting upon the frontier of India with a certain tribe of natives. But England's big task had nothing to do with these trivial matters. An English cricket eleven was playing in Australia. The Australian eleven in their second innings had made an unexpectedly big score, and England's big task was to beat that score.
Price Collier, *England and the English from an American Point of View*, 1909

Money apart, Kerry Packer is not my style. England is my home . . . We put up with the buckets to catch the drips in the dressing-room at Taunton in order to enjoy the wisteria round the door of the George at Bewley.
Mike Brearley, England Captain after Tony Greig deserted to play in Packer's team, quoted in A. Kuper, 'Gentlemen and Players', *New Society*, 9 August 1984

Sport, as a major pastime, would be important to any country's identity, but in the case of Britain it is especially so. It was in Britain that several of the world's most followed games had their birthplace: among them being football, rugby, golf, cricket, tennis, hockey and badminton. Those that the British did not invent, they regulated: for example, the Marquess of Queensberry drew up the rules for boxing in 1865. Even the sport of slalom racing, little practised in the British Isles for reasons of weather and geography, saw its first rules published in the *Public Schools Alpine Sports Yearbook* for 1923. This was appropriate, since it was British skiers who developed these originally Scandinavian races. But then geography was no obstacle to the dedicated sportsman: sport attended Britons throughout Empire. 'The Englishman carries his cricket bat with him as naturally as his gun-case,' observed *Blackwoods Magazine* in 1892. And not just through the Empire. While Petrach was the first man to climb a mountain for pleasure, the modern sport of mountaineering owes its origin to various assaults on mountain-tops made by Britons in the mid-nineteenth century, from Sir Alfred Wills' ascent of the Wetterhorn in 1857 to Edward Whymper's conquest of the Matterhorn in 1865, accompanied by the foundation in London of the first Alpine Club in 1857.

Today, the extent of media coverage suggests that the public is fixated by sport, not just by the action itself but the private lives of players and athletes; there are quiz shows devoted to nothing but sport. People with great sporting prowess become personalities capable of commanding significant fees for show-business appearances; a boxer turns pantomime star. Both Britain's tradition and the enthusiasm of the modern following support the idea that it is a sporting nation.

There is another sense in which this can be interpreted. Sport once defined an attitude to life: it was not only about winning, though to do so was admired. There used to be a distinction – now obsolete – between true sports which, like hunting, were supposed not to be competitive, and games, which result in a winner. Even in games, winning was supposed to be a secondary consideration: taking part, enjoying the challenge, having a good game, were the objects. This attitude acknowledged that chance played a part in any outcome, and also encouraged a respect for one's opponents. The true sportsman did not cheat or even stretch the rules, it being regarded as unsporting for one player to take advantage of another in a way that he himself would not have liked. Being fair was everything, which did not just apply to the opposition but to other members of the team. However dazzling his own ability, the sportsman was expected to allow team-mates – even of inferior talent – their chance to participate. The prima donna was regarded with distaste.

This specifically British idea of sportsmanship found international expression through the resurrection of the Olympic Games in 1896. The man generally credited with responsibility for this achievement was, of course, the French aristocrat Pierre de Coubertin; but by his own admission, De Coubertin's inspiration came from England. An important influence was the reading of Thomas Hughes's *Tom Brown's Schooldays* when he was twelve. Later De Courbertin pursued his passion for the educationalist Thomas Arnold, upon whose teachings *Tom Brown's Schooldays* is based, to the point of self-identification. He believed that the Arnoldian system, if introduced into France, would reinvigorate it after the disasters of the Franco-Prussian War. Were international affairs to be conducted by sportsmen on the British model, their tenor would be greatly improved. De Courbertin was impressed by the curious Olympic revival attempted at Much Wenlock in Shropshire, which he visited in 1889. The symbolism of the international Olympic Games may have been Greek, but the spirit animating it was, if not wholly at least in a significant way, British.

Britain being Britain, it was impossible to dissociate the sporting code from class, for this attitude depended upon the assumption that everyone on the playing field was a gentleman. There was a distinction made between those participants who really were gentlemen and those who received payment. The latter ('players') were listed differently: in the case of cricket, by placing the individual's initials after, rather than before, his surname. As late as 1961 the following correction was broadcast at Lords: 'Your cards show, at No. 8 for Middlesex, F. J. Titmus; that should read, of course, Titmus, F. J.' But even 'players' assumed the role of honorary gentlemen for the duration of the game, and it was expected that they should observe the same niceties of behaviour. For the gentleman himself, sport served as a metaphor for existence. It was not expected that he should try too hard at anything: certainly not making money. It was assumed that he would accept the loss of a fortune with the same composure and unfailing courtesy as he would the loss of a tennis match. To many gentlemen, sport was by far the most absorbing activity in their lives. To all, it provided an illustration of their value system, and the language of sport became their moral language. They played life with a straight bat, which was the British way.

Memories of this gentlemanly ethic linger. Many people who would despise other things that the gentleman stood for still value the air of courtesy and consideration that it bestowed to the sports field. It is easy to imagine that John Major finds it attractive. Certainly he acknowledges other aspects of the historical baggage that sport carries with it, which is why, rather curiously, he assigned responsibility for its well-being to the Department of National Heritage. This was not mere chance. 'Sport is a central part of Britain's national heritage,' he asserted in the foreword to the document *Sport: Raising the Game*, outlining the government's hopes of establishing a £100 million Academy of Sport, in July 1995. Chapter 2 of that document bears the title 'Extending the Sporting Culture' – the word 'culture' being a graceful echo, perhaps, of the old moral and social values that sport embodied. It is typical of the 1990s that it should have been no more than an echo, for the chapter contains no further reference to culture beyond the title; it is entirely about providing facilities to enable more people to play.

It is all very well to be sentimental about the 'Corinthian ideal'; Mr Major, one suspects, is a sentimental man. But it would be better if it were accepted that it was dead. Other aspects of the gentleman have vanished from the stage: it would be ludicrous for anyone to affect a distaste of trade in the modern Conservative party, for example. Chivalry, which lent glamour to the gentleman's self-image, has withered before the fires of radical feminism. Men have become fearful of offering an unknown woman (who would even think of calling her a lady?) a seat on a bus, or the opportunity to go first through a doorway, lest they receive a blast of indignation on grounds of sexism. Yet we persist in clinging to the idea that sportsmanship survives, despite almost daily evidence to the contrary from newspapers and the television screen. The reason has much to do with the fact that sport is, in Mr Major's phrase, 'one of the defining characteristics of nationhood and of local pride'. Reassessment is overdue.

At the end of 1995, the *Independent* published a month-by-month chronicle of the disgrace to have afflicted football that year:

JANUARY
Eric Cantona assaults Matthew Simmons, a Crystal Palace

supporter, with his feet and fists. Mick McCarthy and Steve McMahon, managers of Millwall and Swindon, have to be separated by police during the second half of a Coca-Cola Cup tie. Peter Shilton is sacked by Plymouth over his personal debts. Paul Merson confirms he was addicted to drinking, gambling and drugs. Five police are hospitalised after crowd trouble between Millwall and Chelsea.

FEBRUARY
England fans riot in Dublin. George Graham is sacked for taking a £425,000 transfer 'bung'. Dennis Wise is convicted for assaulting a taxi driver (he is sentenced to jail, then cleared on appeal). Cantona attacks an ITN reporter in Guadeloupe. Thirty-eight arrests and eleven police injured after crowd trouble at the Chelsea and Millwall replay.

And that only takes us to March! It goes on relentlessly. The months I have quoted are not exceptionally bad: the year was not much worse than an average year. It is true that English football's reputation redeemed itself to some extent during the European Championships in 1996, thanks to the English team's superb performance against Germany in the semi-final. The nation rubbed its eyes in disbelief. But the issue is not one of skill – though generally Britain's decline as a world power has been mirrored by its fortunes in sport. It is a matter of attitudes. As mentioned in Chapter One, England's defeat after the penalty shoot-out was followed by riots in Trafalgar Square, during which German-made cars were burnt. It is not enough to say that such behaviour was restricted to a thuggish minority of followers bent on trouble, for whom the match served merely as a diary fixture for violence; their aggressive spirit was not much different from the bellicosity expressed by the tabloid newspapers. The *Daily Mirror* approached Alain de Cadanet to see if he would perform a victory roll in his Spitfire over the German hotel, should England have won. (Mr de Cadanet declined.) It is understandable, perhaps, that the footballers themselves should sometimes behave objectionably, given their youth and the pressures upon them (though to their credit, the

England squad rose impeccably to the occasion of the England–Germany match). But the atmosphere by which football is now surrounded has little to do with conventional notions of sportsmanship. It is about winning, having degenerated from the level of the gentleman to that of the tribe.

Cricket, the game synonymous with the sporting ideal, has changed beyond recognition in terms of the spirit in which it is played. Its nadir was perhaps reached in the summer of 1996, when Ian Botham sued Imran Khan over allegations of racism, yobbishness and ball tampering. Botham's court appearance merely provided George Carman, QC, with the opportunity to level a string of other accusations against him, which pictured the game in an even worse light.

The national team makes little effort to cultivate an image of gentlemanliness through their dress. 'These days, reversed baseball caps, stubbly chins, T-shirts and shorts have become the unofficial uniform of the England team as they perform indifferently around the globe,' commented the *Daily Mail* in March 1997. It was claimed that a lucrative sponsorship deal with Tetley Bitter had been ended because of the team's slovenliness. Sir Ian MacLaurin, chairman of the English Cricket Board, was quoted as saying, after the winter tour in Zimbabwe and New Zealand: 'We were not happy with the way the England team presented themselves. We understand their demeanour was fairly negative and not particularly attractive. Things improved in New Zealand, but there is a long way to go.' It may be coincidence, but the less kempt England's appearance, the worse the team appears to play.

The ungentlemanly tactics of test players are being adopted at humbler levels of the game, too. One might have thought that village cricket would have been impervious to modern influences: the spectacle of players, in whites, moving slowly about the village green is an enduring image of Englishness, which seems to encapsulate something characteristic and admirable about our values. It comes as a shock to learn from cricketing friends that even village cricketers wear the war-paint and helmets that they have seen on television, and bring to bear psychological techniques to undermine their opponents' morale. Opposing batsmen are no longer always clapped to the crease. In 1996, the Woodmancote team, from Hampshire, was expelled from the National Village Cricket Knock-out tournament, for being too professional. It is worth noting that corporate sponsorship has already penetrated the somewhat unlikely arena of the village cricket green, with the National Grid Company plc providing white coats (a short version) worn by umpires. That may seem harmless, and perhaps it is; a big national corporation may be content to allow something of village cricket's folksy image to rub off on it by association. On the other hand, the sponsor may, eventually, seek a more tangible return through the televising of matches and other exploitation in the manner of the 'honeypot' villages of the heritage industry. It would be easy for country informality to be exchanged for the artifice of image-makers.

If is less of a surprise to learn that boxing has shed the last of its always rather spurious associations as a sport of gentlemen. Nevertheless, the scenes that followed the fight for the British bantamweight title in Glasgow on 14 October 1995 should shame humanity, let alone sportsmen. When the challenger James Murray collapsed in the twelfth and final round, later to die in hospital, an element of the crowd erupted into savagery. 'Bottles were thrown and the paramedics rushing to the ring to assist the stricken fighter were hindered by those in their path,' wrote Derrick Whyte in a report published the next morning in the *Independent*. 'Chairs, glasses and bottles were thrown and soon blood-soaked victims were fleeing the part of the banqueting suite transformed into a fighting pit ... Men stripped to the waist and smeared blood from head wounds across their chests in a grotesque imitation of the recent film set in Scotland, *Braveheart*.'

While some doctors speak out against boxing, it is an anomaly of British life that only field sports, such as hunting, shooting and increasingly fishing, should attract organised physical protest and disruption, sometimes involving violent attack. Being true sports as opposed to games, it could be argued that they are the last bastion of the Victorian sporting ideal, now so ill-suited to the times.

*   *   *

As the quotation from Trollope at the head of this chapter suggests, it was, in some small way, ever thus. People have been lamenting the demise of the sporting ethic for well over a century: from the very time, indeed, that it was invented. The main accusation was that participants were taking games too seriously. In its purest form, the gentlemanly code demanded that runners, say, would simply choose a stretch of ground, take off their coats and run. 'The Corinthian ideal of my day never trained, and I can safely say the need of it was never felt,' wrote G. O. Smith. Over-seriousness about sport was in every sense ungentlemanly. The English gentleman inherited the Renaissance idea that he should behave as though life came effortlessly to him – giving the impression of, in Castiglione's word, *'sprezzatura'*. Professionalism was something for the lower orders, and from the earliest days efforts had been made to keep them out. There was a statute of 1542 to prevent them playing tennis, among other games (they encouraged 'idleness and debauchery', which were the preserve of their betters), and another of 1694 to stop 'inferior persons', such as tradesmen, from hunting and fishing. With the growth of industrial cities, the development of railways and the coming of popular newspapers, the best that could be done was to codify the rules of sport, rather as the rules of warfare had been formalised during the Middle Ages. In each case the object was the same: to prevent rude mechanicals taking advantage of the social élite by dint of brute force. Many games had begun life as rowdy village skirmishes. Such brawling behaviour was banished by the Victorians, to be replaced by a framework that encouraged the desirable commercial virtues of self-control and competition.

The better organised the game, the less likely it was to be approached in the *ad hoc* manner of yore. Cricket was an early victim of seriousness. 'There is very little sport in it now,' lamented C. E. Green, a nineteenth-century president of the MCC. W. G. Grace, bearish and beaver-bearded, did not much care about gentlemanliness: he deliberately distracted opponents and tried to bully the umpire. Perhaps he was the first modern? Certainly the crowds reacted to him with something of the appreciation shown to the bad boys of the present day, such as Eric Cantona. As Richard Holt observes in *Sport and the British: A Modern History*, he came to be regarded as a sort of John Bull figure: the Dr Johnson of sport.

The distinction between those who played for the sake of the game (amateurs) and those who got money for doing it (professionals) was made in the nineteenth century. Amateurs who turned professional not only lost caste but forfeited the adulation of the public. Society wrinkled its nose at Fred Perry after he crossed the divide in the 1920s. The distinction was abolished by the MCC (for cricket) and then the International Lawn Tennis Federation (for tennis) during the 1960s. By the decade of the 1980s, when the assumption was that everyone was in everything for the money, it seemed absurd that any sport should persevere with the divide. Anyway, it had become something of a sham, with promoters finding ways to circumvent the rules. Rugby union, with its public school origins, is a largely middle-class game, distinguished for the crowds' ability to remain convivial while inebriated. Even rugby went professional in 1996.

The sporting ghastliness of which Trollope complained in 1868 was, by today's standards, barely worth noticing. Taking things rather too seriously is a scourge of the times. It can be seen in the separation of exercise from sport, which has its origins in the nineteenth century but has now been taken to an extreme. Exercise has acquired some of the elements of religion: people who are feeling low, sullied by the world, perform their devotions at the gym and emerge feeling cleansed. The cleansing element is literal when associated, as in the case of the world's most famous worker-out, the Princess of Wales, with colonic irrigation. Health clubs now perform a function which church-going once provided: social introductions. It was at the Chelsea Harbour Club that Princess Diana met Will Carling, the married former captain of England's rugby team. Their alleged romantic attachment was much speculated upon by the tabloid press. In her choice of Carling, the Princess ratified the new status that sports personalities have acquired.

The modern exercise cult is a long way from the idea of

'muscular Christianity', which helped popularise gymnastics and athletics in the nineteenth century. It can be a hard path to follow: 'No pain, no gain.' But the activity has become narcissistic. The object of worship is the human body: one's own.

Striving for perfection in physical terms still seems foreign to the English tradition, with its acceptance that many aspects of life may always fall short of the ideal. In its present form, the exercise religion comes to us from the United States, a younger culture where such fatalism is unacceptable. The idea that one's body can be made perfect through working out is linked to that other tenet of American life becoming prevalent in Britain – that, in the normal course of events, people may be expected to live for ever. If they do not do so, it must be somebody else's fault, and that somebody can be sued. This is already influencing some sports which involve a degree of unpredictability. For example, riding establishments are increasingly cautious about what they will allow learners to do; yet anyone who rides knows that it is not possible to do so, certainly not to learn, without sometimes parting company from the horse. Most falls are harmless; unfortunately not all. Without a degree of risk, there is no challenge, and consequently no satisfaction. This also applies to obviously adventurous sports such as mountaineering, pot-holing and hang-gliding. One of the most dangerous of all sports, in terms of the numbers of injuries, is rugby. A society in which virtually any level of physical risk is regarded as unacceptable may place more and more constraints in the way of these sports. The obligation for horse-riders to wear hard hats on the road is an example of seriousness that would have struck Trollope, a passionate hunting man, as incomprehensible.

Sport is now serious to a degree that could not even have been imagined half a century ago. It has become more specialised, as one can see in the proliferation of magazines dedicated to each nuance of a discipline. *Horse and Hound*, established in the Trollope era, may seem impenetrable to people who are not particularly horsey; but by aficionados it is regarded as a general magazine because it serves what are now many separate sports. There are specialist magazines on eventing, long-distance riding, dressage, show-jumping, polo and so on. The people who take part in one horse sport may well not know those who ride in another: they have become different worlds. The same is true of other sports, such as athletics. Equally, the number of sports which would once have been considered no more than a bit of fun, but have now achieved Olympic status, grows every four years. Synchronised swimming has been joined by beach volleyball (for which women competitors wear the traditional bikini); in the last Olympics (1996), Britain's honour was maintained by a team from Ruislip Lido.

The hand-maiden of seriousness is science. As understanding of the human body improves, so athletes are able to work with ever greater precision on developing exactly the right muscles for their tasks. World records are constantly being bettered. Such is the competition that top athletes must be totally dedicated to their sport, absolute dedication of this kind being socially admired. Nothing, of course, could be further from the old sporting tradition, in which sport may have been a metaphor for life – but it was only one part of life. It was integral to the sporting code that there were higher values than those purely of sport. The obsession that the sportsmen themselves have with sport is reflected in their followers. 'Eat football, sleep football, drink Coca-Cola,' ran the slogan for one sponsor of Euro 96.

Ironically, the reason for all this seriousness can be explained by the revolution that has overtaken sport throughout the world: it has become entertainment. Relatively few people actively take part in sport (of those people who say they are 'very interested in football', only 14 per cent play); but enormous numbers watch it on television (in the case of football, 98 per cent). We have become a nation of sports voyeurs. Broadcasting has always found sport attractive; the attractions of sports coverage were used to sell radios, then televisions, now satellite dishes. Never before, however, has there been such competition between television stations, each wanting exclusive access to major sporting events in order to improve its viewing figures. Consequently, the amounts of money now being offered for television rights are without parallel. The deal signed by the International Olympic Committee and the American television station NBC for rights to the 2000 Games and 2002 Winter Games was worth $1.27

billion. In England, a £250 million five-year contract from satellite television caused the old Football League to break apart, with the formation of a Premier league of élite clubs, in 1992.

For any sport to compete internationally, it needs money. So to that extent, the new money from television is good news. But there is a price: not every area of sport will have money showered upon it. Television wants entertainment, and it wants stars. Second-rate clubs and players do not command high viewing figures, which puts an onus on the sporting bodies to keep the stars of their sport in front of the public. They cannot afford to lose them. As a result, however dreadful the behaviour of an individual, or a team, or its fans, those people who control sport never take sufficiently effective measures to prevent the offence from being committed again. Their language and their code have not officially been revised since the sports were established. But modern governing bodies show themselves again and again to be supine – like the old-time entertainers that they resemble, their motto is 'the show must go on'. Perhaps it must. But it would be better to admit that the ethos which rules sport is now one of obsessive, selfish individualism rather than self-control, courtesy and sportsmanship. Then there need be no embarrassment about stars such as John McEnroe, whose tennis and even tantrums were too much enjoyed by spectators to be lost to Wimbledon. After his immortal 'pits of the world' outburst, the All England Club withheld his honorary membership and fined him all of £750, but within a year he was an honorary member again! The behaviour of stars is emulated at the lower levels of sport, with the variation that there, with virtually no sanctions that can be imposed against them, players feel freer to abuse and even attack the people supposed to be ensuring fair play. In English football, there is a shortage of referees. 'Local refs are getting assaulted and abused,' the Barnsley referee Stephen Lodge told the *Independent* in December 1995. 'It is hard to attract them into the game. Policemen and schoolteachers are finding it hard to get respect, never mind a young lad in black.'

It would be wrong only to lament sport's new place in the entertainment industry, but let us acknowledge that no continuity exists between the old notion of sport and what we now call sport. It is striking how few sports personalities other than the veteran Sir Bobby Charlton have received knighthoods under Mr Major's newly democratic honours system. We should accept that an Ian Botham, keeping us all amused by the stories about women and drugs that surrounded his foreign tours, is the equivalent of Bruce Forsyth or Michael Barrymore. It is only when one tries to resurrect the image of the sporting hero, admired and beloved by the whole nation, that one's imagination falters. There are Gary Lineker, Sebastian Coe and Jonathan Edwards – I can think of few others. We live in an age averse to heroes, and not only in sport.

It is a funny kind of entertainment. Sport retains its moments of good humour, emblemised by the habit of streaking which has become part of the British system. Of itself, it is not terribly witty or original to see a nude person dashing across a sports ground, trying to evade capture by the police. (One would hardly give such exhibitionism a second glance on a Mediterranean beach, for example.) Its absurdity appeals only as a foil to the seriousness of the sport that is being disrupted. On the whole, sport on television serves only to remind viewers of aspects of society that most would prefer not to recall. Britain has an unenviable reputation as the cradle of football hooliganism, but its repulsive manifestations do not shame the game's authorities, or the government, into withdrawing voluntarily from overseas competition until the boil has been lanced. English teams were expelled from European competition for five years following the riot by English fans in Belgium's Heysel stadium, which left many rival fans dead; but the FA's agitation to have England readmitted before the end of that ban gave the impression that their prime concern was the interest of their members, not the reputation of England abroad. After every example of misbehaviour by English fans, apologists for the sport blame the police in the home country for not responding quickly enough to prevent violence.

It is poignant to read accounts by George Orwell and others of the behaviour of English crowds fifty years ago. Orderliness was a national characteristic; we queued at bus-stops. It only became necessary to segregate fans of opposing teams at football matches in the 1960s. Now it is difficult not to conclude with the Irish journalist Eamon Dunphy, writing in the *Independent* after English hooligans forced an international match in Dublin to be abandoned in February 1995: 'This nation has lost is identity, dark forces have been unleashed, most visibly on Saturday afternoons when the masses come out to play.' The thugs who wreaked this havoc might once have found more acceptable outlets for their aggression – fighting wars or conquering remote territories in the Empire. Now that Britain's place in the world has shrunk, along with it her armed forces, such opportunities are denied them. For these half-educated, criminally violent individuals, football has taken the place of patriotism, some of whose trappings they borrow. Bitter with inarticulate resentment of Britain's decline, they vent their frustration by attacking foreigners. Their anger is made worse by evidence that decline as a power has been mirrored by a decline in sport. The respective British teams' showing in the 1996 Atlanta Olympics showed that decline to have been more drastic than most people had thought – though the vulgarity of those Games would have made success a questionable honour.

There is no denying the prestige that sporting success still lends to a nation. A big football match, such as the England–Germany Euro 96 semi-final, may be watched by nearly everybody in the country: a rare thing given the plurality of choice in television viewing. Nevertheless, we should recognise that the world has changed irreconcilably from the era when sportsmen felt that honour alone was enough to make them play for their country. Sport is now a business (some would call it a racket). It is difficult to see the justification in spending £100 million on an Academy of Sport as opposed, say, to an 'Academy of Ship-Building' or an 'Academy of Vacuum-Cleaner Salesmen'. Acknowledging that sport is just a branch of the entertainment industry might have advantages. At the European level, the government could then ensure that our partners' sporting efforts were not being subsidised to the detriment of our own: the metaphor of the level playing-field would never have been invoked more appropriately.

It is a striking truth that those sports at which Britain excels are also those that receive least official subsidy: these include polo, rowing and pistol-shooting. The day after England's defeat against Germany in Euro 96, I watched the final day of the world Etchells championship at Cowes. Etchells are a class of boat which has long been popular in Australia and the United States, but has only recently gained a following in this country. It is favoured because each boat competing is the same: there is no opportunity for rich sailors to spend a fortune on technological improvements that will give them an advantage. It is the best sailor who wins. On this occasion, in a thrilling race, the winner was Adam Gosling, an Englishman.

This was a remarkable achievement. There was no crowd trouble. Beyond a couple of launches and the new gin-palace owned by Mr Gosling's father, a car-park tycoon, there was no crowd. The men's shop Hackett sponsored the event, in a modest way. But no prize money was offered. It was a perfect English occasion, which received little more than a few paragraphs in the newspapers and no national coverage on television.

The Etchells race was fiercely competitive; in an age which has so little regard for excellence in other areas, at least in sport it remains highly regarded. The result was a British triumph. But John Major's proposed Sports Academy will not just foster competition and the urge to excel. With it will go the aggression characterised by the advertisements run by the sports manufacturer Nike during the 1996 Olympics and European Football Championships. These portrayed the athletic ideal as being not just to achieve a personal victory, but in the process to annihilate one's opponents. Posters for the Championships showed Les Ferdinand (England) and David Ginola (France), both of whom play for Newcastle, under the slogan: 'Friendship expires June '96.' During the Olympics, Carl Lewis appeared with the quote: 'You don't win silver, you lose gold.' Both represent the antithesis of the old notion of sport. Surely these new values are not ones that should be promoted by the government, particularly in the context of 'heritage'.

Assumptions about sport must be challenged. Winning at athletics need not be that important to us as a country. The Prime Minister's objective should be to promote sport in the British tradition, not simply sport *at any price*. The Sports Academy will be élite and centralist. Excellence should always be valued, but the centralising mission is misplaced and a better alternative would be to spread money through schools. Traditionally the British have prided themselves on taking part in sports, not in being a nation of sports voyeurs watching superstars perform on television. This habit of participation has been challenged by the sale of sports fields by schools and the reluctance of demoralised teachers to supervise games which take place outside normal school hours.

'England's big task' – to borrow a phrase from one of the epigraphs at the opening of this chapter – is to decide what sport means to it in the twenty-first century. It is difficult to imagine that the old sporting code can be revivified, since it reflected an attitude to life that went far beyond sport. But there are other values which sport can impart. For example, the sharing of common goals in sport can help to rekindle a sense of collective identity, and this is particularly important for children. For it is in childhood that an individual's ideas of identity are established.

3

Kids Growing Older Younger

*Think what you would have been now, if instead
of being fed with Tales and old wives' fables in
childhood, you had been crammed with geography
and natural history?*
                    Lamb, in a letter to Coleridge, 1802

*The influences of the time are not favourable to
domesticity, and in our progress towards cosmopolitanism the taste for the family life which was once
supposed to be the special characteristic of England
has to a great extent been lost.*
        T. H. S. Escott, *England: Its People, Polity,
                                and Pursuits, 1879*

From time to time, all children write their address in full. They
begin with their house or flat, starting another line with the
street in the conventional way. But they do not feel it is enough
to continue only with town, county and country. In case their
letter was being delivered by a Martian, or possibly God, they
continue with United Kingdom, Europe, Planet Earth, The
Solar System, The Universe. In this way they describe circles
of belonging that expand outwards to infinity. The extended
address is, of course, a joke, which enables them to show off

their newly acquired knowledge of geography and the cosmos. But it is also a metaphor. Unknowingly, they have hit upon the fact that they are surrounded by layers of identity, constructed something like an onion. One of these layers is the nation, which comes towards the outside of the onion.

For most children the centre of the onion consists of parents, the immediate family, then uncles, aunts and cousins. Beyond that lie friends, school and possibly church, together with the organisations that the child may belong to such as the Scouts or Guides. As the individual gets older, so the onion grows outwards. New layers might be college, regiment, trade union, professional association and the clubs or club-like identities that are assumed as a result of particular interests, tastes or enthusiasms. Recently the Internet has begun to service the need of enthusiasts of all kinds to identify with others of the same type, albeit in cyberspace. These are not only child pornographers and other deviants; one of the biggest growth areas of the World Wide Web is fly-fishing. Equally, the gardener who is having difficulty with his parsley can broadcast his problem and receive answers from *soi-disant* parsley experts from around the country, if not the world. Rural clergymen, who live beyond easy range of bookshops, can peruse catalogues posted on the Web sites of religious publishing houses. Children themselves are a particularly active specialist group of Net users. The onion has grown to the size of the globe itself, which only increases the importance of that sense of belonging expressed as national identity.

The habit of belonging begins in childhood. It is essential to the development of character, since it is by testing ideas, by talking to others within the different layers, that the child determines the beliefs and manners of behaviour that shape who he or she is. Identifying with the country to which the child belongs reinforces other tiers of identity, which in turn contribute to it. The most frightening aspect of the development of an underclass in Britain's cities is that the young people belonging to it have few allegiances, other than to an immediate group of their peers. It is commonplace (but nonetheless true) to say that the prime cause for this is the breakdown of family, since it is through the family that most people acquire their sense of attachment to the outer layers of the onion. But it also reflects a collapse of the overlapping institutions and influences that together constitute society itself. Reading court reports of youngsters who have committed heinous crimes – the murder of little children, for example – suggests that they feel little attachment to any group beyond their friends; and their friends are similarly dispossessed. Their individualism has no constraints, and the result is anarchy.

In the face of this, calls by church leaders that morality should be taught in schools – apparently reasonable enough – hardly offer much of a solution to the crisis. Teaching morality does not mean that pupils will internalise it. But the Archbishop of Canterbury is right to ask that schools should reintroduce the practice of assembly; that at least would help to foster a sense of the group identity of the school, a small measure to counteract the tendency towards unbridled individualism. Most people do not do wrong simply because they have an abstract notion that it *is* wrong. They do not do wrong because they lack any strong desire to do wrong in the first place. The attractions of living in harmony with the different layers of society to which they subscribe outweigh the instant gratification of wrong-doing.

If England's sense of itself as a nation is disintegrating, that is partly because those other layers of identity are also breaking up. The most obvious example of collapse is the primary one of the family, where attitudes are in turmoil. The conventional image of a family as having a mother and a father is being undermined not just by the divorce rate (the highest in Europe and rising, according to *Social Trends*) and the number of children born out of wedlock (in the decade up to 1992, that figure doubled to the point where a third of all babies are now illegitimate). Some gay couples do not regard the fact that both partners are of the same sex as an insurmountable obstacle to parenthood. Recently a lesbian couple acquired a baby through the artificial insemination of one of the women with donated sperm. While it is notoriously difficult for older heterosexual couples to adopt children (despite the fact that they are more likely to be stable in their marriages and at a more affluent stage of their careers than younger couples, and may only recently have come to the knowledge that they will not have children of their own), male homosexual couples have been passed as fit foster parents by the social services. Ideas of family structure are being revised, and it is unlikely that whatever new dispensation is reached will be merely a phase.

The forces at work are too profound for an easy return to the old status quo. Structure is only one aspect of the issue; a more pervasive one is the way families of all kinds, including traditional ones, function. Family life itself is changing. Families are like schools: they establish their common identity through regularly coming together in the same place. For most families, the occasion when this is most likely to happen is at mealtimes. But only half of all families now eat together every day, and nine per cent eat together less than once a week; one in twenty families never eat together at all. As family bonds weaken, so do those of national identity; it is through the family that many of the assumptions about what it means to be English are transmitted. Conversely, it could be argued that the decline of identity in families makes national identity all the more important, because it encourages a sense of belonging among children who have little else to belong to.

The consequences of alienation – the absence of any sense of belonging – among young people are reported almost daily in the press. Indeed, both the results and the causes are a cliché of modern journalism. Crime is the most obvious manifestation of the malaise; society is frustrated by its inability to act effectively against persistent criminals who commit unpleasantly grown-up offences, yet by age remain only children. Of equal concern should be the view of child psychiatrists who say that the disturbed children whom they are seeing are more desperate in their actions and mental state than would have been the case twenty years ago. Respectable parents are anxious to erect barriers between their offspring and the delinquency that they fear as endemic among modern youth. Surveys suggest that most parents believe the childhood available to the present generation is worse than their own. Children themselves tend to hold fiercely libertarian views, believing in the right of individuals to determine their own styles of life. This adds to parental anxiety about preserving them from the consequences of their own possible fecklessness, which might extend to drug-taking and unprotected sex. Then there are the horrifying risks of random attack and abduction which seem to be part and parcel of modern life. Parents are right to worry.

Ultimately, though, much of the responsibility for the values held by children must lie with the people by whom such values are transmitted: parents. Often the parents grew up in the 1960s and 1970s, when all symbols of authority were being challenged and patriotism seemed unacceptably naïve and old-fashioned. What was a struggle to the 'Flower Power' generation has become the norm to their children, who take the right to pursue whatever way of life they please as absolute. They have little instinctive pride in the country that they belong to, because their parents' generation has done so much to demythologise the institutions of which it is made. This is self-evident in the case of the pillars that the protest society of the 1960s sought to pull down: the police, the law, the Establishment. But on the whole, children have little more than generalised notions of national structures, and they are more likely to be aware of schools, sports clubs, charities, newspapers and the like – a layer of belonging closer to the centre of the onion. Once it was taken for granted that their identity would be embodied partly through a sense of their own history; these days historical associations are played down and, far from being a source of pride, they are regarded as something of a handicap. It is assumed that history will repel young people, not entrance them.

Since it was the parental generation which created the culture of anything-goes, they cannot be surprised if anything goes for their children, too. But life was easier in the parents' time, when the older generation had a firm set of values to rebel against. Now young people are in a position similar to the Maoist Cultural Revolution, in which the process of revolution must be ceaselessly renewed without any clear idea of the goals it is supposed to achieve. It is tough being a rebel without authority figures to overthrow.

*　　*　　*

One of the areas in which Britain continues to excel is pop music. Any area of national success must be a source of pride, I suppose, but one does not have to be a raging fogey to see that the pop culture so forcefully projected by the music does not help to instil a sense of national identity among its listeners. The message is anarchic. The music celebrates the emotional intensity of the individual; it preaches hedonism, mixed sometimes with violence. Not much to encourage shared values there.

There are some who believe that pop culture is responsible for having driven a wedge between the generations. It is not, of course, merely a question of the music itself, much of which is not very different from the music that the parents themselves still listen to (given the longevity of some rock stars, it might be exactly the same). Rather, it is the values of the culture that perpetuate the gulf of understanding between children and parents. For centuries, the influences that bore down on childhood all encouraged the young person to emulate his or her parents. The object of childhood was presented as becoming an adult. Pop culture continues to be anti-Establishment, and that means anti-parent. The object of childhood, or at least adolescence, now is to stay young for as long as possible. Entry into the adult world is shown to be undesirable: a kind of sell-out, a rite of passage that the young are exhorted to postpone. Their own idols (or perhaps those of a previous generation) steadfastly present themselves to their public as eternal rebels. Recently the pursuit of self-destructive excess has been chronicled by the super-groupie Pamela des Barres in *Rock Bottom: Dark Moments in Music Babylon.* Not everyone in rock overdoes it to the extent of a Jim Morrison, a Jimi Hendrix or a Janis Joplin; but they like to give the impression that they do. And some of them, like Mick Jagger and others, rock on into their fifties, adopting the same posture (literally and metaphorically) as they would have done in their teens or twenties. From their public personae, one would have little idea that in private they live in cirumstances of extreme luxury, often enjoying rather conventional tastes in old furniture and large country houses. Their stage image remains radical.

Anyone who, like me, does not care much for the pop culture

will be tempted by that argument. Perhaps it is founded on ignorance. But one does not have to be a reader of the tabloid press to find plenty in daily life that seems to support it. Certainly this is true of the hype that, in the spring of 1996, surrounded the American film *Kids*, which presents an apparently realistic portrayal of two thirteen-year-old New York skateboarders, one obsessed with deflowering virgins and the other with drugging himself into stupefaction. It caused something of a frisson at the time. But what to me seemed really shocking was that the director of the film, Larry Clark, with his back-to-front baseball cap and ponytail, appears to inhabit the same world. (At least, so one would gather from his depiction in an interview in *Time Out*.) He had the idea for the film while learning to skateboard with his nine-year-old son in Manhattan's Washington Square.

Clark would seem to have postponed growing up indefinitely. To nearly everyone else, the time does come when they must enter adulthood, usually when they get their first job. But having spent their lives resisting the responsibilities of growing up, they are not equipped for them. This extends across the whole range of adult experience; it can almost certainly be associated with the one-in-three frequency with which marriages now end in divorce.

The divide between adult and child is particularly severe in Britain, given that on average people here work longer hours than in any other European country. Also, it is common to find both partners in a marriage working, even when the mother is bringing up the children, which means that even the parents of prosperous families may not have more time to spend with their children than those who are considerably worse off. Moreover, for that time that they can give to them, they may be exhausted. In this, the computer age, allowing more work to be done at home may have been only a partial liberation. In theory, it should allow people to save time by not having to spend so much of it commuting to the office. In practice, the fear of losing a job or promotion through leaving their desk empty (anyone out of the office is assumed by superiors to be on holiday) causes them to stay in the office longer than they need, and then do more work at home. Consequently the division between home and office becomes more and more blurred; this can be seen even in some domestic furniture design which would look more appropriate in an office. All too often in this struggle it is the office that wins.

Ours is not the first era in which the collapse of family and society have been predicted. In 1823, Lord Shaftesbury was forced to conclude that 'domestic life and domestic discipline must soon be at an end; society will consist of individuals no longer grouped into families, so early is the separation of husband and wife, of parents and children'. At the turn of the century, social commentators expressed similar concerns about the development of an underclass to our own. Poverty, which campaigners so often couple with other social ills, bit far deeper in the 1930s than it does today. Over the last twenty years, average incomes have risen after inflation by 174 per cent, according to the Office of National Statistics. Contrary to perception, rates of crime committed by children have fallen since the mid-1980s. As for crimes committed against children, more children are being abducted, but largely by over-affectionate divorced parents rather than perverts. Even church attendance by children seems not to have fallen since 1979. According to a survey by the *Independent* newspaper, most children wanted to enjoy the same level of material lifestyle as their parents: a sign of the extent to which Britain has become middle class. It may be a small consolation to remember that the state of British schools has reached nothing like the level of violence and lawlessness of some of those in America, where pupils queue each morning to go through an airport-style metal detector which the authorities hope will prevent guns being taken into class. There is a popularly held misconception that British society invariably lags behind the American example, which it follows a decade or so later. This is sometimes true, but not inevitably so.

At least part of the reason for the inability of children to grow up in the old-fashioned way lies in their parents' neuroses. Parents are in danger of becoming over-protective. We have already seen that this denies children the freedom to roam over the countryside, exploring at will; this in turn cuts them off from a rich source of the imagery of Englishness. Worries about road safety have also forced more parents to take their children to school by car, thereby increasing the volume of road traffic that was the cause of the problem in the first place. The number of children allowed to walk or bicycle to school has fallen dramatically. There could hardly be a greater condemnation of the way in which society organises itself. Children have become like family pets, living in conditions of comfort but denied the liberty through which they can develop and express their personalities. Strapped into the car, they are unable to run about or climb trees, and do not get as much physical exercise as they should. In the 8 March 1997 issue of the *British Medical Journal*, the Institute of Child Health at the University of London published the result of research into injuries sustained by children as a result of traffic accidents. It concluded that, with fewer children walking and bicycling, accidents on the road had decreased between 1985 and 1992. But it warned:

> While declines in children's walking and cycling may reduce traffic-related deaths, they can otherwise adversely affect child health. Reduced cycling and walking have undoubtedly contributed to declines in overall physical activity, a cause of increasing obesity in British children, and potentially of increased obesity in adulthood with its associated risk of chronic disease and death. The curtailment of independent mobility may also have important adverse effects on children's mental, physical, and emotional development.

In other words, society may have succeeded in reducing road deaths among children, but only at the expense of their general health, both as children and as adults. Of course, parents' desire to protect children from the dangers of the world is entirely understandable: the pity is only that it should felt to be so necessary. But perhaps it would be better if the risks were more equally balanced by a sense of the positive benefits that freedom to explore brings. One might speculate that the tendency for couples to have children later, perhaps after some difficulty conceiving, has inclined to exaggerate the protective instinct.

Growing up should be a continuum, but has become a discontinuity. One of the aspects of adulthood that children do not naturally learn to absorb is what it means to belong to their nation. Parents themselves have lost their certainty about what it means to be British – and children would reject their view of it anyway – which makes it particularly important that schools should hold the transmission of a sense of national identity as a primary object. The discipline into which this naturally falls is history.

The idea that history teachers should be charged with transmitting national identity is not one received with universal enthusiasm by the teachers themselves; many of them have legitimate doubts about what national identity might mean in this context. It is a fluid concept, and a different pattern can be discerned beneath the waters depending upon the personal history of the individual looking at it. Nevertheless, it is easy to agree upon the essence of it: namely, that certain events in British history are communicated to all school-children, giving them a store of knowledge about significant moments of the nation's past which is shared by everyone. These should include the Battle of Hastings, the Dissolution of the Monasteries, the defeat of the Armada, the beheading of Charles I, the Glorious Revolution, the Union with Scotland and so on. They give the structure without which much of British culture becomes a blur.

It is typical of the present drift of teaching, however, that in 1996 the most popular board for history GCSE, the Midlands Examining Group, abolished all five of its British history papers which allowed pupils to specialise in the medieval and Victorian periods and the Tudors and Stuarts. Events such as the English Civil War and Henry VIII's reign have been dropped as specialist subjects. The new emphasis is on world history after 1900; subjects include the demise of apartheid in South Africa. The Board's decision was based on a lack of interest from students; in 1996, the last year it ran, a mere 97 candidates took MEG's Tudors and Stuarts paper, compared with 52,000 for world history. Similarly, the Southern Examining Group is phasing out its two courses in Aspects of English History, 1509–1689 and 1815–1979, in favour of modern world history. Only 270 took the 1509–1689 paper.

The demise of these GCSE papers reflects a reluctance among teachers to promote knowledge of this country's past. Even if they were to do so, they would not celebrate Britain's phases of glory or its virtues as a nation, since it is their habit to deny them. In France there is no such embarrassment about French achievements. In Wales and Scotland, teaching has respectively a Welsh and Scottish cast. The English have become victims of their own over-sophistication. It is modish to regard narrative accounts of history as myths, fabricated for political ends. The teacher sees it as his or her role to help students to 'deconstruct' the myth, removing the superimposed layers of meaning designed to show the protagonist of the story in a favourable light. Nearly always, in the case of English history, the protagonist will be England or an English hero. In the present climate of relativism, every text and viewpoint is seen as having equal validity . . . except that some are more valid than others. In order to promote the foot-soldier's version of a battle, that of the great military leader must be downplayed. It is all too easy for deconstruction to replace one political overlay with another.

While the intentions of great historical figures were not all quite as splendid as they have been portrayed in the past, not all of them were as squalid as they tend to be pictured today either. On the subject of slavery, for example, modern teaching emphasises the horrors of the system and encourages children to imagine what life must have been like for the slaves. But it is inclined to disregard the achievement of William Wilberforce in leading a successful campaign, in defiance of a powerful trading interest, to abolish it. We now know that Florence Nightingale was, in her private life, an impossible character who suffered from what psychiatrists now call Munchausen syndrome. But that should not be allowed to minimise her work in the Crimea. Indeed, were it not for Florence Nightingale's labours as the 'Lady of the Lamp', who would bother with her story anyway? The debunking method – to give deconstruction a straightforward label – is all very well, but only makes sense when children have already been taught the tales that are being shown to be fallible. You cannot demythologise unless you first know the myth.

The country that gave birth to theories of deconstruction was France, but the French know how to deal with intellectual excitement: they enjoy it for what it is and do not let it interfere with their lives. So French school-teachers are not smitten with the same impulse to rubbish national achievements as those in England. The English are often accused of walking with their noses in the air, and perhaps we used to do so. These days, an agonising determination to minimise the worth of our past – a sort of self-disgust – is a more prominent characteristic. Perhaps such an attitude towards a history that is shot through with inspiring incidents of courage, enterprise and humanity helps people to live with a less than heroic present. But it is an example of decadence which we should avoid. Other nations manage to do so.

One of the reasons why GCSE boards now favour modern world history over national history is the assumption that students will be more gripped by recent events than those of a distant past. This ignores the extent to which echoes of the past continue to resonate through contemporary society: an obvious truth, of which events during the 'marching season' in Ulster serve as a constant reminder. That educators should determine syllabuses according to what children want to study is an aspect of the dominant youth culture, which makes growing up more difficult than it should be. If children study only what they want to study, the effect will be much the same as if, at a younger age, they were to eat only the foods that they like: they would be denied essential nutrients; likewise, their ability to take on new experiences, to extend their range in ways that ultimately they might find pleasurable, will be stunted. The culture in which institutions of learning seek to engage the attention of children only by giving them what they want might be called 'kiddism'. Certain national museums are conspicuous in their devotion to it. In the Natural History Museum, displays of fossils in glass cases have been superseded by halls in which young visitors are invited to push buttons and observe answers or effects flashing

70

up on video screens. These techniques are thought to be more approachable and more fun, since they replicate the kind of technology that the children play with at home.

Clearly they are fun – for a certain age group, for a limited time – as can be seen from the children rushing from machine to machine, pushing buttons at random. Whether this enables them to absorb much information about natural science is doubtful; often they are more interested in the kinetic effect than in studying what appears on the screen. But even on its own terms the method fails. It has the uncomfortable feeling of a middle-aged person trying to be hip. Yes, there are computer screens, but the experience is not nearly as enthralling for children as some of the games they play on their own computers. The funfair atmosphere denies them the opportunity of being transported outside their own world by contact with genuine exhibits from prehistory. Not all children would be thrilled by them; some, however, might be captivated by evidence of such enormous antiquity. At least fossils and the like are proper museum exhibits. They are immutable objects which do not change according to theory, though different theories may revolve around them. Push-button and flashing-light displays are not irrefutable facts. They present only the currently fashionable interpretation of how our world developed. They may appear to put 'kids' centre stage, but it is the adults who write the script.

It is part of 'kiddism' to assume that children do not care about what is English and what is not, which almost certainly misreads the children's own instincts. Most children long to identify with groups. They want to see their team, school or form win; they want to believe that the place where they live is better than neighbouring places; they like to boo villains at the pantomime, and they want to cheer for their country. It is perverse that adults should not always encourage them to do so.

'Kiddism' plays only to the modern image of childhood, as a period of electronic escapism. The traditional idea that childhood is the time which young people have to explore, play in the open air and learn a degree of independence has no part in it. Roaming the countryside develops a sense of place and therefore a sense of identity. It is associated with a wealth of children's literature celebrating Britain's Mr Toads, Peter Rabbits, Eeyores and other animals, in an idealised landscape. That literature, more than anything else, transmits a sense of Englishness which is all the more powerful for its overlay of childhood innocence. Many thoughtful parents would like to replicate for their children, at least for part of the time, the sense of freedom conveyed in *Swallows and Amazons* and the like. Now find that they cannot do so. Their ideal is assailed on two fronts. In an increasingly competitive world, responsible parents wish to equip their progeny for the challenges ahead by helping them secure the best possible exam results. In London and elsewhere, there is fierce competition for places at primary school, and from their earliest days in class children are expected to work harder than any previous generation. Equally, the justified fears of road traffic and the statistically remoter risk of attack by paedophile or maniac have put constraints on the modern child that did not exist thirty years ago.

It could be argued that a little less exam success – or at least, exam-obsession – might not be such a bad thing. In August 1996, a survey by the international market research company Euromonitor reflected a phenomenon known in the toy industry by the initials KGOY, standing for Kids Growing Older Younger: shorthand for the tendency of modern children to speed through the gamut of toys at such a rate that they have grown out of them completely by the age of ten. It will not only be the nostalgically inclined who regret this loss of innocence. Since the age of Rousseau the Western world has come increasingly to regard childhood as a special time, which is not just because Freudian psychiatrists have explained its importance in forming later patterns of feeling and behaviour. In an age of failing religious belief, people regard the apparent purity of childhood as the last hope of a darkening world.

It is not, of course, that modern children have fewer toys than their predecessors: far from it. To make up for the lack of freedom to explore in the open air, parents are buying them more toys than ever before. But the kinds of toys that are selling best are those for solitary play, indoors. According to the survey by Euromonitor, sales of outdoor games, such as swings and climbing frames, fell by 12½ per cent in Britain between 1991 and 1995. The worry must be that the avalanche of indoor toys will produce a society even more obsessed by consumerism than the present one. Studies of teenagers already show that they are highly focused on obtaining the material rewards enjoyed by the older generation – another reason why they are determined to do well at exams.

Exam pressure plays its part in causing children to put aside childish things too early. I have heard of the parent of one toddler being told by a concerned teacher that her son could not identify Africa on a globe. After a moment's thought, the mother replied: 'But he can't even speak yet.' As a society, we do not wish to reproduce the conditions in Japan that blight schooldays to such an extent that children talk of the process of 'exam hell' (suicides are not uncommon).

Schools should be encouraged to put a little less emphasis on exams and more on the kind of self-reliant play which parents fear to provide. Not only national character but character as a whole will become increasingly important for those young people who make a success of their lives. Specialised skills may command high salaries for a time, but they can become obsolete at any moment. Adaptability and resilience will be increasingly at a premium; these are attributes of the kind of broad character formed by wide reading. The independence of thought associated with the British tradition will be particularly valued, and must be nurtured as part of national identity.

The essence of identity may not quite be drunk in with the mother's milk, but certainly soon after. Too often, mother's milk gives way to 'Mother's Pride'. The most basic cause of self-definition is food. Probably nothing has undergone such a revolution in the course of this century as British cuisine.

4

Your Beef-eating Britons

M. smiled at him indulgently. '. . . How were the cutlets?'

'Superb,' said Bond. 'I could cut them with a fork. The best English cooking is the best cooking in the world – particularly at this time of year.'
                                        Ian Fleming, *Moonraker*, 1955

The reason why English cookery was allowed to lapse into barbarism was that gradually only one article of diet was taken seriously. That is Steak. This is venerated and idealised. When an ordinary English waiter mentions any other dish, he is a realist and his very tone of voice tells you what that dish really is – muck. But when he mentions Steak, his voice is low, hushed, reverent. First, it is Steak impersonal, the great noble viand. Then, when you have been converted into giving an order, it is Steak personal, your Steak. How will you have your Steak, sir? He's just doing your Steak, now, sir. Here's your Steak, sir. It is as if he were talking about your wife. Name any other item on the menu that is discussed in this fashion. It cannot be done. We live in the empire of the Steak.
                            J. B. Priestley, *English Journey*, 1934

Nothing in England is like the rest of Europe. Everything in Albion has a special character . . .

75

Anyone for England?

Their general style of life does not resemble in any particular that of other peoples: and above all their cooking.

Giacomo Casanova, 1763

'What are these books in your kitchen?' At home in her native Scotland, this question would have struck my friend – to whom it was addressed by one of her new neighbours – as redundant: everyone expects a kitchen to contain a certain number of cookery books. But she had recently settled in a little village near Aracena, a bit more than a hour's drive north of Seville. One of the cultural differences between Glasgow and Los Marines is that, in the latter, the women do not use cookery books; in fact they do not know what they are. There, recipes are inherited from their mothers and aunts like family heirlooms. This conservatism is a cultural strength; in culinary terms, all the people living hereabouts speak the same language. Perhaps it will change: this area of Spain, near the Rio Tinto mines that were a bastion of Republicanism during the Civil War, no longer suffers the impoverishment that Franco imposed upon it. Prosperity has brought satellite television. But as yet the villagers, for all that they are Mediterranean, have not acquired the taste for drizzling virgin olive oil over sun-dried tomatoes. They do not care to experiment. What they have they know, and what they know is good.

In Britain, it is a long time since we ate the kumquat of innocence and fell from that state of culinary grace represented by security within a native tradition. The other day I stopped at a Hampshire pub. It was typical of the revolution in the ordinary pub menu that has been one of this country's greatest achievements of the last thirty years, albeit virtually ignored whenever the subject of British food is discussed. These days, nearly every pub in England (though not as yet Wales, Scotland or Ireland) serves more than the stale pork pies and curling sandwiches which were standard fare twenty years ago.

The drink-driving laws gave publicans a financial incentive by discouraging the consumption of alcohol; the loss of profit on drink is now made up through the serving of meals. At the same time, the microwave provided the technology for this revolution by simplifying preparation and reducing costs. The microwave also makes it possible to offer a bewildering variety of dishes simultaneously. Their inspiration is nothing short of global. In Hampshire, the dish of the day was Mexican pork; ploughman's lunch came with chorizo (appropriate only if the ploughman was called Miguel, one might have thought); and the blackboard showed that Sunday lunch was served with a vegetable called kabosha squash. Nowadays, 'Old English Fare' is more likely to mean lasagne than Lancashire hotpot. Exoticism is to be expected of the new generation of 'gastropubs' in London, such as The Eagle on the Farringdon Road or The Anglesea Arms in Shepherd's Bush, but the remarkable thing is how far foreign dishes have come to dominate the menus of what one would have thought of as workaday pubs around Britain.

Food is one of the unifying forces in a nation. It helps to define us. The British used to have as confident a sense of their own national diet as the Andalusians. They knew its weaknesses: cynics might say that its defining characteristic was its awfulness. But the British could also, rightly, be robust about its strengths. 'Rarely out of England is a first-rate broiled chop to be obtained,' opined a Victorian writer. But neither strengths nor weaknesses are as important in this context as the fact that people knew what it was. It is typical of the present state of Britain that we should have so embraced foreign ways of doing things, convinced that they are better than our own, that the native tradition has become all but submerged.

It used to be an article of faith that British meat was better than that of less favoured lands, a belief which in the 1990s has undergone trial by ordeal as a result of the BSE scare. Nevertheless, the combination of climate and geography that gives us an advantage in animal husbandry has not changed. Even foreigners – particularly foreigners – will agree that these islands are blessed with rain. Of late we have been a little profligate with the use that we made of the consequent water in aquifers and reservoirs, but we still have rain in plenty. Wales and Scotland may rejoice even more in this dispensation of providence than England. Because of the rain, combined with fertile soils, we have an abundance of sweet grass. Consequently, the best of our lamb and prime beef are of a quality to provoke envy in the hearts of farmers whose land has not been so naturally blessed. Sometimes this envy breaks above the surface, or so it would seem when French farmers burn lorry-loads of British lamb.

So the British have good meat, and traditionally those who were able to afford to ate it in quantity. In the 1660s the French traveller and friend of Hobbes, Samuel Sorbière, in *A Voyage to England*, found that the tables of noblemen who did not keep French cooks were laden with little else except meat. Thirty years later another Frenchman, Misson de Valbourg, observed a custom which continued until living memory: 'It is a common practice, even among people of good substance, to have a huge piece of roast beef on Sundays, of which they stuff till they can swallow no more, and eat the rest cold the other days of the week.' In the eighteenth century, we prided ourselves on our carnivorous appetites, attributing to them most of our national achievements, particularly at arms. In the Victorian age, the paterfamilias who did not know how to wield a carving knife and fork with dexterity was regarded as a poor specimen. 'Meat, meat, meat, and no alleviation,' was how the American journalist Price Collier, writing *England and the English*, characterised English cooking in 1909. 'The vegetables are few, and even they, as Heine – how Heine must have suffered in England – phrased it, "are boiled in water, and then put upon the table just as God made them!".' This partiality to meat was given fresh impetus – ironically just at the time when the era of gargantuan trenchermen was in decline – by the advent of refrigerated ships which made possible the importation of meat from the Commonwealth – particularly lamb from New Zealand – at prices that now seem unbelievably low. For carnivores, it was a golden age.

The quality and cheapness of our meat was reflected in the national cuisine. Its greatest strength is the roast, served relatively plain except for such uniquely British accompaniments as Yorkshire pudding or mint sauce. The British middle classes were lucky in the abundance of meat, and could afford the best cuts. Their counterparts in France ate parts of the animal that never would have crossed the plate of a Briton in easy circumstances – they were confined to the unknown diet of the very poor. The French also consumed such unspeakables as snails and frogs and, consequently, they needed sauces and other elaborate techniques of preparation to conceal the vile character of the principal ingredients. Not so the British, where plainness was their glory. History has not much rewarded us for it. Over the years the national aversion to culinary adornment has caused some foreigners to mock British cuisine. The fact that the British themselves have adopted the word 'cuisine' reveals an assumption that the English language lacks expressiveness in matters culinary. Equally, it is an undeniable truth that Britain has little tradition of great restaurants. On the other hand, traditionalists believe that the best food has always been eaten either in people's homes or in certain clubs: only there, generally, can one find such incomparable delicacies as roast grouse served with breadcrumbs and fried bread, along with all the other game birds from wild duck to widgeon. Game, as it happens, is relatively unregarded in the market-place and remains surprisingly cheap, even in those supermarkets which think it worth-while stocking it.

But a food culture that depended upon excellence of produce, particularly meat, available at lower prices than would have been the case in other European countries, was clearly vulnerable when British prices rose in line with those elsewhere in Europe. Joining the Common Market, as it was then called, was a disaster for British cuisine. Suddenly, prime cuts of meat became the luxury that they already were in neighbouring countries. Rather than pay more, many people made do with poorer quality, without the skills necessary to elevate these second-rate ingredients through culinary art.

That is not all. Supporters of the indigenous cuisine might well think that fate had conspired against it. Elizabeth David first opened British eyes to the delights of French cooking in the 1950s; for a while, the only dish served at London dinner parties was coq au vin. The years that followed Britain's entry into the EEC, paradoxically, saw its taste-buds tantalised by produce and styles of cooking from all over the world. The proliferation of first Indian, then Chinese restaurants was a legacy of Empire. London's earliest Indian restaurant, off Leicester Square, opened in 1919. But there was still no more than a handful in Britain after the Second World War. In the 1960s and 1970s, their enterprising, hard-working owners established themselves in every town in the British Isles, from Stornoway to Bangor. In some places the only restaurant is Indian or Chinese – certainly it is likely to be the only one open when you want it to be. Then the 1970s saw the arrival of American fast-food chains, such as McDonald's and Kentucky Fried Chicken.

Formerly, the English staple had been the fish-and-chip shop. Fish and chips are, indeed, identified with this country through-out the world. Ten years ago I sat in the library of a celebrated historical society in Massachusetts, distracted from my manu-scripts by listening to the two genteel voluntary librarians as they planned a visit to London. Much excitement followed the discovery, in some guidebook, of a fish-and-chip shop (as it happened, just around the corner from where I then lived). In that learned setting, far away from home, I had hardly expected to hear talk of fish and chips. But again, at a time of increased competition, fate threw obstacles in the way of the chippy success. First, urban renewal destroyed the old intimacy between proprietor and customer. Traditionally, in the north of England, fish-and-chip shops operated from the front rooms of terraced houses, as a sideline for the wife while the husband was at work. With the comprehensive redevelopment of the 1960s and 1970s, these informal outlets were swept away: five or six little shops would be replaced by a single big one, in a new precinct. Customers remained loyal to the product, but perhaps their resilience had been weakened in advance of the sea change, so to speak, that overcame this market when the price of fish rose. Overfishing had depleted the North Sea, cod was becoming almost as expensive as some luxury foods. Then in 1984 Nigel Lawson, as Chancellor of the Exchequer, decided that indeed it was a luxury, and the ailing fish-and-chip industry was made subject to VAT. According to experts, this spelled the demise of mushy peas; this traditional accompaniment cost about the same as the new tax, and people stopped buying them. Often the place of fish-and-chip shops was taken by Mexican or pizza establishments – sometimes, ironically, by sushi bars. One craze for an exotic fast foodstuff follows another.

It could be argued that, say, a doner kebab outlet in the Earls Court Road bears only a passing resemblance to authentic Turkish cuisine. Certainly, anyone who has visited China will realise that Chinese restaurants in England are a hollow echo of the real thing; they have even taken on obviously native characteristics, and some sell fish and chips. In other words, they themselves have become, to some extent, the new vernacular – only it is a more cosmopolitan vernacular, as regards eating out, than of old. There is some truth in this; besides, it is inevitable that people should now thirst after different types of cuisine, given the freedom with which they travel to far-flung places on holiday. It is difficult to lament the decline of fish and chips when the product so often fails to satisfy the principal requirements of good food: that is, to be tasty and health-giving.

What should be of more concern is evidence that British consumers are losing touch with the superb ingredients for cooking available from their own country. For a nation that once prided itself on its agriculture, it is extraordinary that we should have a £6 billion trade imbalance in food with the rest of the world. Some of this is caused by imports from other northern European countries, such as Holland and Denmark, who grow much the same things that we do – they just market them better. But another part of the deficit is the result of our appetite for year-round delicacies, flown in from every quarter of the globe. It is depressing to think of the resources being squandered as mange-tout from Kenya and asparagus from Peru are flown to us from around the world. Supermarkets have not heard of the seasons. Often out-of-season produce, such as strawberries, is greatly inferior to the home-grown version eaten at the right time of year. More fool the consumer. The pity is that such a cornucopia of foreign produce seems to have driven out of the public mind an intimate knowledge of the food that we grow best here. Recently, there has been a modest revival in the sales of speciality English apples, produced in smaller quantities than cotton-wool rivals such as the infamous French Golden. But 2p for every pound of English apples sold goes towards the sticker that names its type; without this, the check-out girls would be unable to make the correct identification. One wonders whether they would have this difficulty with, say, kiwi fruit. In 1997 the Ministry of Agriculture revealed that bananas have replaced apples as the nation's most popular fresh fruit.

In some areas of gastronomy, the cosmopolitanism of the English market is a blessing, if not a miracle. The range and sometimes quality of wine available in supermarkets is astonishing, while any half-way decent high-street off-licence offers wine from a dozen different countries. By contrast, the selection available in the French equivalent, selling mostly wine of the region, is meagre. Though the value, if not quality, of the wine actually made here is ambiguous, England can claim to be the wine capital of the world. As a trading nation, we have always been open to foreign influences and foreign produce. In the present global market, however, the bewildering variety of geographical sources is apt to deprive English food of a specific identity. (It can no longer even be assumed to be awful.)

That a section of the public yearns after an indigenous cuisine has been recognised in various quarters. It is noticeable that the 'super chef' now fulfils the role that the photographer did in the 1960s, the hairdresser in the 1970s and the bond-dealer in the 1980s: cooking is now the number-one glamour occupation, at least for men. (An intriguing contrast to the feminine equivalent: the self-denying, matchstick-thin supermodel.) These stars of the English kitchen are receiving international recognition, even from France, and the Michelin guide has started to scatter rosettes like petals on an autumn lawn. Most Michelin-rosetted restaurants in England serve variations on English or regional dishes such as bangers and mash, stuffed chine (shoulder of pork) and black pudding. Perhaps such fancy versions of what were otherwise humble dishes may help to reinvigorate a tradition of everyday cooking that is on its last legs. On the other hand, they may be of little wider application than a Mozart variation on 'Three Blind Mice': amazing, but not very relevant to the nursery.

There has in recent years been a striking revival in the availability of British produce. In the 1960s and 1970s, small shops fell victim to the first wave of big supermarkets. Then supermarkets inside towns succumbed to the superstores being built on the outskirts; these offered convenience for the car driver, and in some areas an improvement in quality. Now, though, surveys suggest that consumers prefer shopping in high streets. Shopping itself has become a leisure activity, and there is little pleasure to be extracted from pushing a trolley along the aisles of an overlit warehouse. Those speciality shops which survived the retailing revolution are now doing well. There are some aspects of food that even the ritziest superstores have not managed to get right: for example, fish, cheese and anything that requires individual preparation by the shop-assistant. I am well aware of the appeal of the alternative shopping experience – by chance, I happen to live in a street which has an extraordinary concentration of specialist food shops. They are here because part of the street contains an open-air market, mostly for vegetables, and the kind of people who frequent it also like the rest of their shopping to have an old-fashioned character. Parking is free on Saturdays, but such is the popularity of this street that it is rare that you can find a place; for most of its length, cars are double-parked. Some of the best shops are Italian or Spanish, but there is an exceptional cheese shop, a fishmonger whose family have been there since the eighteenth century, and a butcher selling organic meat.

Nothing, of course, stays the same. It would be pointless to imagine that the goods sold in these shops are the same as those on offer one hundred years ago, or even thirty years ago. One would not want them to be. It is sad that the fishmonger cannot sell kippers that flop off the side of the plate, as they used to once: the herrings do not come that big any more. But there have also been gains. Thanks to the efforts of one or two pioneering shopkeepers in the 1980s, such as the Neal's Yard Dairy in London, the last small producers of the cheese 'territorials' – Stilton, Cheddar, Cheshire, Double Gloucester, Lancashire and Caerphilly – were rescued, often from the brink of closure, and now have dedicated markets. The more adventurous supermarket chains, having tried in vain to force them to alter their production methods to make cheeses that could be pre-cut and cellophane-wrapped, are now trying to devise means of stocking them. They have not done so yet, and among cheese connoisseurs there is a suspicion that they are less interested in supporting small producers than in being seen to stock a quality range. Quality no longer exclusively means traditional. The last decade or so has witnessed an extraordinary boom among what might be called boutique cheesemakers, many of whom are middle-class escapees from the city. Their success has been in signal contrast to the government's one attempt, through the old Milk Marketing Board, to expand the range of British cheese: the now defunct, little-lamented Lymeswold (easily lampooned as Slime's Mould). Typically the official aim, bolstered no doubt by a realm of market research, was to produce something for the mass market which, while not actively offensive to most people, did not seem specially pleasant to them either. What the experience shows is that they should have gone for quality and individuality – but whenever did a government-sponsored body think of that?

The products of the boutique cheesemakers are part of the movement being called 'modern British' food that has become evident in the last couple of years. They espouse traditional values as regards quality of ingredients and scale of production, but what they make is an invention. This is also true of some of the breweries now making traditional beer – or rather, beer in the traditional style – following the triumphantly successful Campaign for Real Ale, now over twenty-five years old. Every year between fifty and a hundred new small breweries open. There is still nothing like the diversity that existed a century ago, but the situation is infinitely better than could ever have been predicted in the 1960s, when big breweries were buying up and closing their smaller brethren, and supplanting traditional bitter with the gaseous, easy-to-look-after swill in kegs.

'Modern British' food is all very well: more than that, some of it is very good. But one would not want Britain's identity in matters of food to depend solely on boutique producers.

Traditional producers labour here in the face of obstacles that do not confront them to the same extent in other countries. The first is distribution and marketing. Of all countries in Europe, Britain depends most upon supermarkets and superstores for the purchase of food. They are owned by large chains, and large chains centralise. Recently some of these chains, responding to press criticism, have begun to explore ways of introducing greater regional variety into their stores. Previously, they rejected any product whose volume and continuity of supply could not be guaranteed, even though its quality might be higher than the equivalents they stocked. They also said that they could not cope with products that could not be put into all their stores at the same time. In other words, specialist producers could not penetrate their important outlets. However, there are now the first signs of a change of policy – the supermarkets having recognised that some of their customers – particularly the big-spending ones – are becoming increasingly sophisticated about their demands in food. Unlike the villagers of southern Spain, they are reading more cookery books. As a result, supermarkets no longer feel that they can ignore accusations of arrogance in their dismissal of anything that does not conform to their distribution system. But it is early days. So far, the results have been modest. Perhaps those people (apparently most of us) who continue to appreciate shopping in the high street should be grateful. The weakness of supermarkets allows other shops to thrive.

The second obstacle facing traditionally produced food in Britain is this country's mania for regulation, some of which was born beneath the bright full moon of the European Union. It is frightening to hear the European Commissioners address their special subjects. If you had imagined that they would use their breadth of responsibility to deliver inspiring ideas about the European destiny, you would be wrong, for their one over-riding obsession is with harmony. Harmony in other contexts is a pleasant concept, but not in this. Bringing each member state into harmony with every other, to achieve 'social and economic cohesion', is like making the Ugly Sisters' feet fit Cinderella's glass slipper. As regards food safety, harmonisation required countries in the north of Europe to adopt uniform standards that were equally applicable in the south. And, of course, vice-versa. This is why Britain, a country where bakingly hot weather is a rarity, found itself adopting regulations for refrigerating food in shops that would have been appropriate for Sicily. Except that everyone knows they would not have been implemented very rigorously in Sicily; but in Britain, despite their idiocy, they were.

Ask a Frenchman whether over-regulation is altering the character of local food production in France, and from my experience he will not understand the question. Officiousness has become an unattractive characteristic of the British. Colston Bassett, the last maker of unpasteurised Blue Stilton, ceased production of this cheese (though it continues with a pasteurised version) after the salmonella scare in the late 1980s. Although salmonella has not proved to be quite the scourge predicted, it would now be too expensive to re-equip with the plant necessary for traditional production. Traditional methods of curing ham are under attack from health inspectors who insist that the meat should rest on stainless steel rather than wood. According to Richard Woodall of Cumbria, whose family have been curing on wood for four generations, the use of stainless steel impairs the flavour. Without a special licence, it is now forbidden to send fish, such as kippers or smoked salmon, through the post. Norfolk shrimpers are being driven out of business because of regulations insisting that the equipment for sieving and cooking the shrimps on the decks of their boats is made from stainless steel, and that expensive refrigeration machinery is installed. Equally, enjoyable local variations in flavour are being ironed out of the Welsh cockling industry by diktats seeking to control the water temperature and salt content in the cooking process. Needless to say, these demands are accompanied by an insistence that the latest in cockle-boiling technology is installed.

Since the 1994 Deregulation Act, Michael Heseltine has promised to make a bonfire of red tape, with Roger Freeman appointed the minister responsible for stoking it. So far the results of the initiative have abolished some seventeenth-century statutes relating to the proofing of gun-barrels; altered the rules for registering deaths; and axed the Long Pull Order, which made it an offence for a barman to give a customer more than a pint. This campaign against bureaucracy has not, however, repealed the measures which have prevented the shop in the Northamptonshire village where my horse is kept from serving ham off the bone, or from serving home-baked cakes on any day of the week except Thursday. Perhaps he could turn his attention to those too? For those of us who used to enjoy those products on a regular basis, their disappearance has materially diminished the quality of our lives.

One way to help hard-pressed traditional producers would be to allow those of proven reputation to label their wares with a disclaimer, which should read to the effect: 'This product has been prepared to a traditional recipe but does not necessarily accord with the latest environmental health regulations.' After all, what amounts to a disclaimer appears on packets of cigarettes in the form of the government health warming: it is known that there is a risk associated with smoking tobacco, but the practice is not banned. Obviously, in the case of food, the people entitled to use the disclaimer would have to be registered as traditional producers, or else it would prove an escape clause for any dubious supplier. And equally, producers would have to be sure that the disclaimer protected them from unreasonable prosecution. But it could still provide a simple means of enabling the most saporous of British speciality foods to be enjoyed by those members of the public brave enough to take the risk of consuming them – just as their forebears have done, without ill-effects worth speaking of, for centuries.

As yet, the revival of good English food is a stratified phenom-enon, for which there is only a niche market. This is not strictly a matter of class, at least not in the most obvious way. I have been offered abysmal fare in the opulent and indisputably upper-class surroundings of country-house dining rooms. Traditionally it was regarded as bad manners to comment on the food – even to draw attention to its possible excellence. That must have reflected the sheer difficulty of producing anything at all in an antiquated kitchen, miles away from the place of consumption. The difficulty persists. But the foodie generation is dominated by a class: that of professional people living in cities. These are the kinds of people who follow modern lives, with the husband sharing many of the household duties with the wife – those, that is, which are not accomplished by the daily. Between them they have far more time for food than their equivalents in a country house, who may not be (from the woman's point of view) so liberated. The country-house wife may even relegate her responsibilities in the kitchen to a cook, with uncertain consequences. To an increasing number of young professionals, quality of food is a passion, which does not always seem to be the case with cooks.

Not all of the new foodies are young professionals: the cause having been espoused by television, it attracts adherents at every social level. But the impression that good food must be élitist is encouraged by superstar chefs who charge hundreds of pounds for a meal. It is a harsh fact of British food that, for the majority of purchasers, the only determinant is price. Why else, in the first wave of a panic about the safety of beef, were supermarket shelves cleared as soon as prices were reduced? Despite recent publicity for the organic movement, supermarkets persist in maintaining that customers will not pay a premium for the undoubted nutritional and safety benefits of organic produce – though the growers themselves say that the demand for what they sell is so high that they cannot satisfy it.

To an extent, food is a great leveller, in that we all need to eat. But in Britain we are less likely all to want to eat the same things as would be the case in most other countries in Europe. Like so many other things here, food has always had a class dimension, but the gulf between the classes in eating is becoming wider. This is partly a matter of obvious practicality: the poor cannot afford to buy the same food as the rich. As the rich have become richer in relation to the poor, so the difference in spending power has been exaggerated. Not that necessity is the only determinant, for there are very few people so poor that they are not able to make some choices. Money can be found for cigarettes, chocolate bars and drink, but nourishing food comes low in the order of priorities – reflecting an attitude that seems to be universal throughout British society. That we do not spend so much money on food as some neighbouring countries is probably as true for the rich as for the poor, though the consequences are particularly sad for the latter. The British rich can afford to spend relatively less on food than their French counterparts and still enjoy a good diet, but not the British poor; their diet of white bread, crisps and chips has little to recommend it in terms of either taste or nourishment. The divide between rich and poor has been exacerbated by the obsession with healthy eating that beset the middle classes in the 1980s. Butter vanished from the tables of the well-to-do, but remained on those of the less affluent. Almost certainly, another factor in widening the contrast in diet between the classes was the rise in the cost of food that followed Britain's entry into the Common Market in 1973.

The foodie movement shows that the public has experienced an awakening about taste, but it is depressing that the British have become so remote from the process of production. In primitive times, we used to hunt food, kill, cook; then cook only; now not even that. We shop. This is borne out by statistics showing that over the last decade the time spent shopping for food has risen, but the time spent actually cooking it has gone down.

But for a nation of shoppers – formerly shop-keepers – we are remarkably bad at the activity. As a nation, we have less concern for quality than Continental neighbours, and less interest in the origins of what we eat. A salient characteristic of British food used to be that it achieved a certain standard of quality: in a word, it was safe. The best food still is safe – but that is also the most expensive. With a public that makes few distinctions about food beyond price, a new class divide is in danger of opening up – between those who can afford safe food and those who cannot.

*   *   *

What the mad cows are telling us

Should the French dare invade us, thus armed with our poles,
We'll bang their bare ribs, make their lantern jaws ring:
For your beef-eating, beer-drinking Britons are souls
Who will shed their last blood for their country and King.

Drinking song, c. 1757

There could hardly be a greater symbol of British identity than beef. Indeed, the French know the English as *les rosbifs*, in acknowledgement of the national dish. To British patriots, the eating of beef epitomised the vigour of a yeoman people with their feet planted firmly on the soil. It could be served plain, without the sauces needed to disguise the inferior, possibly intestinal ingredients tolerated in less favoured lands. Foreigners could only salivate in envy at its quality (the consequence of so much good grass).

In William Hogarth's painting, *O the Roast Beef of Old England*, a French cook staggers beneath the weight of the side of beef which he is carrying to an English pub in Calais. It is being ogled by under-nourished French soldiers, as well as a corpulent monk. The moral is that only under the perfection of the British system can ordinary people hope to feast themselves upon the supreme viand. Impoverished, at the mercy of a greedy church, the French have no such sustaining fare. As a result, they are puny weaklings, likely to be knocked down by a puff from a British grenadier; the English, fed on beef, epitomise the manly virtues.

It was not only Hogarth who took beef to symbolise the bounty bestowed by nature on true Britons, but the cartoonist Gilray and others. The essential nobility of the meat had long been acknowledged: Charles II had knighted Sir Loin. But its more general ascendancy in culture and availability on the plate derived from the benefits of agricultural improvement in the eighteenth century. Beef was expensive. The French, still ploughing with oxen, could not afford it so often. In the arcadian landscapes created around country houses, grazing cattle symbolised plenty, peace and prosperity, amid an agricultural system created to promote their husbandry. Beef is more than a dish served roast with decreasing frequency at Sunday luncheon. It could almost be said, in a metaphysical way, that the English *are* beef.

Equally, when disaster hit the British beef industry, with increasingly dire scientific findings about the disease Bovine Spongiform Encephalopathy, the crisis was more than a localised issue, affecting an industry that few people understood. It was – and is – a paradigm of the British condition, which forced a painful examination of many deep-seated assumptions about ourselves. In April 1996 Franz Fischler, the European Agricultural Commissioner, imposed a worldwide ban on the export of British beef and beef products. Most people in Britain were horrified to discover that he was able to do so and it turned out that, strictly speaking, he was not, but the ban was soon confirmed by the whole Commission. This was the first vivid illustration of the supreme powers accorded to the European Union, in the face of which the Parliament at Westminster has been revealed as impotent.

Naturally the first (and for the press, enduring) reaction was to attack Europe for high-handedness, hypocrisy, commercial knavery and ignorance. Sublimely, after an initial hesitation checked by a price reduction, the British carried on eating beef. But as the year progressed it was impossible not to start searching the British soul. Our own sense of patriotism, our national competence, our reputation for tolerance, even that most fundamentally British quality – our respect for animal life – was called into question. All danced around the maypole of that most absolute of late-twentieth-century values: the preservation of health. It used to be said that the English disease was bad industrial relations. Now the English disease is BSE: the sickness in our cattle is the sickness of the nation.

History may yet come to regard the BSE crisis as an outbreak of mass hysteria. The Germans are thought to be especially liable to it, just as the British are known for their phlegm and the French for their arrogance. One of the striking aspects of the affair is the degree to which each nation reacted according to

91

stereotype. From the beginning, it seemed extremely unlikely that the few occurrences of Creutzfeld-Jakob disease in young people – whose possible link to BSE caused the scare – would be harbingers of an epidemic. Even now the link remains speculative. In the case of another degenerative brain disorder, Alzheimer's disease, there are known to be at least fifty variants, all of which cause the same symptoms. It may yet prove that the rogue strain of CJD, a very rare disease, is a mutation which occurred naturally and is unconnected to BSE in cattle.

It is at least conceivable that the British beef and diary industries have been punished because of something Britain has been rather good at: namely, researching CJD. There were British scientists studying this disease even before BSE appeared in cattle in the mid-1980s. Concern about BSE caused the government to fund an entire unit to investigate CJD. Before the scare, most doctors knew almost nothing about it and would have been unable to diagnose it. Since it occurred principally (if not exclusively) in old people, it was easily confused with other afflictions of late life. The rogue strain, in young people, appears on present evidence to be even rarer than the classic form; it could just be that it was spotted in Britain because scientists were especially dedicated to looking for it. In other countries, such as France, it would also have been difficult to collate information about the different cases: again, epidemiology happens to be particularly advanced in Britain. As yet, no study has been undertaken into the incidence of CJD in young people in countries other than Britain.

So there was every reason to treat the findings of the Spongi-form Encephalopathy Advisory Committee – made public by the Agriculture Minister, Douglas Hogg, and Health Secretary, Stephen Dorrell – with the caution that SEAC itself advised. Caution, however, is not a quality deemed to sell newspapers or attract television audiences. The media immediately assumed the worst, and bludgeoned the public with a scare. In April, one front page of the *Daily Telegraph*, traditionally positioned as the newspaper most sympathetic to the country interest, carried a heartrending picture of a straw-hatted young girl, Vicky Rimmer, now in a coma, whom her grandmother claims to have been struck by CJD. Since Miss Rimmer had worked in a kennel, she might not have contracted the disease (if she has it) from eating beef, but from handling fallen stock – if indeed beef was the source of infection. But because CJD can only be diagnosed by autopsy – and at the time of writing Miss Rimmer is still alive – it is as yet unknown whether she has CJD at all. The next day the *Daily Mail* stoked the flames still further by a front-page headline asking if CJD could be 'worse than Aids'. On the BBC, John Humphreys grilled Stephen Dorrell (who withstood cross-examination well) against a background montage of John Gummer attempting to feed a hamburger to his daughter Cordelia and cows being led to slaughter. The hamburger incident had been Mr Gummer's attempt to interpret SEAC's then assurances about the safety of beef for human consumption. Its use on what one would have hoped would be an impartial programme prejudiced viewers' minds, by persistently reminding them of how government and scientists had previously got it wrong.

The media love a scare; so do opposition MPs. Naturally they delight in any discomfiture that will embarrass the government, whether or not it is of the government's own making. But traditionally it was accepted that legitimate criticism should stop short of damaging the national interest. In the House of Commons, the Labour health spokesperson Harriet Harman repeatedly challenged Mr Dorrell about feeding beef to children. 'Does the Secretary of State acknowledge that public confidence on this issue is hanging by a thread?' she shrilled. It was a thread she helped to snap. The more generous of her parliamentary colleagues took the 'poor Harriet' view: 'She has been under a lot of pressure since sending her son to a selective school.' Soon the Labour Party's position on BSE was being fronted by the more considered Gavin Strang, its agriculture spokesman, though even he declared that the French acted 'prudently' in imposing a national ban before Europe took action. Perhaps Ms Harman's attack on the quality of a British product was no more than a personal error of judgement, or perhaps it reflects the general erosion of certainty about national capabilities.

It is unimaginable that a French politician would have attacked the fitness for consumption of French beef. On the contrary, in France – where the consumer was not so protected from contaminated meat as in Britain, and the number of cases of BSE is almost certainly far higher than has been officially reported – all sections of the community unite in denying that the French product is anything less than perfect. And apparently for one simple reason: it is French. Ms Harman's stance suggests that national pride is no longer second nature to the British, and this impression is confirmed by the surprisingly small degree of censure her remarks received in the press. Even in Parliament, little attempt was made to burden her with blame for precipitating the EU ban. Yet on 18 April 1996, Franz Fischler was reported as saying that he felt he had no alternative but to impose the ban, since the safety of British beef had been questioned in our own House of Commons. Of course, the public, the press and even quite a few Tory MPs felt that Ms Harman was likely to be right.

A subtext to the scare was the feeling, both in Parliament and the country, that the farmers had done too well for too long. Even farmers are aware of their own unpopularity – in fact, it would be difficult to think of a profession that is more anxious about its public image. Their dilemma is that they are constrained to build their businesses upon the bogs and marshes of the Common Agricultural Policy. For individuals who are already rich to receive immense payments from the Ministry of Agriculture for allowing their land to lie fallow – now even, in some cases, just for owning land – is not good public relations. But the farmers themselves cannot change the world in which they operate. It is a mad world – one in which the markets are rigged – but it is not a world of their making. Still, the public felt that the farmers had it coming to them, and this was probably an element in the hyping of the scare. It may reflect the uncomfortable fact that Britain has become an envious nation, in which the majority detests the success and prosperity of any individual or group. In the United States they rejoice in producing highly motivated, well-rewarded businessmen; in Britain we stigmatise them as being fat cats. Since there are relatively few people employed in agriculture in Britain, they are an easy target for hate.

Now the farmers were getting their come-uppance, and for a moment the rest of the population rubbed its hands. There was a measure of truth in the view that British farming had brought the crisis upon itself, since farmers had been responsible for the unpleasant practice of feeding ruminant animals the rendered remains of other animals, including some of their own species. But only some farmers had done so, and of these even the scientifically educated claim to have been unable to discover what the protein in the protein-enriched cake that they were buying comprised. The distinguished *Times* columnist Simon Jenkins argued against farmers receiving compensation for their plight. Perhaps he failed to consider that the farming industry is not monolithic, and that not all farmers behave in the same way. Many farmers feed their cattle nothing but grass and silage; their animals have never suffered BSE, except sometimes those bought from other farms, but they are enduring the same loss as the intensive producers who fed high-protein cake. And of course it is not only farmers who have suffered, but abattoir workers, auctioneers, haulage contractors and everyone else whose livelihood is linked to cattle. These people's businesses and jobs have been blighted by a fiat from Brussels which the government of the United Kingdom regards as unjust. The government had no option but to support the industry. When it was realised how much the crisis would cost the country – £2 billion, £3 billion, probably more – it began to be taken seriously.

One might have expected the BSE crisis to provoke a re-evaluation of Britain's food industry. Most people do not know a lot about intensive agriculture; but when it is brought to their attention, they find it instinctively unattractive. BSE did bring it to their attention; there was a flurry of newspaper articles on modern farming techniques. Perhaps this will lead more people to question the desirability of other high-tech practices whose consequences over time cannot be known. Ostensibly, though, it was not long before the public managed to put the subject from its mind. Within a few weeks, beef sales were back to 85 per cent of their level before the European ban, while political and media interest moved to the confrontation between Britain and Europe.

The opportunity to analyse the industry – to ask what kind of food the public needs – was passed over. The government began its political offensive against the European Commission, in an attempt to restore exports. It became a matter of patriotism, tinged with machismo, for public figures to eat beef on every possible occasion.

In its handling of the crisis, the government approached the issue from the perspective that Britain must be right. This consorts with an old-fashioned concept of national identity, and perhaps it is touching that the Prime Minister and his colleagues should still adhere to it, but it was woefully inadequate to the occasion. The British government had just proved themselves to be spectacularly wrong: they had persistently declared that BSE could not possibly offer a threat to human health, and now the findings of the official committee forced a revision of the official line. This in itself could have been forgiven: scientists can change their minds. However, there were two aspects to the government's predicament that make it extraordinary. First, the scientists, some of whom obviously knew the explosive nature of the material they would discuss in their meeting, did not trouble to tell the ministers of the likely outcome before the meeting took place. Second, the government was so sure of its own position that it had no contingency plan. If anyone had thought the unthinkable, they had dismissed it, whereas routine disaster planning should have told them to do otherwise.

In Europe, it scarcely mattered whether or not Britain was right in theory, when the deportment of ministers and officials showed that they were not prepared to accommodate the genuine anxieties of other countries. The Agriculture Minister, Douglas Hogg, was not a well-known figure in Brussels. It is a deficiency of the British system, in contrast to the French, that politicians can reach high office without much experience of working in the EU. Mr Hogg had no friends around the conference table; he could make no small talk. It is rumoured that the chief veterinary officer arrived at meetings of the European veterinary committee wearing a bowler hat – which signalled insularity, an indifference to convention and the opinion of others. Mr Hogg also chose to distinguish himself by his headgear: for some reason a round

Australian hat. Admirably, he continued to wear it, despite daily ridicule in the press. Stubborn independence has its place, but what the European ministers wanted to hear was that Britain would do everything possible to alleviate their fears – which was not what the hat seemed to say. A little contrition would not have been out of place.

Instead, Britain made it clear that it would do the minimum possible to allay other countries' concerns. The government viewed the matter politically, as a negotiation, hence it wanted to sacrifice – and pay compensation for – the smallest conceivable number of cattle. In the cold light of reason (and Mr Hogg is a highly rational man) there might seem no need to sacrifice any cattle at all, but from the beginning it was obvious that reason had little to do with this health scare. The foreign media had taken the lead from Britain's own. In time, wiser counsels prevailed in the British newspapers, advising caution. Furthermore, it is clear from the fact that the British public resumed eating beef that they pay scant attention to what appears in the press. In Germany, the newspapers are not regarded as a kind of entertainment but purveyors of fact. There was no incentive for editors of foreign newspapers to publish stories overturning the early hysteria. When Chancellor Kohl of Germany was served beef at No. 10 Downing Street, Germans believed he was playing Russian roulette. In Aberdeenshire, a school-teacher leading a group of children to visit a farm would not touch cows in the prime Aberdeen Angus herd because she thought CJD could be caught by contact.

The British position would have been more tenable if its record of treating BSE had been one of competence. Ministers must have known that it was not. As time went on, it became clear to anyone following the story that the Ministry for Agriculture, Fisheries and Food (MAFF) is a smugness wrapped within a complaisance, inside an indolence. This revelation was such a blow to national self-esteem that some people found it hard to accept. For years it had been a British myth that our problems in Europe in part derive from the efficiency of our own bureaucracy. Our officials are sufficiently motivated and organised to implement any legislation, however misconceived, whereas those on the Continent simply ignore it. Britain, we believed, was the place where regulations were effectively enforced, sometimes to our own detriment. If only this had been true in the case of BSE! The British beef industry would not have been brought to the point of disaster if the regulations introduced in 1988 and 1989 to stamp out BSE had been properly policed. These regulations banned mammalian protein – the ground-up carcasses of sheep and cattle – from cattle feed. Thereafter, the epidemic began a steady decline, suggesting that the correct course of action had been identified. In particular, the number of young cows affected has decreased dramatically. But in the summer of 1996 new cases of BSE were still occurring at a rate of 200 a week. Why? One reason may be that mammalian protein was not banned from the feed of poultry and pigs until 1996. Significantly, the highest number of new BSE cases in cattle occur in areas where there are also pig and poultry farms. Incredibly, it was only in 1996 that farmers were compelled to destroy old stocks of possibly contaminated feed. Evidence that measures introduced to prevent the brain, spinal column and offal of cattle from entering the food chain were not being properly observed in abattoirs further dented public confidence, both in beef and in MAFF. To introduce measures but not to police them seems cavalier to the point of lunacy, but it would appear to be a lamentable truth that human nature is as fallible in Britain as in other parts of the European Union.

Following the 1996 crisis, tests that had been under way since the late 1980s to establish whether BSE could be transmitted vertically – that is, from a mother cow to her offspring – were accelerated. Previously, word had it that preliminary results seemed to show that vertical transmission did not occur. Then came the official report revealing that, in a very small number of cases, it did. This provided another – though not complete – explanation of why BSE had not died out with the measures already taken. Since it was possible to speed up the tests in 1996, it seems regrettable that they were not hastened before. The results made a nonsense of the government's cull policy; they showed that the progeny of diseased cattle should have been slaughtered from the outset.

In sensationalist television programmes, accusations were made about cover-ups in the 1980s. Those seem far-fetched, but the evidence of incompetence is only too palpable. The implementation of the slaughter policy after April 1996 was a fiasco. MAFF is in the unusual position of representing only two industries: farming and fisheries. One of the arguments for this privileged position (there is no ministry representing the interests of, say, the gas industry, or journalism) is that agriculture is particularly complex, and it is necessary to have a specially dedicated ministry to understand it. It quickly became apparent that MAFF's understanding of it was about what one would expect from Whitehall civil servants who rarely venture outside their own fastness: hopelessly limited. During the early summer, I visited one beef farmer in Somerset who showed me no fewer than nineteen briefing papers sent him by the National Farmers Union, attempting to keep up with official pronouncements. By the end of the year that number must have approached a hundred. The farmer had recently been told that compensation would be offered for the slaughter of male calves under ten days old. Why ten days? Regulations forbid the transport of calves under seven days old, leaving only three days when slaughtering could take place. But in many areas abattoirs are not open every day of the week, therefore it simply might not have been possible for a calf born at the weekend to be slaughtered within the prescribed period. That is only a small example of the confusion surrounding the scheme. In August, there was still a backlog of 180,000 cattle waiting to be slaughtered. One problem was that the Ministry did not foresee that the big supermarkets would insist on using only abattoirs not participating in the government slaughter scheme, lest consumer confidence was damaged.

The Prime Minister appeared to operate on the principle 'Do little, then panic'. During the summer he personally took charge of the crisis, and instigated a policy of non-cooperation within Europe, designed to bully Britain's beef back on to menus around the world. Believing the universe to be ruled by logic, he had reached an extremity of frustration caused by his European partners' failure to appreciate the reason of the British approach. However, he had failed to take account of the value put on health throughout the Western world. With the decline of religion, health has become the new moral absolute. The richer the country, the less inclined its citizens are to admit that the earthly paradise can ever be invaded by disaster and disease. Germany never imported much British beef, but such is their antipathy to risk that the sales of all beef collapsed. While sales in Britain recovered, those in Germany remained depressed at about half their previous level, despite the fact that no British beef at all was on sale there. It was obvious that Germans would not allow the ban to be lifted until such time as they were certain that British beef posed absolutely no health threat whatever. This time could only come with the total elimination of BSE from the British herd. Bully as he might, John Major could not force his beef into mouths clamped shut against it. (In March 1997, discussions were underway to allow exports to resume from herds certified as never having experienced BSE. The success of even this initiative is far from certain.)

As a master of the political fix, he secured an agreement at the Florence summit of June 1996 which meant one thing on the Continent and another at home. At home it meant that a framework had been established by which, logically, British beef could be exported after a series of agreed conditions had been met. He led the Euro-sceptics in his own party to believe that something might happen by October – a ludicrous ambition, given the state of the slaughter policy. On the Continent it meant that the future of British beef exports had been left effectively to the discretion of the notoriously hostile European veterinary committee, which had been given wide powers of interpretation. Anyone who really believed that the Florence framework meant that British beef would be exported one day sooner than would otherwise have been the case was deluding himself. When, a month later, it was discovered that BSE could be passed from cow to calf, Germany – a reluctant signatory to the agreement – rushed to question its continuing validity. Powerful voices within the EU, including President of the Commission Jacques Santer, held that it would be five years before Britain could export beef again. Five years, a decade – a time-scale of that order could have been predicted from the start.

There has been skulduggery within Europe; the suspicions of the Prime Minister and his colleagues were to some extent right. The majority in Europe have acted to protect their own national interests at the expense of Britain. Their own national interests include (a) maintaining the price of beef, since sales of all beef – not just British – have suffered during the scare; and (b) keeping British beef, some of which is recognised to be excellent, out of home markets. There has also been bad faith. It is inconceivable that the level of BSE cases in France, Holland and elsewhere is as tiny as official figures indicate. Merely from the amount of tainted animal feed and the number of calves exported from Britain, it is obvious that the rate of incidence should have been much higher. If BSE really does pose a threat to human health, the EU acted shamefully slowly in imposing upon the whole of the Union the measures against BSE (removing the specified offals from slaughtered cattle) introduced by the British government in 1989. The European Union did not introduce its ban on the use of animal-derived protein in cattle feed until two years after Britain, in 1990. The EU Scientific Veterinary Committee in Brussels only announced that it would instigate a surveillance programme for BSE in all European herds in 1996. Given that, in Britain, BSE has been a notifiable disease since 1988 and farmers have been required to keep cattle records since 1990, these European measures were overdue.

The Germans and others also over-reacted; but for all that, it is impossible not to admit that they have a point. That the British herd developed BSE is a national calamity. That it has not been eradicated swiftly is a national disgrace.

Agriculture used to be an area of British expertise. In the eighteenth century, Britain was the seat of the Agricultural as well as the Industrial Revolution. Since the Second World War, it has been an astonishing success story. Our isolation during that war, when all imports ran the danger of U-boat attack, revealed the doldrums into which farming had fallen during the Depression. Successive governments determined that our survival should not again be put at risk through over-dependence upon food from overseas. They made agriculture the number one priority in the countryside; they lavished money on grants. The spirit of past agricultural reformers – Jethro Tull, Coke of Norfolk, 'Turnip' Townshend – was revived and British farming became mechanised. It was not, by and large, a sentimental activity: there was no money in hedgerows and scenery. But by its own standards – which were also those of both Conservative and Labour governments – it worked. By the 1970s the British looked down with a degree of contempt upon the Continental farmers, for whom Europe's Common Agricultural Policy had been forged. They were inefficient: little better than peasants. Like most foreigners, they were corrupt. By contrast, the British farmer was a businessman doing well in a perfectly regulated industry. Doing well was his line; he did well out of the CAP, even though every effort was made to treat our farmers, with their larger landholdings, unfairly. Ironically, it is at least arguable that one policy of the CAP – the restriction of milk production by a quota system – encouraged the practices that caused BSE, since quotas caused farmers to resort to ever-more intensive methods of production in order to maintain their profit by keeping fewer cows. But it was only in Britain that the regulations affecting the rendering of carcasses (the process by which they are made suitable for inclusion in cattle feed) changed, allowing the work to be done at a lower temperature which permitted the scrapie agent (in sheep) or BSE agent (in cattle) to survive. Since Britain has one of the most intensive agricultural systems in Europe, it was natural that, should intensive practices go wrong, they would do so here.

They *have* gone wrong: BSE should be a warning. The present crisis will shake the public's already insecure faith in high-tech farming practices – and with reason. People are right to distrust methods that they cannot understand. Most ordinary men and women, if they visited some high-tech operations – a dairy unit stocked with huge-yielding Holstein cows fed on 'rocket fuel', for example – would instinctively feel that these went against nature. The fallibility of scientists during the BSE crisis does not inspire confidence in their assertions about the irradiation of vegetables, the genetic engineering of plants and animals, and the use of extra hormones to generate ever-greater volumes of milk – all might be held to be perfectly safe today, but who knows what scientists will be saying tomorrow? In the forty years after the end of the war, British farmers were outstandingly successful in meeting the objectives set them by government (if only other British industries had been able to match their performance!). Neither government nor the Opposition have rethought those objectives to accommodate the rightful concerns of the public.

The response to BSE should have been for the British government to accept that foreign markets would be closed to us for several years. It should have used that period to re-establish the British beef industry as a synonym for excellence. MAFF is now so compromised that it should be abolished and replaced by a ministry that represents all the interests of the country-side, including those of consumers. The first object of this new ministry should be to devise and police its own scheme, guaranteeing quality in both the product and the means of production. Consumers should know, for example, that the use of antibiotics has been kept to a minimum. Part of this endeavour would be a system of labelling that gave the buyer authoritative information about the product. At present there is distrust of the premium-grade labels in supermarkets, since careful wording can bamboozle the unwary. The meat trade has not been sufficiently rigorous in maintaining the authenticity of labels such as 'Scotch beef'. The new labelling system should allow the consumer to trace the origins of his or her food, in the manner pioneered by Safeway.

We must establish a new national beef herd, providing a nucleus of BSE-free breeding stock, supervised by a British Beef Council. These should be only beef animals, without calves imported from the dairy sector. Meat from old dairy cows should be sold under a different name from prime beef. None of our competitors then could boast an industry of such guaranteed quality. Ultimately, the collapse of confidence of beef sales in France and Germany – proving that consumers there have little faith in their own farmers – should represent an opportunity for Britain. We are being made to suffer grievously for the incompetence of our officials, but from the ruins we must rebuild a system of agriculture that is acknowledged to be the safest and most humane in the world.

What has been particularly distressing about the BSE crisis is to discover that Continental consumers both understand more about food than the British, and are prepared to pay more for quality. They are closer to the production of food than the urbanised British; they also spend more time in their kitchens. Britain has never much prided itself on fine cuisine, but it has done so on wholesomeness. If it comes hard to think that such pride may have been misplaced, it comes even harder to realise that we seem to be incapable of formulating a vision to do something about it.

5

Le Style Anglais

When he walks in a waterproof white,
The children run after him so!
Calling out: 'He's come out in his night-
Gown, that crazy old Englishman, oh!'
Edward Lear, 'How Pleasant to Know Mr Lear'

(Of English society immediately after the First
World War:) *Well-born young women seemed to*
have taken for their models the cretinous little
oddities of the film world.
John Buchan, *The Dancing Floor*, 1926

The last chapter dwelt on what might be called the crisis of the
inner man (or woman): what we eat. There is less of a crisis
affecting the outer man (or woman), in respect of what we wear.
Still, it is an area where the sands constantly shift beneath our
feet, and few things are so self-defining as how a person, or a
nation, chooses to dress.

When my wife was young, she had a collection of dolls from
other countries, dressed in the costumes of those lands. Perhaps
there is still a vogue for such dolls among little girls. I doubt that
they have ever reflected the garments actually worn as a matter of
course by the compatriots of the traders selling the dolls, though

a memory of them was preserved and finery would be paraded, as it still is, for saints' days and other special celebrations. The dolls commemorated the fact that the peoples of different countries like to distinguish themselves from one another by how they look, though this is not only a matter of dress. Anyone who visits Antwerp will be aware that facial hair is as much a characteristic of modern Flanders as it was in Rubens' day: even taxi-drivers wear flaring moustaches in the style of the 'Laughing Cavalier'. Equally, there is geographical dimension to hair: purely in terms of coiffure, it would be difficult to mistake a resident of Belgrade for one of Bel Air. But most of the words in the language of appearances are provided by clothes; they offer a more flexible, varied vocabulary than moustaches or hair-dos, neither of which can be changed very frequently. One of the messages that clothes send is that of belonging. They indicate that the wearer wishes to associate himself with a certain group, or class, or generation. Above all, sometimes subliminally, they indicate the degree to which the wearer wishes to proclaim membership of that larger grouping of individuals: the nation.

These days, it is difficult to think of any developed country where people wear national dress – in the tourist doll sense – without a degree of self-consciousness, though no doubt the fact that they wear it at all, for weddings or other special occasions, has a symbolic importance that helps to remind them of their shared identity. They can all feel silly together. As it happens, however, the English have never been conspicuous for their national dress. While the Scots have their tartan kilts, the Welsh their shawls and pointed hats, and the Irish their plaids, the English are rare among the countries of the world in having no universally acknowledged folk costume. We can boast the jingling bells and flying ribbons of Morris dancers – but not everybody in England is a Morris man. There are Beefeaters, wearing a distinctive uniform, in the Tower of London; but no one outside that body of men is entitled to wear it. The same applies with the red frock-coats of Chelsea Pensioners. Probably the most enduring national stereotype is the bowler hat and rolled umbrella of the City gent – again, not a style of dress ever favoured outside a narrow band of professions, located in a specific area of England. It is also of relatively recent origin, dating from the years after the First World War when former members of the Brigade of Guards took to stockbroking. There are, of course, other regional variations: the Cornish tartan, for example. But they are not as codified or as instantly identifiable as, say, Montenegrin national dress would be in Montenegro.

While the English have no national dress, we do have some distinctive ways of dressing. Simply from her clothes, no one could mistake Her Majesty the Queen for anything other than an Englishwoman. With her twinsets, her taste for country clothes and a stout handbag invariably on her arm, she is apt to cause despair among that section of the *beau monde* which prides itself on the sophistication of its eye. They say she looks dowdy and frumpish – how typical of the British mania for self-denigration – but the great couturier Hubert de Givenchy sees the matter differently: 'She dresses like a Queen – *that* is style,' he says. Some of the traits in clothes that identify the nationality of the wearer are a matter of instinct as much as conscious choice. The English tend to prefer a softer palette of colours than that, say, of Spain, reflecting that of the English school of painting. We do not have the fierce sunshine of the Mediterranean; most people seem intuitively to feel that muted shades – the beloved eau de nil and taupe of the fashion pages – look best beneath water skies. These soft, rather washed-out colours could lose their appropriateness if the recent run of hot summers keeps up. Bright sunshine requires a vigour of colour which the British would not know how to use. It would not suit their complexions. If climate change becomes a reality – as it seems likely to – a whole aesthetic, which British people acquire by instinct, would have to be overhauled. Some people would welcome the exchange, and there would be something to be said for it. But I suspect it would engender a sense of loss.

Textile manufacturers say that, for some reason, the Germans prefer patterns which, in Britain, would look aggressive. It goes, perhaps, with their penchant for hard-edged modernism. Traditionally, the English have been more likely to fade into the background. Here the quintessential English garment must be the slurry-coloured waxed Barbour jacket. Barbour stands in a peculiarly British tradition of robust outdoor clothing, all of it in earthy hues, that stretches back to the tweeds of the Victorian era – Barbour itself was established in 1894. The tweeds may have been boldly patterned with checks and overchecks, but the colours were such that the wearer could still merge effortlessly with landscape of a Scottish glen.

In clothes, the British national character displays itself in precisely the opposite way to the French. The highest expression of French style is to be found in the elegant Parisienne, shopping in the Place Vendôme. Her English equivalent, by contrast, is not the figure who most fully epitomises the special attributes – one might say oddities – of British dress. They are not feminine, not metropolitan, not chic; they are masculine, they operate by their own laws (mostly traditional), not those of the fashion world, and they achieve their finest flowering in the country. In an age which does not much value formality, they can look awfully like uniforms: indeed, many of the people who maintain these habits of dressing served in the armed forces, where a familiarity with showy ceremonial dress goes hand in hand with an obsessive attention to detail.

The taste is deep-seated. 'In his heart of hearts every Englishman is a lover of uniforms,' wrote the perceptive German observer Karl Silex in *John Bull at Home*, published in 1931. While England has no national dress, English people have plenty of opportunity to garb themselves in distinctive clothes. Livery company dinners, courts of law, East End funerals, state openings of parliament – all require the participants to put on a show. Perhaps this love of ritual, combined with finery, explains why the cause of national dress has never got very far in these islands.

When Karl Silex said that the Englishman loved uniforms, he also meant the English woman, with, at that period, her wardrobe of 'tailor-mades'. But in the world of English clothes – at least those which are most distinctively English – women have never dominated the stage. Early this century, writers put this down to their husband's control of their finances: they were not expected to shine in the manner of their Continental counterparts, and they were not allowed the money that would have enabled them to do so. Since then, much has changed.

British women have independence; in 1988 they spent £10.5 bn on clothes, in 1995 £14.5 bn. While few, perhaps, scale the ultimate pinnacles of chic occupied by a few rich people on the Continent, a glance around the capitals of Europe shows that most dress with as much brio as those in Paris or Madrid, Bonn or Rome. There is an active British fashion industry, with London shows that emulate those in Paris and Milan; these occasions are taken increasingly seriously. But women's clothes in Britain tend to be metropolitan and international. In the London collections, it is difficult to distinguish specifically British themes. The great exception is Vivienne Westwood. Once celebrated for the rubber skirts and safety-pins of punk – itself expressing a self-hatred which seems peculiarly British, though it found resonances around the world – Ms Westwood now feasts on English fabrics and fashion history, regurgitating them in bizarre, fantastic transmogrifications of the originals, perhaps incorporating a tiny bowler hat or the knitted dress material popular at a time of textile shortages in the 1940s. Call them baroque, call them witty, call them absurd, call them crude, they must nevertheless be called deeply English, if only because Ms Westwood personifies that most celebrated of all English characteristics: eccentricity.

The whirligig of women's fashion spins too quickly for traits of national character to be observed as more than a blur. Traditionally, by contrast, men have been less mindful of fashion than clothes, and on them more thought is expended than one might imagine. Few British women have ever been internationally recognised for their style; today, even our most media-celebrated icons of femininity, such as the Princess of Wales or Liz Hurley, cannot be said to have won international acclaim for their dress sense. On the other hand, the English style of men's clothes has a worldwide following. In Britain, the tradition of the dandy is enduring. Successive Princes of Wales – the future Edward VII, Edward VIII and the present Prince Charles – have personified *le style anglais*, an idiom that has been transliterated on to the smartest streets throughout Europe and the Americas. Ralph Lauren claims that the greatest moment in his life came when he discovered the Duke of

Windsor's wardrobe, now preserved in his house in the Bois de Boulogne. Indeed, the vogue for the English style is stronger than ever. The canny men's outfitters Hackett, who have capitalised on this taste, now have shops in Paris, Madrid, Berlin and Tokyo.

If, these days, British men are sometimes thought to lack the dress sense of their French and Italian counterparts, that is only because most people tend to compare one metropolitan example with another. In the country, men rejoice in ways of dressing that are unique to these islands. Their particularity about what to wear – for example, on the hunting field – can be traced to the fact that many have served in the Army. The ceremonial of the British Army remains something that we in this country do supremely well.

In the nineteenth century, the Army both allowed and encouraged the British male's taste for peacockery: the evidence exists in those dozens of little-visited regimental museums. Military ceremonial is still something that Britain does particularly well – better, possibly, than any other country in the world. But military uniforms, like most other areas of life, have now become more codified, allowing less room for self-expression – though their wearing still inculcates an appropriate respect for self-parade. Consequently, it is in what used to be called the manly pursuits of the countryside – some with obvious associations with military values – that this urge finds its outlet. Hunting dress bears out Karl Silex's observations about uniform's: any deviation from the rules or failure to keep up appearances would incite the displeasure of the hunt committee, as dispelling some of the *braggadocio* that allows horsemen to risk their necks in pursuit of this sport. But it is nevertheless a uniform on which variations can be played. Equally, shooting men vie with each other in the extremes of tweed and check. Perhaps it is because field sports are not in themselves competitive that this degree of rivalry can be observed in dress.

It could be argued that commercialisation is tending to distort the individuality of the original – marked, if not quite by unselfconsciousness, at least by a complete disregard for the fashion pages of magazines and the windows of high-street shops. For example, now that gunmakers Holland and Holland are owned by Chanel this has possibly given a greater sharpness to the shooting clothes now sold there. On the whole, though, the clothes associated with field sports, and the way they are worn (a degree of shabbiness is thought to add patina), remain distinctively English. The same is true of other manifestations of gentlemanly attire in the country. Visit the Game Fair and observe the number of regimental ties and panama hats being worn. Recently, following the example of some American firms, some employers have issued the injunction to 'dress down on Fridays': the wearing of casual clothes, associated with home, is thought to promote bonding within the business team, and presumably Fridays were chosen as preceding the weekend. If those weekends were to be spent in the country, however, in some circumstances it would be good advice to dress up. At London dinner parties, men tend either to wear the kind of suits they might have had on at the office or, by contrast, something completely relaxed. In the country, such events are an excuse for parade: otherwise quite sober individuals sport extravagantly checked trousers (tartan, of course, in Scotland), flamboyantly frogged smoking jackets, opulently embroidered slippers – even the ultimate absurdities of Victorian-style fezes and tasselled caps are not completely unknown. Guests may have travelled long distances to reach the party, they are not inclined to let the opportunity slip by.

These conventions are worth comment because they are unique to Britain. They are not driven by the dynamics of the fashion industry; in fact, these are not the sort of men's clothes that fashion editors publish. They have much in common with the Vivienne Westwood school of the baroque and self-parody. It cannot be denied that they are a rite of what are popularly deemed the upper classes, but they are not exclusive to members of that caste: while James Knox, writing his series 'The Modern Dandy' in *Country Life*, has identified the Duke of Devonshire as one of the greatest dandies of the age, another is the boxer Chris Eubank. Here indeed is a cause for rejoicing among those who fear that something of the special savour of Britishness is evaporating from national life. That is not to say, however, that even in the country – that last redoubt of individuality in dress – life has not provoked changes to some of the apparent classics of the wardrobe. It has.

Take that quintessentially British cloth, the stalwart of a million sports jackets: Harris tweed. The story of Harris tweed encapsulates much of the social evolution of the twentieth century. Originally it was a very heavy fabric, woven by crofters in small quantities and coloured by dyes made from naturally occurring materials such as lichen. Its weight gave it a certain impermeability, and it began to enjoy a vogue among Victorian sportsmen. The trade in Harris tweed was systematised when Kenneth Mackenzie founded a business to market it in 1896. There was a legal battle over the right to use the name, and now the *appellation contrôlée* is protected by the Harris Tweed Authority, which specifies the standards that the cloth must meet if it is to be sold under the Harris Tweed trade mark (in the form of an orb). It must still be woven by crofters in their own homes. Consequently, it remains an essential ingredient of the economy of the island, which has few opportunities for employment. That is why the European Union provides 70 per cent grants towards the costs of the new type of loom which Mackenzie's regard as necessary for the modern trade.

The old looms wove the cloth to half the width of that used commercially; that did not matter so much in the days when jackets were generally made by tailors, but nowadays the cloth is nearly all sold to 'makers-up': big garment manufacturers whose products can be seen in multiple clothes shops throughout the world. This internationalism has forced another development. Gone is the palette of natural colours: the last native weaver to use them, Marion Campbell, died in 1996. Today, the global demand – Harris tweed is big in Germany and, of all places, Japan – can only be satisfied by patterns suited to the markets in which the cloth is sold. This year, Germany has gone for bold checks. Among the plain colours on display in the Mackenzie's showroom are duck-egg blue and bubble-gum pink. Clearly, the customers for whom these patterns are intended are not the sporting types who valued the tweed for its warmth and ability to withstand all weathers.

Once famous for its water-resistant hairiness, Harris tweed is now made of different mixtures of wool to achieve a softer feel. Above all, for most people – except the very poor, who cannot afford the heating bills, and the very rich, who live in country houses – the private world is a much warmer place than it used to be. They move from centrally-heated home to air-conditioned office, perhaps going between the two in a motorcar that is well insulated from the elements. They want lighter clothes. So the immensely heavy weights of the past that gave Harris tweed much of its character have gone out of production. Even the so-called standard weight accounts for only 10 per cent of the volume. Mackenzie's have found that their featherweight sells well, and they are now experimenting with a super-featherweight. The Harris Tweed Authority still insists on a certain density of thread to the square inch. But it remains to be seen whether, in its lighter weights and softer wool, this hand-made, relatively loosely woven fabric will retain its most conspicuous virtue: that it would never wear out. Tailors doubt it.

The decline of Harris tweed reflects a shift in British values. We used to be thought of as a nation who lived in the fresh air. At the turn of the century, fresh air was held to be, literally, an elixir of life, being an antidote to tuberculosis and the other ills of smog-ridden, congested cities. Now, the great fear of the middle classes is heart attack, Alzheimer's, Aids – not TB. So fresh air has been excluded from many areas of life. Pollution causes some people to regard unfiltered air as positively dangerous. Even in the countryside, there is a perception that fresh air is not as fresh as it used to be. Walk past a battery chicken shed and it is difficult not to agree. As a result, there is a hostility to exposing the person to the elements that would have puzzled our parents and grandparents. In some pockets of the country, the old values persist – neglected and out of fashion, like Roman Catholicism in the days of the Commonwealth. A tell-tale sign of their survival is the assemblage of impermeable, slime-hued garments that clutters the hallways of traditionally minded houses in rural parts, where the owners are likely still to be loyal to the ritual of the country walk.

For many people, a walk on Boxing Day used to be as much of a gesture towards tradition as attending church on Christmas Day. Even people who never otherwise walked liked to remind themselves that they were still part of the walking classes. For some, the ritual retains its potency, but observation suggests that generally it is losing it grip. It is not that walking does not take place at all – far from it. But the activity, among devotees, now has a fearsome earnestness about it. Too many people are – to borrow the phrase coined by Michael Howard about village patrols – walking with a purpose. Ramblers are politicising the activity. Despite Britain's 120,000 miles of footpaths, and the Countryside Commission's target to ensure that they are all marked and cleared by the year 2000, the principal pleasure for the fanatical rambler would seem to lie in finding paths – however little used – that are blocked. Walking has evolved from a gentle pleasure into a single-minded, rather aggressive pursuit – the change being expressed in the clothes people wear for it. In common with many other activities, it appears walking cannot be properly enjoyed when participants are dressed merely in variations, perhaps warmer, of the clothes they would wear at home. Increasingly it requires its own specialised dress, its own apparatus. The state-of-the-art walker, or rambler, does not make his determined way across the Lake District, or some other ravishing landscape, in clothes that merge with the scenery; on the contrary, his brightly coloured cagoule is intended to stand out. Walking is coming to be regarded as a junior branch of mountaineering, ideally practised by people wearing clothes designed for more testing conditions.

Really to appreciate a good walk, in the old-fashioned sense, required something of the leisurely attitude to life summed up in the art historian Joe Mordaunt Crook's *Who's Who* entry, where for recreations he simply lists 'strolling'. In the exercise culture that has grown up since the 1980s, there is no place for strolling. Exercise can, of course, be taken in many forms; in the nineteenth century almost any activity in the open air was regarded as exercise, even though it might not have been very strenuous. Nowadays, exercise carries within it an idea of exertion: it must be vigorous and single-minded, or it hardly counts. Equally, for some people exercise has become an end in itself – or rather the means through which a number of other self-referential ends (thinner thighs, a longer life) are fulfilled. In the rush of modern life, people want to get their exercise over quickly – an attitude, so inimical to that of the old-fashioned country walk, which has its origins in the United States.

The roots of the exercise obsession lie partly in the muscular Christianity particularly associated with nineteenth-century British public schools, and partly in the activities of ardent American health campaigners such as S. D. Kehoe. In 1866 this advocate of the Indian club echoed the fears of many when he warned against the deleterious effects of excessive 'mind work, by the ambitious student, the covetous and care-worn merchant, or the adventurer in political life'. The antidote was vigorous physical exercise. That prescription has become increasingly fashionable, and not only among people whose mental faculties are in danger of being over-stretched. Diana, Princess of Wales, is a conspicuous champion of the *in corpore sano*, if not necessarily *mens sana*, approach, which is wedded to a range of style garments such as baggy sweat-shirts and thigh-tight lycra running shorts. The gym has become a place of resort, in much the same way that Turkish baths were in the last century. The advantage of the gym, however, is that it can be frequented by members of both sexes. Just as there is a thesis waiting to be written on the connection between central heating and sex – in the 1950s, this necessary adjunct of the Scandinavian life-style may have formed an essential prerequisite for the permissive society that followed – so too the nexus between the gym and what, in old-fashioned parlance, would have been called the boudoir deserves exploration.

The point about exercise is not clothes but what lies underneath them. This literally naked celebration of the body has found an expression in magazines such as *Tatler*, where female celebrities are increasingly persuaded to reveal themselves to the camera in the nude. They know they look good, and they are encouraged to believe that their husbands will be proud of them for showing off. This is hardly remarkable. At almost every European seaside resort, women sunbathe in a condition close to almost total nudity every fine day of the summer. The problem for the British is not the absolute absence of clothes, which absolves the individual from decisions of sartorial taste, but what might be called the penultimate stage in clothes reduction. The British generally have lacked style in summer clothes, largely because traditionally we never had much of a summer. Now that summers are frequently hotter than they used to be, it is noticeable that *savoir faire* in this respect has not kept pace. In the excessively hot summer of 1995, people stripped to their underwear in St James's Park.

That illustrates the fundamental shift in attitudes about dress. The British have never been good at taking their clothes off. Traditionally we have been a buttoned-up nation, in every respect. All classes used once to dress with a formality greater than would be found generally in other European countries or the United States. Something of this formality persists in the City suit. It is another example of the British love of uniforms. In an age of individuality, people no longer want to be regarded as uniform, or to wear them. The new freedom is expressed through the imagery of exercise and sport, often borrowed from the United States. The potency of this imagery can be seen in the footwear favoured by teenagers: designer trainers have achieved the status of icons. For the middle-aged, it has made track-suits and jogging bottoms acceptable as garments to be worn every day. These clothes are sanctified by association with the cult of the body, glorified by fashion magazines, yet their effect is at odds with this celebration of physical beauty, since no garment could be less flattering.

In the old days of the uniform, British people did not have to think about the appropriateness of their clothes: there were codes that told them what to do. Now there are no codes, outside the military, the county set, the royal family and certain ceremonial occasions. It has brought a greater informality, which is attractive, but at the expense of style. There is still a *style anglais*, but only a limited number of English people subscribe to it. Perhaps in time the clothes of the exercise culture will become naturalised, giving a British character to the way people dress. But it has not happened yet.

* * *

As regards dress, the very emblem of British identity was the uniform of the police force. It was the uniform of uniforms, given that it was the one most people were likely to encounter on a daily basis. Traditionally the British have been proud of our police force. Recently stereotypes have been challenged with the realisation that the avuncular Dixon of Dock Green era of policing was, on some occasions, rather too cosy for the public good: the 1970s in particular saw several appalling miscarriages of justice due partly to a culture in which police officers protected one another and knew their villains rather too well. Nevertheless, the public manner of the police force can still cause prickles of gratification, when foreigners tell us of the courtesy with which officers have treated them – so different, they say, from their sullen, gun-toting equivalents back home. We rather like the fact that our constabulary is smarter than that of other countries. It is, we are inclined fondly to believe, the outward sign of an inward discipline.

Of late, however, this uniform, which plays such a part in the British scene, has become, so to speak, less uniform. Variations have been played on it. In some forces, the jacket has been discarded almost entirely, as a result of which officers wear as their top garment either pullovers or a short nylon raincoat. During a state visit in early 1997, the streets of London were lined with policemen and traffic wardens wearing coats of fluorescent yellow with silver bands. This is an outfit designed for directing traffic at night. As a matter of fact, the effect was visually dramatic – but the individual coats, not having been made for ceremonial purposes, were soiled and tattered.

Then there is the helmet: not only the symbol of the British police force – or rather forces, since it is subject to subtle design variations around the country – but one of the universal symbols of Britain itself. It was a symptom of the malaise that caused me to write this book that proposals to redesign the bobby's uniform in the style of a supermarket security guard or zoo attendant, replacing the helmet with a flat cap, did not cause a surge of national indignation that overwhelmed the committee of senior policemen that recommended them. Instead, they were accepted, in most places, with a weary resignation, as though they were inevitable. As though they did not matter.

So far the only force to have broken cover on this issue is Greater Manchester. Since, historically, Manchester is the home of the Gradgrind school of utilitarianism, some people may have thought that the move was merely a local aberration. Alas, no. It was apparently intended that nearly all the policemen's helmets throughout the land would be replaced by peaked caps (though I am pleased to say that *Country Life* has published a letter from Sir Paul Condon, the Metropolitan Police Commissioner, saying that at least the force under his command is safe). Outside London, only those officers on ceremonial duties – for example, outside Windsor Castle – will continue in their present attire. But by then they will be freaks, parading for the tourist industry. Like the red telephone box, the policeman's helmet is important through ubiquity, not singularity.

Why does the British public believe that developments it does not want, developments which diminish Britain's sense of itself, must be accepted? In this case, because of some spurious arguments mounted by certain policemen. Apparently some officers claim the helmets to be inconvenient. If so – and asking a number of police officers on the street suggests that many of them do not agree with the anti-helmet faction – that by itself should not provide sufficient grounds to stop wearing them. There are many ways in which the garb people wear every day falls short of total comfort and practicality. In some circumstances, the ultimate in convenience would be to wear no clothes at all. This, on the whole, we refrain from doing in public. No doubt the police would find shell-suits more convenient than even the vestigial uniforms they are proposing. Convenient perhaps, but not appropriate.

They say that helmets can be awkward when officers run after villains – which begs the question of how often an officer is seen running after a villain. I do not remember having ever observed a policeman run at all; usually, even in moments of crisis, they approach at a stately pace. According to the police's own figures, a beat officer can be expected to apprehend a malefactor red-handed on average once every three years. For the rest of the time the role of the police on our streets is less glamorous – which does not make it less vital. Police officers are visible symbols of authority, who reassure the public that society is properly ordered.

Just because the helmet has imperfections does not mean that the only alternative must be a cap. Almost incredibly, with a traditionalism that would be laudable in other circumstances, the helmet is still made from layers of rabbit skin, cork and felt, according to a *Times* leader of August 1996. These materials are hardly state-of-the-art, and make the helmets both heavier and hotter than they need be. Yet in recent years there has been a revolution in the making of protective headgear: for example, the latest riding hats are a fraction of the weight of the old ones. The use of modern materials would revolutionise the practicalities of the traditional helmet, but I very much doubt that this option was considered. The public might like the impression of solidity given by the policeman on the beat, but to the police service itself this image is less than glamorous. They would much rather that they were perceived as the fast-moving, chance-taking heroes of *NYPD Blue* (and similar British programmes, such as *Thief Takers*) than as mere bastions of respectability. The point could hardly be made more effectively than by a recent cover of the magazine *Police Review*, which showed a crew of armed officers from the Special Boat Unit, Britain's only armed-response marine unit. The picture, sanctioned by the police, was thought sufficiently shocking to occupy the whole front page of the London *Evening Standard* on 7 March 1997. The black-clad officers aggressively aim their weapons at the camera, while their features are hidden behind frogman-style masks and military-looking helmets. To policemen, perhaps this sort of image seems state-of-the-art, but to the public it is terrifying.

In the countryside, the loss of the village policeman is widely lamented by people who live there; but even in those areas where they still exist, recruitment is difficult. Village policemen do not get easy promotion, however effective they may be at preventing crime and reassuring the local population. Nor does that sort of policing make the adrenalin flow. It is as though senior police officers want their forces to live up to their television image. Targeting high-profile crimes such as those involving drugs and violence is obviously important; but most people would prefer at least to think (whatever the reality) that the British way of policing has not been abandoned in favour of a more aggressive style from overseas. The helmet should express that continuity.

It may be signicant that the move to abandon the helmet was made at the same time that CS gas canisters became available to police officers in some parts of the country. The CS gas sprays were intended as a means of last resort, to be used against violent individuals attacking the police. Predictably a study soon showed that they were being deployed against anyone who stood in an individual police officer's way: for example, a mother refusing to surrender her baby to the social services. I do not know whether the officers concerned in these outrages wore helmets or caps. My strong suspicion is that they would have wanted caps, whether they actually had them or not. There is, indeed, what might be known as a cap school of policing in Britain. The peaked cap, with its overtones of officiousness and authoritarianism, could be the symbol of modern Britain. This could be called the flat-headed tendency.

Pointy heads might describe those of us who favour the old-style helmet and all it stands for. Pointy heads arise! We must not allow the flat heads to oppress us.

6

In Affluence, Austerity

The fields from Islington to Marybone,
To Primrose Hill and Saint John's Wood,
Were builded over with pillars of gold;
And there Jerusalem's pillars stood.
                    William Blake, 'Jerusalem', *c.* 1804

Public penury, private ostentation – that, perhaps,
is the heart of the complaint.
                    C. F. G. Masterton,
                    The Condition of England, 1909

In its external trappings – the kind bought mostly in shops – a part of Britain has undergone nothing less than a revolution. The British have never been noted for their visual discrimination. In this aspect of the art of living, the French and the Italians have for centuries managed to manoeuvre the rest of Europe into the assumption that they were the ones who knew about style. The British subscribed to this myth. In their case it was, indeed, rather more than a myth: most fair-minded English people would have agreed that the French and Italians certainly were more elegant than themselves. (Those of Celtic descent, with their long visual tradition, may have been more sensitive on the point, but on the whole Welsh, Scottish and Irish visual taste was little, if any,

125

better than English.) The English, being stubborn, converted an innate lack of flair into a virtue. The middle classes gloried in their philistinism. Matthew Arnold made this observation in *Culture and Anarchy*, and it would have been no less true a century later. All that has changed: the English have opened their eyes.

It is incredible that even in the arena of fashion Paris and Milan are being jostled, if not yet quite toppled from their pedestals, by London. In the realm of the home, the contrast is even more marked. During the 1980s, the surge of British interest in their sofas and curtains can be charted through the explosion of what have come to be known as shelter magazines: publications devoted to nothing but rooms and their furniture. *The World of Interiors* led the way, astonishing devotees of such things by its novel way of photographing and presenting the houses it featured. The houses, too, were different from those shown in other magazines, the editor having a particular fondness for those of the 'Sleeping Beauty' type in which every drawing room looked as though it had been sprinkled with talcum powder. By contrast, no kitchen in *The World of Interiors* would have been complete without its artfully placed basket of carrots, hinting at the wholesome and informal life of the occupant (though the carrots probably arrived with the stylist from London). The magazine, as its title indicated, embodied a world. Its success spawned rivals such as *Country Homes and Interiors*, *Period Living and Traditional Homes*, *Elle Decoration* and *Country Living*. On the back of a booming property market, longer-established titles – such as *Homes and Gardens* and *House and Garden* – prospered. Rising house prices persuaded people to move house more often, and each time they did so, they decorated. Advertising poured into editorial offices; at *Country Life* there was serious concern that the quantity of advertising would compromise its prestige. That was in the 1980s. The 1990s have been a quieter decade, less given to exuberance or big expenditure in decoration. But as people have felt compelled to go out less, either because they do not have so much money or do not want to be seen spending it, the home has become even more important. In 1827 the Italian Count Pecchio observed:

'To an Englishman, his house is his Gibraltar; he must not only be inviolable, but absolute, without dispute or *fuss*.' Never have those words been more true.

With the magazine boom came a 'look' – an interpretation of the airy, grand, deeply comfortable style of the country-house drawing room. This was the moment when the country became a consumerist value, through its association with the good life. Rural images were used to sell any number of products on television. But the 'country-house look' was not confined to rural areas: Agas and pine kitchens were installed throughout the smarter residential areas of London; flounced Venetian blinds ('knicker blinds', as the supercilious liked to call them) could be observed everywhere, including the windows of council houses that had recently been sold to their owners; the *Country Living* Fair, with its celebration of traditional rural manufacturing and crafts, took place in Islington. Like any style, that from which the country-house look derived was itself an invention. In the early years of this century, chintz was used only in bedrooms; in the drawing room, the curtains might well have been velvet. The person responsible for liberating chintz from the bedroom and throwing open the doors of grand country houses to a new freshness was Nancy Lancaster. Born in Virginia, she had come to Britain in 1920s. In America, styles of decoration, particularly in the country, had always been lighter. So it is not surprising that what came to be thought of as the immemorial English country-house look should have appealed to Americans, and became a significant cultural export. In New York cosmopolitan decorators such as David Easton made an expensive speciality of it. At a marginally less exclusive level, Ralph Lauren bottled it, promoted it throughout his chain of shops and sold it back to England.

That again was the 1980s. Since then the focus of Ralph Lauren shops has shifted to sportswear: healthy, not stuffy, is the image. In Britain, decorating has similarly tightened its belt, preferring simplicity in muslin curtains to the opulence of brocade. Decorating has become a less public art, and in a decade of individualism, there is no dominant style. But a definably English taste survives in areas where one would hardly expect it.

Take soap. The number of British luxury soap manufacturers is now remarkable. Floris and Penhaligons were joined, in the 1980s, by Crabtree & Evelyn, a triumph of packaging as much as fragrance, founded by an American in association with an Englishman who were called neither Crabtree nor Evelyn. Their flowery style, echoed by many less expensive manufacturers, has now been superseded by Jo Mallone, a young Englishwoman with an eponymous shop in Walton Street. There, as befits the sober 1990s, the packaging is styled entirely in cream and black. The growth in the market for soap shows how far the national taste for *la dolce vita* has developed.

It is not coincidental that the eye should light upon soap as an indicator: the bathroom is now an English preserve. We are not the only nation to make bathroom products, but ours have a special quality which some people like – a quality that is, above all, distinctively English. This extends from unguents such as the hair oils made by Trumpers, the barbers to George IV, to the robust taps and shower-heads of the bath itself, which will be in nickel or chrome, not gold. The demand for such unadorned bath fittings can be measured by the prices in Czech and Speake, the Jermyn Street shop, which are high. They seem oddly consonant with that humblest and most enduring icon of the English bathroom: the cork bath-mat. So unknown is this utilitarian commonplace to Americans that one transatlantic friend made buying one a prime object of his visit to London.

The reputation of the English bathroom, at least in England, itself represents a revolution of taste. Historically the British were rather slow to catch on to the merits of bathrooms; certainly they did not much associate them with luxury. As in dentistry, most advances in plumbing this century have come from the United States, where householders have always demanded a high level of efficiency from bathrooms, and those rich enough have topped it off with a degree of flamboyance. Both in design and equipment the American bathroom celebrates the sensuous pleasures of bathing. These days English bathrooms emulate them. What might be called the cork bath-mat aesthetic is a style choice, not influenced by cost. It perhaps reflects the degree to which the National Trust (with its membership of over two million) and historically based television series (*Upstairs, Downstairs* and the like) have put the British back in touch with their past. People who would never have visited a country house thirty years ago now know, almost instinctively, what it feels like to live in one. Naturally they would like their own houses to resemble, in some respects, those that they have seen, which has been a powerful incentive to the upscaling of domestic ambitions.

The English, with their floriferous suburbs, have always been gardeners, but during the 1980s this enthusiasm came close to becoming a mania. The garden centre, a phenomenon of the decade, was the new temple of Flora. Gardening combined within itself three potent themes of the era – health, environmentalism and money. Money sometimes looked like the dominant member of the triumvirate, since the garden industry took hundreds of millions of pounds in sales each year. Plants and potting compost were only a part of it; gardening expressed a way of life. Sitting in the garden was as important as tending it, and much of the profit from garden centres came from exorbitantly priced garden furniture. From sitting, thoughts turned naturally to eating. The barbecue – so foreign to English experience – became a rite, its mysteries not always understood by those male acolytes making burnt sacrifice of steak and sausage upon its embers. The economic cycle may have caused sales from garden centres to fall off during the recession that began in the late 1980s; but the evidence of book publishing, television and one's own eyes suggests that the gardening passion continues to rage.

One feature of the 1980s garden craze was that it kindled an interest in the historic character of gardens. This was partly academic, partly conservationist, but it also found expression in the demand for old varieties of plant which average gardeners were coming to prefer over more blowsy modern versions. To that extent, the English tradition was recycling itself. But that does not obscure the fact that gardening is, and always has been, an eclectic art which takes its raw materials – plants – wherever it can find them. Paradoxically this makes it all the more English. The most English of all English emporia of taste is the Conran Shop, with its sophisticated blend of

Indian wastepaper baskets and Italian glass. In the garden, terracotta pots, made in Mediterranean countries, have become naturalised; indeed, with pink and blue flowers spilling over the rim, they could hardly look more English. There are some elements of garden craft to which England can lay special claim: the garden gnome, for example. (The father of John Major, a prime minister who has made a particular parade of his Englishness, was at one time a manufacturer of garden gnomes.) But these purely national individualities are rare. Gardening is, indeed, a lingua franca, uniting enthusiasts around the globe who may not have any other language in common. What is distinctively English is the passion and extent to which gardening is practised.

Kipling took the 'glory of the garden' as an emblem of all Britain. In terms of taste, garden influences stretch into every recess of the British home. The manufacture of pot-pourri has become quite a substantial industry, and it would hardly be possible to think of a more English product than transfer-printed china, generally decorated with floral or botanical motifs. More generally, it accords with the English fondness for the outdoors. The great rush for the countryside will be described in Chapter Eight; perhaps it is not surprising, given the strength of this impulse, that the English should be particularly good at making clothes and equipment for the outdoor life. Often this is extremely practical; at its best, it has the stylishness of any object that is particularly well made and suited to its purpose. Sometimes it is well made but not suited to its purpose; there was something of this about the Range-Rover, the car that most symbolised the 1980s on English roads. Cramped, noisy, fuel-hungry and with a low top speed, many versions of the Range-Rover failed to meet the demands that their owners – as likely to drive them on motorways as across country estates – placed on them. They were laughed at as a style accessory, yet retained their cachet. By contrast, as *Harpers & Queen* pronounced in August 1996, 'the Rolls-Royce, once a motorist's dream, has become indescribably naff'.

The English have developed a genius for what Peter York describes as 'roughing it in style'. Their rejection of the old status symbols as being too obvious is a concomitant of their new attention to visual taste.

This revolutionary interest in matters aesthetic may, paradoxically, result from an abundance of the one thing that the old-fashioned aesthete most professes to hate: namely, money. There is much more of it around; Britain is richer than at any time since at least 1929. Further, the redistribution of wealth means that a lot of people have the ability to make judgements not just on grounds of utility, but of taste. The British, on their travels, may respect peoples who are not faced by so many choices; who know who they are and what belongs to them because they can afford nothing else. But they have long escaped that state of innocence, and they would not really want to go back. Shopping is too much fun; it is the principal leisure activity.

It is a symptom of the British malaise that the middle classes do not recognise, let alone celebrate, their own prosperity. Of course there are still two million people unemployed, but that section of the population which is in work continues to benefit from an expanding economy. That expansion may only be gradual: a rate of 2¾ per cent a year. But it is worth remembering that if that rate of growth were to continue for a century, the economy would have expanded to fifteen times its present size. To gauge the increase in prosperity (and therefore expectations) that has taken place in the last few decades, it is enough to compare the range of goods offered by Habitat when it opened in 1964 and today. It used to offer a dab of cosmopolitanism at budget prices. It still does, but budget now means bedside tables costing £500 and sofas priced at £2,000. For householders, the recession has brought benefits in terms of the availability and price of labour. Tradesmen turn up when they say they will – a boon beyond the dreams of all but the richest and most optimistic of their employers ten years ago. Prices have also become more affordable.

The rise of expectations in line with money can be seen in the kind of parties some people are giving. Conventional wisdom has it that the 1980s were synonymous with champagne and

131

celebration: modish types could be heard using the word party as an intransive verb in the American way, as in the expression 'let's party'. The urge to throw parties did not die with the decade. There are now fewer, but the hosts who give them are more demanding – if they are spending money, they want the result to be memorable. There also exists a type of person who does nothing but organise parties for other people. These professionals, like estate agents, say that location is everything. Naturally, the more people who are looking for singular venues, the more difficult it is to identify places that have not been used before. *Harden's Champagne Mumm London Party Guide* is a handy index of possible locations, but to the purist, of course, it makes dismal reading: everywhere in it, from the Fan Museum in Greenwich to the Old Operating Theatre at St Thomas's Hospital (complete with old surgical instruments and a display of pickled internal organs), has been done before. For this reason, a couple of specialist companies – one in Docklands, another in Spitalfields – have recently started selling one-off locations that are guaranteed never to have been seen before. The companies create an ambience, then hire it out for a series of nights after which they destroy it. By comparison, the 1980s were predictable.

In the 1990s, no one wants to be seen showing off, though this is not entirely a question of money: not long ago a private American client at Spencer House, in St James's (a glamorous house restored as a location for parties and launched in recession-struck 1990) spent £18,000 on flowers alone. But even the rich have a different idea about money, and they want it to work harder for them; or rather, they want the people organising the party to work harder for them. Today's added value is imagination. Ten years ago a host might have given an organiser a budget, and some weeks later turned up to a party that was almost as much of a surprise to him as to his guests – if indeed anyone at all was surprised, since the formulae for parties tended to be similar. Now, say the organisers, clients want to be involved. They demand hand-crafted events without a detail out of place – which will be, if possible, unique. The florist Stephen Woodham, who finds that he can be called upon to arrange more in his clients' lives than just flowers, recalls a party he created at Claridges for a passionate fisherman. It was his fiftieth birthday, and his wife asked that fishing should be the theme. 'There were ice-sculptures of fish in the reception,' Woodham recalls. 'The tablecloths were printed with scenes of the Lake District, and we put goldfish swimming in bowls on each table. The bowls stood on drifts of pebbles and a base of blue scabious flowers which coloured the water blue.' The point of such *jeux d'esprit* is not the expense but the amount of thought that goes into them – though expense, too, has its place. The discretion of the 1990s is not only the mood of the times but perhaps more in tune with English taste than the extravagance of the previous decade.

The new importance of the florist may be a symptom of increasing visual sensitivity. It was when my son was born that I noticed the revolution that flowers have undergone; the most fashionable arrangements now include dark colours, overblown blooms and contrastingly spiky textures – the effect is baroque. 'Soft colours are out,' says the doyen of florists, Kenneth Turner. 'Now it's vibrant, clashing colours.' Recently Turner converted the ballroom of the Grosvenor House Hotel in Park Lane into a jungle: 'Even the chandeliers were growing.' Apparently no one still wants to see anything as banal as flowers displayed on a pedestal. Clever flower arrangements can be made to seem even more sophisticated by good lighting, and again a mini-industry has sprung up to supply it – able to draw upon the technology developed for rock audiences who demand ever more spectacular effects. Because rock bands travel all round the world, their lighting equipment must be easily portable; now the most advanced lighting systems are computer-controlled, with one lamp serving a number of different functions and oscillating rapidly between each.

There has even been a revolution in the party nibble. In the 1980s the caterer Lorna Wing pioneered the mini-meal: doll's-house-sized portions of bangers and mash, fish and chips, and roast beef and Yorkshire. She believes that the idea has not lost its appeal, particularly since there are so many national dishes that lend themselves to witty reduction. But she also spots a new taste developing for Thai canapés. 'Food is moving in a lighter direction. It is more aromatic, fragrant and pungent,' she says.

These refinements of party-throwing taste show that con- spicuous consumption was not defeated by the recession – it just became less conspicuous. The luxury goods trade confirms this observation. When *Country Life* surveyed the market in October 1993, it found that some Bond Street shops were flourishing despite the glacial temperature into which other trades found themselves plunged. Quality counts. For some people, luxuries have come close to necessities. Therefore they have become more discriminating in their purchases, not more frugal.

This has helped to keep alive a class of goods that are special to England: those made by craftsmen. Even a very rich man would now be unable to build and furnish a new Chatsworth. But quite a swathe of the middle classes is sufficiently prosper- ous to support rocking-horse makers, bowyers, basket-weavers, damascene barrel engravers and flint-knappers. Four years ago, we began a weekly series on such people in *Country Life*; we called the feature 'Living National Treasures', after the system for honouring great masters of hand skill in Japan. Originally we thought we might keep the series going for a year or so, but the supply of 'Treasures' seems inexhaustible. Some of them fear that their skills will not be passed on to the next generation. Not all the workshops, one suspects, would meet the strictest standards of health and safety officers, but people want to buy the things that they make. Often our editorial office is besieged with enquiries for information from readers.

The number of specialised skills in Britain defies the trend of so much manufacturing towards globalisation. Most motor-cars now contain parts from different countries and are built for sale around the world. There is less and less that is distinctively French about a Citroën, and nothing that is especially English about a Rover. But the finishing of a Bristol, a Morgan or an Aston Martin proclaim their origins in this country. (The Bristol motor is the closest living approximation to the vehicles of which my father would have approved, except that the Bristol is not a regular production model but a curio.) The skills of the people who make such things should be nurtured.

They not only give an identity to Britain, but help keep alive some of that fugitive reputation for quality which I remember British products enjoying when I was a child. With the prospect that Western economies will never return to full employment, it makes no sense for the government to support industries which are constantly becoming more efficient through the use of technology. It would be far better if they invested in keeping alive skills that can only be done by hand; such jobs can never be rationalised out of existence. At present there is a mismatch between unemployed young men in northern towns, who say that their self-esteem depends on finding work with their hands, and craftsmen around the country who are unable to find the modern equivalent of apprentices to work with them.

It warms the heart to see a packet of Fisherman's Friend throat lozenges, an old-fashioned (but new) Roberts radio, a bottle of Lea and Perrins sauce or Robinson's barley water: these are products that time seems to have forgotten. They have always been popular enough, and for some reason they have avoided the attentions of image men – though one hears with regret that Fisherman's Friend are embarking on an advertising campaign designed to promote their sex appeal. But it warms the heart more to enjoy the work of craftsmen who are adapting their ideas to meet new market demands. What they make continues to evolve, and something special about this country is kept alive.

It is a remarkable thing that so many craftsmen still flourish in Britain, but more persuasive evidence of a general rise in visual awareness comes from popular culture. The most popular of all culture is television advertising, which has to be popular or the product does not sell. Britain's TV ads are probably the most sophisticated in the world. In other European countries, the genre has not developed beyond the smiling-man-offering-a-pizza stage, which to a British audience would seem obvious, banal and hamfisted; they might just win a cult following as embodiments of kitsch or high camp, but otherwise they would be dismissed with contempt. Many of Britain's advertisements are shot with a skill equal to that of the most prestigious feature films; sometimes, indeed, they are made by the same directors. They are so fast-moving and allusive that it seems almost vulgar to mention the name of the product. The bank NatWest ran a series of black-and-white vignettes of everyday life in which the services being promoted appeared for a fleeting moment, apparently as the merest incidentals to the story. The makers of that advertisement anticipated a very high level of cognitive ability on the part of the viewers.

It would be too much to say that such advertisements acquire the status of art, but they challenge the mind in the same way as contemporary art – a sphere in which Britain excels. As Nicholas Serota, director of the Tate Gallery, commented to me: 'If British tennis players were as successful as British artists, it would be a cause of national celebration.' It is an area of achievement which does not receive much credit in the media. Critics who lampoon the work of such artists are given disproportionate space in which to unfold their views, and not just in the popular press. Yet the galleries in which such work is displayed are thronged. So many people crowd into the Tate Gallery on Sundays that sometimes it is forced to close its doors.

This is partly a reflection of the astonishing museum boom that has been such a phenomenon of the last twenty years. Blockbuster exhibitions continually break new attendance records; they are so crowded that fatigue and claustrophobia tend to be more perceptible emotions than aesthetic elation. But still the public come, as though in pursuit of a devotional rite. It has been said before that museums have assumed some of the functions formerly associated with churches. On Sundays, people flock to them in search of transfiguring experiences, leaving the churches deserted. All types of art have benefited from this emotional transference. It is perhaps particularly surprising in the case of the most avant-garde art, which one would have thought required a degree of exegesis which most gallery visitors would not trouble to give it. Avant-garde art tends to be a cerebral affair, in which the artist talks to critics and other artists while the public looks on in mystification. For many spectators it is enough, one suspects, to feel that they are part of a happening experience – that they are at the cutting edge of something, even if they do not know what it is. No doubt the Tate's new gallery of contemporary art, to be located in the former Bankside power station, will be packed.

To me, by origin an architectural historian, it is still a source of some amazement that architecture in Britain has become controversial. Twenty years ago it was just disliked. At that time there was very little discussion of it in the press: virtually none at all beyond some rather tired columns on the arts pages. Now a new building, or even a dispute over the preservation of an old one, can be front-page news. Much of the credit for this change in status must go to Prince Charles. Critics who do not sympathise with his vision of architecture should nevertheless be grateful for the fact that architecture is now debated, and that it is a passionate debate, with invective flying on all sides. That the debate is taking place at all, at the popular level, must be good for architecture. It sharpens minds; the instincts of patrons and planners, as well as architects themselves, are honed. As it happens, British architecture is going through a similar renaissance to that of British contemporary art. The panoptic historian Alan Powers believes this to be its best period since the 1890s.

From all this one would have expected that the British should take pleasure from their surroundings, and that these surroundings would help to reinforce their sense of themselves. But it does not happen. When they look about them in the streets, they do not like what they see. Personal affluence contrasts dismally with too high a level of public austerity. The streets of Britain have been allowed to become miserable. The symbol of their impoverishment is the number of people huddled in doorways in major cities, who continually affront our sense of inhabiting a humane and civilised society. The phenomenon is not restricted to Britain, and is probably no worse here than in most other Western countries. The difference is that in Britain, relatively prosperous and endowed with one of the most developed welfare systems in the world, we had grown unused to the parade of human degradation. It seemed new in Britain in a way it did not in, say, Spain or the United States.

Emerging from opera house or restaurant, the middle classes

are distressed to discover that the problem still has not been solved. They tell themselves that there must be an answer. But if there is, it may be more complex than they suppose, since the rough sleepers include psychiatric cases, alcoholics, drug-takers, job-seekers from other parts of the country and a small proportion of young people for whom dropping out is a fashion statement. Ideas of what constitutes self-respect have changed; begging seems a more acceptable activity than it did in eras of greater destitution earlier this century. Also, society itself seems to have lost a degree of self-respect, to have become a slut, prepared to tolerate streets strewn with rubbish and tawdriness. The bundle of rags in a doorway, which to one's horror one finds to conceal a human being, may not be so much a symbol as a symptom of a nation whose sense of civic dignity has withered.

When I was growing up, spitting was an activity practised – to the Englishman's amusement or disgust – by the French and other foreigners, but hardly known in Britain since the time of Dr Johnson. Spitting is now back, and seems to be regarded as rather chic by young people and acceptable by others. People spit even in the foyers of office buildings and such places. Like habitually swearing in conversation and arguing in the street, it is a sign that the habits of civilised life, so hardly won from barbarism, are slipping away. The Englishman is losing his self-control.

We have reverted to a condition that would have been familiar during the Regency period and before. Then, one of the objections to the columns gracing Nash's Regent Street quadrant was the prospect of men urinating against them. The Victorian age engulfed the cities in a tidal wave of improvement. By 1900, urinating against pillars, at least in the West End, was not a habit commonly indulged in. With their lamp-standards, post-boxes, statues and imposing public architecture, the streets had a grandeur that seemed to preclude it. Above all the streets had an identity; and that identity was not merely the preserve of one class or group of residents, but of everyone who belonged to the city – perhaps one might say everyone who belonged to Britain. To offend against the city was to offend against oneself.

Some people did so offend, by acts of vandalism and the like. But the aura of permanence and respectability exhaled by the details of the street scene provided some measure of discouragement. That sense of permanence has now evaporated, partly as a consequence of privatisation. Privatisation reflected the prevailing Conservative belief, forcefully articulated by Mrs Thatcher, that private endeavour, regulated by market disciplines, was necessarily more efficient than public institutions. In some areas, history has proved this theory to be correct. Most obviously, the telephone service was revolutionised when British Telecom became detached from the Post Office. The types of telephone service available to the public multiplied; the waiting time for the installation of new lines vanished; pay-phones that seemed invariably to be out of order worked again. But equally British Telecom typifies the brashness with which a fledgeling organisation throws old traditions out of its nest. The Post Office, for all its failings, radiated the dignity of a public utility, owned by the nation. In its ponderous way, it sought to maintain the standards expected of it; it sought out the best artists to design its stamps, for example. British Telecom had a different sense of itself. It did not want to appear cautious, slow-moving and dignified; its senior executives believed that the sophistication of modern communications should be expressed in a zappy, twenty-first-century image. If they had had their way, they would have scrapped every one of the indestructible old red telephone boxes throughout Britain. A public outcry, which persuaded English Heritage to list a few thousand of the boxes, restrained them; but every box that was not officially listed went. Their replacements were flimsy structures, more booths than boxes (in some cases mere hoods), based on versions seen in America and on the Continent. In London and other cities, these tacky impostors were immediately covered in cards advertising prostitutes. It was private enterprise, but not as the country wanted to know it.

Ten years on, British Telecom have tacitly admitted their mistake. They have added bits to their new booths, and these bits, which include a dome, are coloured red. Whether or not the result is actually worse than boxes without bits is open to question, but certainly it is a vulgar mockery of a design. It would, of course, be better to replace all the old red boxes, ripped out at a cost of over £50 million. As yet, that logical conclusion has been too much for British Telecom to swallow – though there are signs that BT has started to salvage and reinstate such red boxes as it can find.

The old boxes had their imperfections. They could smell sometimes of urine, and the telephones in them did not work. Much was also made of the dislike of them evinced by the disabled lobby. But these objections could have been overcome. For the old boxes also had their advantages. Made of cast-iron, they are virtually impossible to destroy. Above all, they are classics of their kind. When they were first introduced in the 1920s, the Post Office behaved responsibly and held a competition. The authorities knew that there would be an outcry against telephone boxes, as an unwelcome intrusion of technology and sameness into areas that were resistant to change, but they took what trouble they could to make the new boxes worthy of the beautiful landscapes, villages, hedgerows and streets in which they would be placed. They acquired an immemorial air; their classical proportions add dignity to city streets. Nor do the red boxes seem out of place in remote locations. By contrast, a modern box in the Outer Hebrides looks as though it has come from outer space.

More than all this, the old boxes were a symbol of Britain. They are still used on tourist postcards, in advertisements and in any portion of a film which the director wishes immediately to place in the British Isles. Symbols of this kind are not easily manufactured. The replacement booths have no national quality, and will not acquire it with age. Such emblems should not be lightly cast aside, but the red telephone box has been so treated. If it had been sacrificed to efficiency or cost, that would have been distressing but understandable. In fact it succumbed to the promotion of a rival image – the go-getting corporate image of British Telecom.

The demise of the telephone box personifies the collapse of civic spirit among the utilities and other public bodies. It was an erosion of dignity, and we have become used to our dignity being eroded. What used to be red double-decker buses – another symbol of Britain – took on new liveries when their routes came to be operated privately. Black London taxi-cabs, or some of them, are smothered in advertising. The capital now gives the impression of a place that no longer troubles to take care of itself. It looks like a man who used to go into work, dressed smartly in a suit, but now slops along anyhow. The neighbours notice, and say he is on the slide. Nobody quite knows why, but the evidence is there in his appearance. It is the same with London, which was never as self-consciously grand or beautiful as Paris but had its self-respect. Now that is ebbing away, and it has become a city which cannot get anything right. It is unable to fund its museums properly, to make more than a noisy traffic island out of Trafalgar Square, or to prevent Parliament Square from being choked by pollution. Even the Queen Mother's gates, sagging like an old cardigan, were a fiasco.

Outside London, expectations are lower: there is no call for pomp and circumstance in country towns. Nevertheless, their streets should still radiate a decent pride in themselves. But they rarely do. Wherever the civic soul makes itself evident – through bus shelters, road signs and the like – it reveals ugliness and impermanence. Objects which look temporary call out to be vandalised, and vandalised they are. The phenomenon is not new. In the 1950s John Betjeman led a campaign against the erection of concrete lamp-posts in the towns around Wantage, where he then lived. He was unsuccessful, and over the years we have become accustomed to them. But that does not make them more lovely, and it would be better if they were not there (Betjeman championed the alternative of attaching lamps to the walls of buildings in historic areas).

Part of the trouble is the 'Age of Utility' through which Britain has been living since 1979. Private affluence has been accompanied by public meanness. Perhaps this helps to account for the absence of the feel-good factor which has so far eluded Mr Major. In the present austerity Britain we are unable to maintain a body of gardeners for the royal parks, or to train bandsmen to play in military bands. Publicly owned forests, through which people have been able to walk their dogs at will, have been sold off without provision for access. The same has happened to land surrounding reservoirs. The royal yacht *Britannia* is thought to be too expensive to run. A great institution such as the Victoria and Albert Museum is given barely enough money to mend the roof. While No. 10 Downing Street and the Foreign Office have been restored, and nothing less than a palace has been built for the Department of Social Security in Whitehall, most official buildings where the public needs to do business (the Passport Office, for example) radiate gloom and despair of Dantesque proportions.

More taxpayers' money is being spent by some government departments, such as Health, than before the Tories came to power; but at least during Mrs Thatcher's premiership, such expansiveness was lost to view beneath a deluge of rhetoric about cuts. The public believed the rhetoric; it ignored the increases in expenditure which might have made the world seem a less Gradgrindish place. Under John Major there has been less of the dogma, a bit less of the Gradgrind, but the image daily relayed by our streets and public architecture is of unremitting poverty of spirit. It is in sharp contrast with Britain's increased visual awareness in other areas. It takes its toll of national self-confidence. These were once things that we did well; they were the lasting physical embodiment of a land which prided itself on the longevity of its traditions.

7

Tradition: Trick or Treat

*They keep their old customs, costumes, and pomps,
their wig and mace, sceptre and crown. The middle
ages still lurk in the streets of London, the Knights
of the Bath take oath to defend injured ladies: the
gold-stick-in-waiting survives. They repeated the
ceremonies of the eleventh century in the coronation
of the present Queen. A hereditary tenure is natural to them. Offices, farms, trades, and traditions
descend so. Their leases run for a hundred and a
thousand years.*
Ralph Waldo Emerson, *English Traits*, 1856

I was brought up to believe that Britain was the land of tradition.
This was partly embodied in such immemorial institutions as
Parliament, the Law and *Mrs Dale's Diary*. A child could more
easily appreciate the notion through watching the Lord Mayor's
Procession, the Trooping of the Colour and the Braemar Games.
The survival of these events, along with livery company dinners
and the many peculiar rituals associated with the ancient universities, reflected the massive continuity immanent in a country
whose mainland has been free of battle for over two centuries.

Later I came to realise that other countries, with more tur-
bulent histories, had rather good traditions of their own. In the

metro in Brussels, I collided with an orange thrown by a man in an Andy Pandy costume, whom I discovered was a Gilles from Binche. It was never clear to me what this folkloric manifestation was doing in Brussels; the true Gilles, it was explained to me, did not leave Binche. In Perugia, where I went in an only partially successful attempt to learn Italian after leaving school, my first evening was turned into an enchantment by the carnival mounted by students of the university. I remember groups parading past in masks and cloaks, and carrying guitars, as though they had strayed from the set of a Rossini operetta.

Later that year I witnessed the race of the Ceri, immense oaken towers carried swaying up the hill at Gubbio: the men who were half-running, half-staggering beneath these burdens had gritted teeth and bulging eyes. It was no joke, that *festa*, though the really memorable part was the rustic meal served at long, bare tables into which my friends and I had somehow managed to inveigle ourselves, though it was intended only for townspeople and served free. Also, from a largely recumbent position following a morning of over-indulgence, I witnessed the Pallio at Siena, the famous bareback horse race in which both riders and horses are quite often killed. These occasions seemed to have a popular dynamism which even our own Guy Fawkes night, around a precipitous bonfire in a local field, hardly equalled. Perhaps life in Britain had already become too regimented, having lost touch with its rural origins, but the dionysian element seemed to have vanished from its folklore.

Much later, once I had learnt to ride – in fact, as I was to discover, rather before – I made up my mind to try fox-hunting. Hunting must seem to foreigners the most British of British traditions. It is the one that a large proportion of the population, who have generally not troubled to find out much about it, would like to see abolished. To rehearse the arguments about hunting would be tedious. My own magazine *Country Life* has always presented it as a great pageant of the countryside. It is also an emblem of community: one of the pleasures of hunting, even in the Shires, is the variety of country people who take part. It is something of an irony that 'New Labour', for whom community is a watchword, would make parliamentary time available for a Bill to ban it.

One of the legacies of Thatcherism is that tradition is no longer a concept to be proud of. This does not apply just to hunting, of course. But the willingness of senior Labour politicians to preside over its destruction – without even having visited the hunts that take place in their own constituencies – illustrates the hatred that traditional practices now attract. (In Sedgefield, Tony Blair's constituency, the South Durham is, the Secretary assures me, devoid of toffs among the followers. It is a farmers' pack. But not of the scale it once was, because the country is rapidly disappearing to development. That problem is an issue for anyone who loves the countryside, and yet fails to arouse the passionate emotions generated by the hunting debate.)

There were other traditions that bound people together. One of relatively recent origin, as mentioned earlier, was the ceremony called 'Watching the Nine O'Clock News'. In that distant era, the television set was a domestic altar around which the whole nation gathered at certain times, for acts of living sacrifice. 'Watching the Nine O'Clock News', a daily ritual, prepared one for the greater, but rarer, tedium of the Queen's Christmas broadcast, a yearly penance that seemed a necessary and seemly corrective to the orgy of feasting that preceded it. Both the Nine O'Clock News and the Christmas broadcast continue, but they are not the almost compulsory viewing that they were. Newspaper editors no longer regard the embargo on publishing the contents of the Queen's Christmas speech as sacrosanct. The taboo has been broken. The Queen is apparently so cross with the BBC that she now allows her message to be carried by the 'vulgar' commercial channels. The viewing figures have plummeted.

As the number of television channels proliferates, the power of the medium to create national figures declines. The fact that some popular entertainers such as Michael Barrymore command enormous fees is itself evidence of television's loss of authority. Stations need star individuals to maintain their ratings. There was a time when television itself was enough: when anyone who appeared on it became famous, simply by virtue of appearing.

No more. Television has become omnipresent: there are sets not just in living rooms but in kitchens, bedrooms, bathrooms, even motor-cars. But while the medium has multiplied, its audience has necessarily fragmented. The quality of most television journalism is now little better than the local newspaper or free-sheet. The medium has about the same amount of glamour, too.

When England played Germany in the semi-final of the Euro 96 football championship, the nation suffered a convulsion of nostalgia. The comparison with another England–Germany match – the final of the World Cup in 1966 – was inescapable. What seemed to complete the throwback was the sense that nearly everyone in the country had their eyes fixed simultaneously on a television set. Those who did not participate in the activity were generally making a point. For the rest of us, it was hard to avoid some contact with the experience. I found myself watching because my wife was watching, though neither of us has any interest in football as a rule. When the distraction of putting our son to bed made me realise that I had an urgent domestic errand to perform outside, the street was empty. But I could still follow the match, by the roars and groans emitted from the pub. It was an extraordinary moment, but of a kind that once would have been almost commonplace.

It is not merely television which has fragmented, but the subjects it reports. Football now battles for attention with a plethora of sports which most people would not even have heard of twenty years ago. This was reflected in the proliferation of sports now held to be worthy of Olympic status: at Atlanta in 1996, every form of competitive activity, save only backgammon and mah-jongg, had its day, lauded (or larded) with the same hysteria of commentary. (I heard a Finnish competitor in the javelin being described as a 'particularly exciting thrower'.) After what one hesitates, for reasons of political correctness, to call the normal Olympics came that for athletes with disability, which was reported almost as fully. An ordinary Saturday afternoon's *Grandstand* would once have featured little more than wrestling, racing and a few football matches. Now it is impossible to imagine which of an infinity of minority sports will follow darts and snooker into prominence on the viewing schedule. The one sporting fixture to have declined in terms of the coverage given it is the 'Horse of the Year Show' at Wembley. This does not seem to reflect the popularity of show-jumping among those who practise it, since all the horse sports attract more participants every year. Perhaps the programme controllers reacted against its following as a British institution.

It is not always the nature of an institution to be fascinating. Some, like the monarchy, are dull, and that is as it should be. The important thing about them, for purposes of national identity, is that they are shared. Formerly, the British Sunday was about as exciting as the Nine O'Clock News. But its longeurs had an immemorial quality about them; seventh-day life had been like that for well over a hundred years.

> Sunday in London in the rain: the shops are shut, the streets almost deserted; the aspect is that of an immense and a well-ordered cemetery. The few passers-by under their umbrellas, in the desert of squares and streets, have the look of uneasy spirits who have risen from their graves; it is appalling.

So wrote Taine in his *Notes on England* of 1861–62. To J. B. Priestley, seventy years later, the savour of Sunday was still as stale as the odour of cabbage in a boarding-house corridor. 'Even the weather is different,' he noted gloomily.

Priestley was one of the rebels. 'Bluntly, the position is this,' he wrote in *English Journey*:

> The good old-fashioned English Sunday – the Sabbath, as it is called by a great many people who do not seem to realise, first, that they are not Jews, and secondly, that anyhow they are a day out in their calculations – is still being imposed upon large numbers of people, especially younger people, who no longer want the good old-fashioned English Sunday, any more than they want the good old-fashioned English side-whiskers, thick underclothing or heavy meals.

That was in 1934. It took another half-century for the British Sunday to be abolished, with the Sunday Trading Act of 1994 which allowed shops to stay open, for the first time in centuries – just as they have always done on the other side of the Channel. This encouraged the trend for more sporting events to be held on Sundays, in competition with church services. I am told by the Bishop of Dorchester that it is the rise of alternative activities – rather than any decline in faith – which has caused church congregations to fall on Sundays. The total number of people attending church, according to this view, has not fallen; it is just that they go less frequently and perhaps on other days of the week. (Congregations at Christmas get bigger every year.) It may be that the liberation of Sunday has been to everyone's benefit, except a few religious fundamentalists and possibly those shop workers who feel compelled to work on Sundays to the detriment of their family life. Certainly it is very convenient to be able to buy groceries at the time that one wishes, and it would now seem positively cruel to the many people for whom the act of shopping is an essential therapy for that restorative activity not to be available on both days of the weekend. Let us simply note that while the British Sunday has been gladly sacrificed as a shared experience, nothing has replaced it. The variety of choice of entertainments now available on Sunday itself shows how cohesion has dissolved.

By contrast, the British Saturday seems, in some respects, to have evolved remarkably little over time. It was in 1862 that Dostoyevsky described Saturday evenings in London, when

> half a million workers, men and women, with their children, flood like a sea over the whole city, gathering principally in certain districts where till five in the morning they celebrate the Sabbath, that is to say, guzzle and get bestially drunk – drunk for the whole week . . .

Still, change has overtaken even the sale and consumption of liquor. England's draconian licensing laws, introduced so that munitions workers would maintain productivity during the First World War, were revised in 1988 to allow pubs to stay open from eleven in the morning till eleven at night. Although even these extended hours do not equal those of equivalent establishments

150

on the Continent, they have encouraged a different attitude to the consumption of alcohol, characterised by the appearance of tables on London pavements even where conditions for imbibing or dining *en plein air* are rarely propitious. The new table-on-pavement habit marks a significant development of the British psyche. Pubs used to be wombs: dark, furry and inward-looking. Now they are becoming flowers opening their petals to the sun. Only there may not be any sun, and publicans and restaurateurs have not learnt how to separate drinkers and diners from passers-by as effectively as in Paris or Rome.

Table-on-pavementism reflects the extent to which the world has been worn smooth. The excrescences of regional difference are being rubbed away by global communications. Once it was explicable that Australians should be brought up to associate snow scenes and heavy, winter food with Christmas Day, 25 December. The majority of the white population descended from families for whom those traditions had a relation to living experience. It is much stranger to go to Singapore, which has little Christian tradition, and see much the same images decorating the streets. They have borrowed Father Christmas from television. What is so odd is not that the Christmas imagery has lost any religious overtone – it is heading that way in the West – but participation in it is purely optional: Christmas is a consumer choice. In Britain, Christmas remains inescapable; those who ignore it can hardly do so without self-consciousness.

Kissing is another practice to have crossed national boundaries. Thirty years ago the British did not do it much socially; the accepted greeting between all but close family was the handshake. The French kissed; so, more extravagantly, did the Russians. It all appeared very curious and laughable. Shaking hands seemed integral to the British idea of themselves, expressing their bluff, no-nonsense approach to the world, which they kept at a distance; this nation of hand-shakers kept their emotions to themselves and did not invite easy intimacy. It was how we liked it. Above all, it was what we understood and felt comfortable with.

Barristers did not shake hands at all. The historical point of a handshake was to show that the limb which might otherwise have held a sword was empty; barristers regarded each other as men of honour, so dispensed with the formality. Now, members of the Bar tell me, no end of handshaking goes on around the Inns of Court. Barristers have always been a breed apart; just as they have taken to shaking hands, the rest of Britain seems to have abandoned it in favour of kissing. Almost everybody seems to kiss-greet – including, in some instances, men with men. Rather like the use of exotic ingredients in the kitchen, it is one thing to do it, quite another to do it properly. We do not naturally inhabit a kiss culture, nor one in which emotional support between strangers is expressed through hugs and strokes. Yet so far have things gone that the Oxford diocese of the Church of England has had to issue instructions on intimacy to its clergy. Without common rules, mistakes can be made: 'One touch can lead to another,' warns the fifty-page manual of guidelines. Indeed it can. Equally, not to touch at all could be interpreted as stony-hearted. And there lies the dilemma: the English no longer know where they are with body language. Apparently some people in Britain interpret a kiss as the equivalent of a cheery wave, others as not much short of a proposition. The Church of England must itself take some of the blame, having introduced the handshake of peace into its liturgy. It is admittedly only a handshake, not an embrace, but a handshake where there wasn't one before. There can be no true Englishman or woman who does not find this a dreadful moment, the approaching embarrassment of which can overshadow the preceding section of the service. Presumably it came about when the Church decided that the traditional English *froideur* of its congregations discouraged feelings of community. Something touchy-feely, it was thought, would help overcome inhibitions. What they failed to realise was that inhibitions are essential to the English personality. Take them away and what is left? Nothing but a floppy upper lip.

Liberal opinion seems to smile upon the liberation of that tactile urge which the British successfully kept repressed since the Victorian period. On the other hand, it is a sign of the ludicrous confusion into which we have fallen that hardly any adult would risk giving a cuddle to a stray child found crying on the street for fear of having to answer for it in court.

The more intimate body language now in vogue derives from Continental practice. The French, as everyone knows, are always at it, but the difficulties of adopting Gallic customs are much the same as imitating their cuisine. Lots of people now have olive oil and garlic in their kitchens, but precious few know how to use them properly. It might be hoped that an increased use of garlic will lead, naturally and inevitably, to a decline in physical endearments among acquaintances. In the meantime, we are at sea. One imagines that the Latins regard our miserably graceless kisses and hugs with the contempt that teenagers feel for their parents' attempts to dance to pop music. Some people no doubt find a misplaced kiss positively offensive. It is the sort of behaviour that deserves a European directive to establish the rules, but that is the trouble with European directives: there is never one when you want it.

The perplexity over kissing reflects a more general malaise. For example, people arrive at job interviews dressed as though they might be going to the beach. The globalisation of culture, through television, has led to the import of folkloric customs that are not indigenous to this country. Throughout the land families will soon turn their mind to celebrating Guy Fawkes Night. Before that, however, inhabitants of cities – the practice does not yet seem to have penetrated rural areas – will be subject to that licensed extortionism by young people, 'Trick or Treat'. It is very much like kissing. In the United States, where 'Trick or Treat' originates, householders know what to do. They have on hand a suitable, usually edible 'Treat'; presumably they are able to quantify the hazard of the potential 'Trick'. In Britain, we have no natural instinct for the dynamics of this imported custom. The way to observe Hallowe'en here is to hollow out a pumpkin, carve a face on it and put a candle inside; the smell of scorched pumpkin remains, for me, one of the most profoundly evocative in the world. But I do not think British children have ever, until recently, made much more of the occasion, no doubt because of the proximity of Guy Fawkes Night. Perhaps both practically and metaphorically, the correct British response to any such uncomfortable novelty is to pretend not to be at home.

Part of the trouble with our native folk traditions is that many of them relate to a rural way of life, based on the land, with which only a small percentage of the population now have contact. When most people experience God's bounty by selecting something tinned, frozen or polywrapped from a supermarket shelf, 'Harvest Festival' loses meaning.

It is in the country that tradition has more adherents than elsewhere. Perhaps because there are fewer opportunities for meeting each other, rural people make more of an effort. They will dress up for a dinner party, then drive half-way across Scotland to go to it. Men wear panama hats and regimental ties to the Game Fair, women summer dresses. The same uniform is worn for county agricultural shows and puppy shows. In fact, the word 'uniform' is not out of place, since many of the men controlling these events derive their image of what it is proper to wear from their time in the armed services; it could not be described as unbuttoned. The other factor at work is that country people are inclined to feel themselves a beleaguered minority. Knowing that their values are not those of the urban population, they adhere to the annual rites of the countryside as though to an article of faith. In their panamas and flowery dresses, they parade at them with something of the stubbornness with which a section of Ulstermen every August don orange sashes and follow the beating of enormous drums. ('What do people do here in the summer?' I asked a contact in Northern Ireland, expecting to hear about country activities. With mordant Belfast humour he replied: 'They march.') Maybe some rural people, as they see their way of life pressed ever closer to the edge of extinction, will develop similarly aggressive habits.

However staunch the country interest has been in defending the shoreline of its way of life from the encroaching seas of urbanism, it is powerless to prevent erosion. Take the language. Earlier in this book, I commented on the unexpected tenacity with which regional dialects have survived, despite the ubiquity of television and other levelling influences. But the *Atlas of English Dialects* also records losses, the most conspicuous of which is of old-fashioned farming terms. Now that horses no longer draw ploughs, the words referring to details of harness and other forms of equipment have vanished from use. That is hardly surprising; probably one should not even regret it. But it is worth reflecting on the implication of society's growing unfamiliarity with rural imagery in terms of understanding what was the universal store of reference in the past. For example, the teaching of Christ was couched in terms easily comprehensible to an agrarian community in the first century, and his parables would have remained graphic to most people in the world throughout nearly all of the next two millennia. Now their imagery has become opaque for a generation of British city-bred children, unused to growing crops, raising animals or watching trees multiply a hundredfold.

People no longer commonly enrich their language with Biblical expressions or quotations. Instead, the shared reference is likely to be soap operas, pop music or computer-speak. It is no good railing against it, however sad one privately thinks it to be. Traditions evolve. Sometimes they die, and their replacements may be just as good in some ways. But they lack the centuries-old connection with the prayer book and King James Bible, and therefore do not fulfil the same role in forming a national sense of ourselves.

The idea that most characterised the 1980s, and has not yet been replaced, was privatisation. Economically this meant chipping functions and industries away from the megalith of state ownership. But another kind of privatisation was taking place in the home, where individuals and groups were splintering off from the collective mass of principles and activities that form a community. With videos, computers and compact-disc players, many people now prefer to entertain themselves in the most private of settings: their own living rooms. The English used to be particularly good at group activities, such as team sports, standing in orderly bus queues and running Empires. Now habits, manners, morals, codes of conduct, ways of life . . . these have similarly been privatised. In deciding which to adopt, the individual has never been more on his own.

The irony of all this is that it seems to have created not more diversity and richness in life, but an even greater uniformity. Look at the people who are the most obvious beneficiaries of economic privatisation: the 'fat cats' in the corporate board-room. There has been much talk about their enormous salaries, but little on how they spend it. In this age of unparalleled choice, these new millionaires achieve a consistency of dullness that one would hardly have thought possible. The 'English Eccentric' – another tradition – seems to have perished in the face of plurality. Few business people are now collectors or great connoisseurs. The distinguished arts magazine *Apollo* used to appeal to a reader-ship drawn from business people, committed to the highest ideals of civilisation, as well as those professionally concerned with the arts. Now it is more or less restricted to art dealers, museum directors, Ph.D. students and a handful of international collectors for whom their purchases are an investment. This represents another aspect of the fragmentation of Britain. In the 1960s there was still a Society, kept alive by hostesses at whose soirées the worlds of theatre, business, museums and politics would intermingle. In the early years of their marriage, the Prince and Princess of Wales could have kept this tradition alive, but did not. Now it has died. The different elements have separated like curds and whey, and rarely meet on equal terms. 'The vision thing' is not just a problem for politicians; it is difficult for any eye to sweep the far horizon when the hillocks of sectional interest keep obscuring the view.

I was also brought up to believe that tradition to some extent governed behaviour. In our household, this would never have been overtly expressed – we did not talk much about abstracts – but there was an assumption that standards of behaviour were inherited and immutable. That was because they were English. In other words, some things were done, some not done, because this was the timeless dispensation. It was an orderly world.

One was encouraged to behave like a gentleman. It was thought a good thing that children should give up their seats on buses and trains. There seemed to be less emphasis on winning a match or a game than on avoiding conceit when having done so (in my case, hardly a problem, since I never did win). It was always encouraged that a boy would put other people's interests over his own, and that the individual would give precedence to the group. Chivalry had not entirely perished. It was expected that men would walk on the outside of pavements to shield what was thought of as the more delicate sex from the horrors of road traffic. The code of honour of a nineteenth-century gentleman was not regarded as wholly laughable. We had modernism in architecture, modernism in the freedom of sexual relations, but modernism in ethical values had yet to arrive. Now it has . . .

I use the word modernism to denote sets of principles developed in the twentieth century, and promoted to overthrow those of tradition. It is not simply that they lack the authority of centuries of past human respect, but they seem to be established in active opposition to it. Architecture was the most visible manifestation of modernism. Its towering blocks of flats sought to impose an alien way of life on people who had formerly lived in terraces, a way which had never been tried before but which its advocates were certain would be better. It was contrary to common sense, but good on paper. When people objected that the results were hideous and impractical, they were told that they were too ignorant to judge; in time, they would come to appreciate its rightness and beauty. Except of course that they never did. The public hated the modernism of high-rise construction, and has not changed its mind. After thirty years of unbridled destruction, it forced the élite thinkers who believed they could impose their values on everyone else to respect society's opinion. The planners changed their minds, and architecture has now altered course. But exactly the same process has started in other areas of life. Modernism has caused a discontinuity between the way people have lived and regarded each other over centuries, and the way they are supposed to do now. Feminism and political correctness are the equivalents of the 1960s tower blocks now being blown up, or sometimes collapsing through their own structural faults. People can be talked out of their common sense for a while, but usually it reasserts itself. That, at least, must be the hope.

The reason why so many notions, apparently contrary to common sense, have been able to take hold is because of the general view that all values are relative. Any one creed or way of life is thought to be as good as another, and it does not matter which you choose. This attitude is an article of faith – perhaps the only one – among most young people. There are exceptions to this ethical laissez-faire: for example, their universal tolerance is suspended when it comes to alien practices such as hunting. Otherwise life comes *à la carte*. You look at the menu and choose what dishes you want. This approach – not exactly value-free, but judgement-free – is not confined to the young. The extent to which it has penetrated British life can be gauged instantly by seeing its effect on that subject which seems genetically programmed into the metabolism of any normally functioning individual from these islands: namely class.

It has always been said that class divisions were the equivalent of the semi-permeable membrane: people filtered up and down by a sort of osmosis. Yet it was clear what the classes were; there was a structure. Now that structure has decomposed to the extent that people can pick and choose their class-associated activities. All sorts of people shoot, all sorts of people hunt, all sorts of people (including posh ones) go to football matches, pop festivals, prison. Class is now only in small part a matter of birth; it has much more to do with taste, inclination and self-identification. The aristocracy still enjoys certain advantages: Lord Snooks may find it easier to book a table at a restaurant than plain Mr Snooks. But these privileges are of course nothing compared with those enjoyed by stars from the film, music and media industries. Birth alone does not guarantee entry to the social élite celebrated in the pages of *Tatler*. In the words of an upmarket estate agent, there is now no such thing as old money and new money; only money.

This state of affairs may lack romance, but otherwise represents an attractive development of British society which should allow the best of the old tastes and ways to survive happily alongside the new. I cite it here only to illustrate the pervasiveness of the culture of relativism. In other respects, relativism is not so benign. We have reached a stage where ordinary people, the middle-class and the middle-aged, do not feel able to say 'this is wrong' or even 'this is disgusting' when their personal values are challenged. The arena in which this is most discussed is that of art. Part of the function of art is to act like a toddler: it must push at the boundaries of society, test its patience, continually threaten to self-destruct. Art shocks. To the extent that the shock heightens awareness, provides novel and challenging insights, that is good. But to be shocking is a currency soon spent, and there are now hardly any taboos left to be broken. Gilbert and George were prescient in introducing their own persons into their art. Now we can expect more of this kind of verismo. Carcasses of animals have been used in distressing ways, famously in Damien Hirst's bisection of a cow preserved in formaldehyde. There are some boundaries yet to be crossed, but not many. One may be the mutilation of animals or people (perhaps the artist) while still alive – though the fashion for body piercing suggests that we are already half-way there. The depiction of sexuality in children, at a time when child abuse and paedophile rings are in the news, remains the one subject that society cannot stomach. A minor flurry stirred the newspapers in February 1997 when it was announced that works from the Saatchi collection would be shown at the Royal Academy. The thirty artists on show included Marc Quinn, notable for having made a cast of his own head which he then filled with his own blood and plasma, and Marcus Harvey, who has made an eleven-foot high portrait of the Moors murderer Myra Hindley. It is difficult not to presume a degree of desperation on the part of artists who are finding it increasingly difficult to *épater les bourgeois*, when the bourgeois have become resistant to shocks.

But that is the art world: a foreign country, where one expects strange things to happen. In this respect, however, the art world seems only to be reflecting the value of society at large. It is not only avant-garde creative types who feel unable to make moral judgements, but respectable middle-class publishers whose firms may have long histories of handling very eminent authors. I shall not name the publisher of a new sexual politics list for personal reasons: I have a family connection with that publisher, though not with that list. If it were not for that connection, I would never have noticed it. It was not intended for me or for people like me. Having had it brought to my attention, however, I can only say that the contents cater in the most explicit way to a depraved taste. Works of an ancient publishing house set the norms of society. In this case the norms, at least as purveyed in the most vivid works on the list, are those of sexual aberration, celebrated in explicit terms. Men urinating on each other, erect penises bound in leather, scenes of buggery – these are all shown in striking photographs, as though they were perfectly acceptable reading matter. Once when one of these volumes found its way into my house, I was forced to act with the sort of discretion that I had previously imagined belonged exclusively to another age, before *Lady Chatterley's Lover* was tried for obscenity. I hid it from the au pair.

The individuals responsible for this tide of filth defend themselves with a two-word argument: it sells. That they feel this justification to be adequate perhaps reflects a decade of Thatcherism, in which we were encouraged to believe that most things in life were best regulated by market forces. Margaret Thatcher herself was a figure of towering convictions, but her philosophy of the free market led the morally vacuous to slough off their responsibility for moral decision-making.

Relativism means that it is no better to be English, or to act in an English way, than anything else – which is partly why we have lost faith in our institutions. The prestige of our legal system, which we proudly exported around the Empire, now seems so stiff in its joints that a Zimmer frame might be a more appropriate emblem than a wig and gown. It seems incapable of evolving to control the big scams of modern life, perpetrated in the world of the City. In the 1990s, a series of miscarriages of justice has come to light, culminating in the release of three men wrongly convicted of the murder of the newspaper boy Carl Bridgewater. This case, like that of the Birmingham Six and Guildford Four, dates from the 1970s, a time when police resources were more than usually stretched by the threat of IRA terrorism. It is now realised that some officers were over-zealous in responding to the public's desire for convictions. Some were simply corrupt. These miscarriages of justice largely turned on unsound confessions from defendants, and the rules under which confessions are taken were changed by the Police and Criminal Evidence Act in the mid-1980s. In addition, forensic science is now far more sophisticated and reliable than it was twenty years ago. So there is reason to hope that standards of policing have improved since the gung-ho era of the 1970s. Nevertheless, the impression that this succession of legal catastrophes gives to the public is of general rottenness – an impression which their low opinion of authority makes them all too inclined to endorse.

Basing itself upon precedent, which was supposed to embody the accumulated wisdom of ages, the English legal system had about it some vestige of robust common sense; that was what made it seem English. In a succession of libel awards and cases for damages, the threads of common sense have broken. The judgements of the courts reflect the degree to which we have resiled from the old-fashioned culture of responsibility. Instead we seem to have moved towards an acceptance of the assumption, common in the United States, that the natural condition of man is to be perfect. When anything mars this perfection – illness, accident, personal tragedy – it is against the supposed natural order of things. So someone, or more likely some company, must be to blame. That person or company can then be sued. The notion that Western man was intended to live for ever, in circumstances of unalloyed peace and prosperity, has its charm, of course. The associated idea that someone else must be at fault when this dispensation is not fulfilled helps to explain why the culture of personal responsibility has collapsed.

The English used to pride themselves on being gentlemen, even when they were not. Part of this code of honour was to resign from positions of authority when things went badly wrong. To hold such positions was regarded as an honour and a duty, as well as a source of emolument. Merely to mention this set of values now seems ridiculous, as remote as the age of duelling and periwigs. To quote A. J. Davies' history of the Tory party, *We, The Nation*: 'Cabinet ministers simply do not resign.' The last great unforced resignation was Lord Carrington's, when he took personal responsibility for the Foreign Office's failure to predict the Argentine invasion of the Falkland Islands in 1982. It is difficult to imagine any circumstances under which a Cabinet minister would now resign, other than to advance his or her own career interests. Neither Britain's chaotic exit from the Exchange Rate Mechanism nor the 'arms to Iraq' scandal caused resignations.

Then there was that other tenet of the gentleman: his word was his bond. As a matter of fact, this assumption used not to be confined only to gentlemen. To Ralph Waldo Emerson, the English hatred of dissembling flowed through the veins of the whole nation. It could be traced back to Saxon times, when King Alfred was called the 'truth-speaker':

> The mottoes of their families are monitory proverbs, as *Fare fac* – Say, do, – of the Fairfaxes; *Say and seal*, of the house of Fiennes; *Vero nil verius*, of the De Veres. When they unmask cant, they say, 'The English of this is,' etc.; and to give the lie is the extreme insult. The phrase of the lowest people is 'honour bright', and their vulgar praise, 'his word is as good as his bond'. They hate shuffling and equivocation, and the cause is damaged in the public opinion, on which any paltering can be fixed.

Cynics will rightly protest that crooks, fraudsters and sharks have always been putting their hands up the skirt of the City of London, whose decorum should most have been protected by the rule. No matter. It was a state to which business people, liking to believe they were gentlemen, aspired. However much her undergarments were fingered, the City still maintained an expression of po-faced rectitude to the world. Then came 1987's 'Big Bang', when the libidinous goats were let out of their cages and the City lost her reputation for rectitude. She has been subjected to the indignities of the Lloyd's débâcle, the Barings crash and other public revelations of board-room complacence, if not complicity. There is media and parliamentary clamour against the lack of restraint. With every scandal, the City looks less like a virgin queen than a bordello-keeper. Attempts to push the poor old matron of the City back on to her pedestal look, to the outside world, increasingly grotesque. Whether they succeed or fail is a matter for the markets, and no doubt means of regulating the City will be found if without them its potential for money-making is diminished. The point here is the extent to which a sense of shared values, the myth on which generations of English people have been brought up, has now perished.

It is not merely that the City authorities seem to have outgrown the old code of behaviour. What is more shocking is that they do not appear even to be competent in establishing a replacement. There used to be areas of life in which it was taken for granted that Britain did things well. One was finance; another the armed forces. While so many British institutions seem on the point of breaking down, if they are not already on the hard shoulder with their bonnet up and the red triangle displayed, the armed forces are still well-tuned machines, purring with efficiency. It is a joy to watch them in motion; they are a source of national prestige. But even here, damp seems to be getting into the spark plugs. Look at the attempt to dispose of the Royal Hospital site at Greenwich. Admittedly the decision was forced upon the Royal Navy, which would have preferred to continue using it as a staff college (in the Senior Service, tradition bites deep). But Britain has withdrawn from colonies more easily than the Navy is extricating itself from Greenwich. The attempt to form a joint services staff college at Camberley has been a fiasco; the plans to do so have been abandoned as too expensive, and a new site is being sought, but the new building will not be ready in time for the originally intended date of withdrawal. The cost to the nation will almost certainly be greater than if the Navy had kept Greenwich. The likely new main user of the Greenwich buildings – the most magnificent baroque ensemble in Britain – is a former polytechnic, now called a university, which will not be able to occupy the place in the style and dignity it deserves. Withdrawing from Greenwich is made more difficult by the little inconvenience of a nuclear reactor, about which the authorities seemed to have forgotten when they laid their first plans. Not only is this no way to treat Wren and Hawksmoor's great complex; it is a colossal bungle from beginning to end.

The British used to be famed and respected for running a tight ship. As mentioned earlier, the proprietor of Harrods, Mohammed Al-Fayed, is fond of recalling his childhood in Alexandria when he watched British ships, the officers on the bridge dressed impeccably in white trousers, making their way through the Suez Canal. They seemed a symbol of the order, incorruptibility and efficiency that Egypt lacked. That was the image he formed of Britain, and it made him wish to come here. Now, after a public battle with both Lonrho and the British government, he may view the British Establishment differently. But then, his perception was far from unique. It was the view that many foreigners shared of us.

At a time when it is difficult to compete industrially against the tiger economies of the Pacific Rim, reputation should be all the more important to this country. Yet we do not cherish it. We have a Department of Heritage, the very title of which implies the defeatist assessment that the best of things belong to the realm of the past. What we should have is a Department of National Culture, to revivify and celebrate our waning sense of identity.

8

Our England is a Garden

England is a garden. Under an ash-coloured sky, the fields have been combed and rolled till they appear to have been finished with a pencil instead of a plough. The solidity of the structures that compose the towns speaks the industry of ages. Nothing is left as it was made. Rivers, hills, valleys, the sea itself, feel the hand of a master. The long habitation of a powerful and ingenious race has turned every rood of land to its best use, has found all the capabilities, the arable soil, the quarriable rock, the highways, the byways, the fords, the navigable waters; and the new arts of intercourse meet you everywhere; so that England is a huge phalanstery, where all that man wants is provided within the precinct.
    Ralph Waldo Emerson, *English Traits*, 1856

Our England is a garden, and such gardens are
    not made
By singing: – 'Oh, how beautiful!' and sitting in the
    shade . . .
    Rudyard Kipling, 'The Glory of the Garden'

During the Second World War, a series of posters was issued under the heading of 'What We Are Fighting For'. They showed

167

images of the British landscape, on the assumption that most people would respond to them as symbols of shared identity, certain to trigger a patriotic impulse. It is interesting to speculate whether, after fifty years, a Minister for Propaganda – if we had one – would choose the same images to tug at the heartstrings of the nation as were produced during the Second World War. I suspect he would. For while many of the threads of the gentle old tapestry of the landscape have been pulled out by modern agriculture, the degradations suffered by our towns and cities have on the whole been worse. We have a genius for landscape, enshrined in protective legislation. One has only to visit Paris, or an Italian hill town, or one of the charming little towns in Holland, to realise what opportunities we have missed over the last half-century to make our towns and cities beautiful. By contrast our landscape remains extraordinarily varied and comely, for all the pressures upon it.

The British countryside retains an emotional significance even for people who do not visit it very often. We almost take this for granted. Few other nations are possessed of such a yearning for the rural idyll. In most other European countries, the pursuits of rural life are a necessary inconvenience to support the real glory of civilisation, expressed in towns and cities. There rural populations are still falling, as people quit the land in favour of urban areas. In Britain, this position is reversed: more folk are settling in the countryside than leaving it. In those Continental countries where the balm of nature is regarded as a necessary antidote to the city, people like to take their landscape in the raw. They walk in forests and climb mountains, seeking those areas that most correspond to their ideal of wilderness. Our countryside is not like that, for there is nowhere in the British Isles whose present character has not to some extent been shaped by man's intervention. Even a seemingly remote, little populated and wild place such as the island of Harris has been inhabited for millennia. The Lake District has been refused European designation as a wilderness because it takes many aspects of its appearance from farming. In England and Wales, most of the beauty spots that tourists flock to see are farmed, if only for sheep. We are unusual in this sympathy for farmed landscapes.

Certainly few people would regard the farmed landscapes of, say, the United States as conventionally beautiful. In England, in particular, we actively like to see the results of husbandry – or certain types of husbandry – in the shape of hedges, copses and the occasional building.

Traditionally, the English have presented themselves as a nation of country people. Our emblem, still alive in the pages of the tabloid press, is John Bull: a stolid, stout, no-nonsense sort of individual of yeoman stock, in the robust, unfashionable clothes of a farmer. His virtues are reflected in the bull dog that accompanies him: a tenacious, aggressive creature associated with a particularly brutal country sport. John Bull assimilated some of the characteristics of an older stereotype, John Barleycorn, in whom the farming interest was even more plainly embodied. At the time of the Napoleonic Wars, when John Bull solidified as a character, it was flattering to the English to think of themselves as, at bottom, country people – even though, ironically, England was already the furnace in which the Industrial Revolution was being wrought. Country people seemed to be obstinate and independent, and that was just how we wanted to be seen by our neighbours on the European mainland; we found the imputation of rough, outdoor manliness perfectly acceptable. (We did not much care for the epithet 'nation of shopkeepers' sneeringly bestowed by Napoleon.) By contrast, all foreigners, particularly the city-loving French, were regarded as disease-ridden and effete.

Partly in reaction against the unattractive condition of the towns, well-to-do people developed a taste for living in the country which became an art in itself. The charm of this country life and the surroundings amid which it took place forcibly struck Washington Irving when he visited Britain in 1820:

> The foreigner who would form a correct opinion of the English character, must not confine his observations to the metropolis ... It is in the country that the Englishman gives scope to his natural feelings. He gladly breaks loose from the cold formalities and negative civilities of town, throws off his habits of shy reserve, and becomes joyous

and free-hearted. He manages to collect round him all the conveniences and elegancies of polite life, and banish its restraints . . .

The great charm, however, of English scenery is the moral feeling that seems to pervade it. It is associated in the mind with ideas of order, of quiet, of sober, well-established principles, of hoary usage and reverend custom. Everything seems to be the growth of ages of regular and peaceful existence.

Washington Irving was seeing the landscape through the eyes of the well-established Picturesque movement, which both anatomised its various beauties and ascribed to them the moral qualities developed in the iconography of landscape parks. People were viewing rural England as though it were a painted scene. Landowners became artists, improving its attractions through the planting of woods and streams to form lakes. Fortunately – though not by coincidence – what was thought to be beautiful in landscape corresponded to what was efficient in agriculture.

For centuries, the works of art that seemed most typical of Britain drew their inspiration from landscape. Most obviously, the English School of painting celebrated the particular beauties of the countryside, pioneering the habit of direct observation of nature. There was a taste for the unpretentious, which fuelled the careers of watercolourists such as Samuel Prout and Peter de Wint. Even a portraitist such as Gainsborough won a special place in the British pantheon for his affection for landscape. This seemed to make him more English than Reynolds, with his aspiration to the 'grand manner'. Later, under the influence of Ruskin, the British public came to see that the great moral themes beloved of the Victorians could be expressed through representations of landscape, in the work of Turner and some of the Pre-Raphaelites. In the early twentieth century, this stream of English visual art diverged from the river of Continental modernism, but in their leafy backwater artists such as Graham Sutherland, John Piper and Paul Nash continued to reinvent the landscape tradition for their own times. Their spirit continues to hover over an array of painters, working in a representational idiom that receives little critical notice in the press, preoccupied as it is by the supposed avant garde, but bought eagerly by a surprisingly large body of collectors and the general public, who find that these are the sort of works that look well in English homes. Every year the number of tiny, meticulous woodcuts shown at the Royal Academy's Summer Exhibition astonishes me. One would have expected the technique of woodcut to have vanished from the earth, if the opinion of modernist critics was anything to go by. Yet the skill flourishes. The subjects of these woodcuts are invariably rural; they celebrate what appears to be the unchanging spirit in English landscape.

Landscape and the natural world also permeate the music of the most British of British composers. Today, this is as true of Peter Maxwell Davies, living in the Orkneys, as it was of Vaughan Williams. The horrors of the First World War gave the mood of dreamy pastoralism, into which composers had already been beguiled, a new significance. In the case of Vaughan Williams, the building of the Dorking by-pass was felt almost as deeply. Despite the thriving musical tradition of the northern cities, expressed in choral societies and brass bands, it is difficult to think of an English composer who captured the spirit of industry or even city life. Even a composer such as Britten, keen to emphasise his international and modernist credentials, established the Aldeburgh Festival to celebrate his music on the Suffolk coast. No complete account could be given of his musical personality without an understanding of the haunting landscape of this area. Even today, most composers prefer to live amid the relative tranquillity of the countryside or in university towns, rather than the noisy bustle of a big metropolis.

So the landscape permeates British culture and our sense of ourselves. Its hold over the national imagination was vividly demonstrated by the reporting of Dutch elm disease and the great storm of 1987, both of which were portrayed as national calamities which would sear the British soul. Not everyone believes that the special place accorded to country tastes in British culture has been entirely positive. Some revisionist historians disapprove of the tendency of industrialists and businessmen to demonstrate their new wealth by setting up as country gentle-men, which they associate with Britain's economic decline. If only those country-house types had kept on being industrialists and businessmen, and their children after them, industry and business would be accorded higher status and the nation would be more dynamic. Perhaps. Here it is enough to note that the pleasures that can be derived from living in country houses, gardening, running estates, keeping horses and taking part in the sporting activities in the countryside are potent. The economic contribution of the retired industrialist does not end when he withdraws to his country paradise; his presence may stimulate the rural economy. The countryside is not necessarily inimical to business: indeed, now more new businesses are started in rural areas than in towns.

However, it would be difficult to deny the central charge that this affection for the landscape encourages a spirit of nostalgia. There is a poignancy associated with the countryside, as though it were an Eden continually being lost and forever in need of recapturing. This is a condition of pastoralism; perhaps it appeals particularly to that taste for melancholy which has been associated with the English. It probably owes something to the images of the countryside so potently conveyed by children's literature. For most of the classics of British childhood have the country as their *mise-en-scène* – this is as true of *Just William* or most of Enid Blyton's *Famous Five* and *Secret Seven* stories, as it is for *Wind in the Willows, Winnie the Pooh* and *Swallows and Amazons*. The idea of the countryside in British culture is inextricably associated with that of the innocence of this literature. For many people, the move to the countryside is, one suspects, at least subliminally linked to the desire to recapture – or capture for the first time – the idyll of childhood.

Landscape is part of a shared dream, but the landscape of the modern countryside is changing. In itself this need not cause either surprise or fear, since the countryside has always changed. Farming practices have developed, populations have moved, and economic circumstances have varied. Whole villages have disap-peared beneath the sod; open fields have been enclosed, enlarged and subdivided again; families have prospered for generations, only to be ruined. What should concern us about the present changes in the countryside is the extent to which they are waking us from the dream. The countryside is more than just a place, with a physical shape and existence; it is a cultural construct, a product of the imagination, which both lives in the English psyche and helps define it. Even to people who do not dwell there, who may never dwell there, it has traditionally offered the hope of a more wholesome, safer, less regulated way of life than that available in cities. It could be argued that this way of life, which finds its fullest expression in the country house, is more completely civilised than most others in the world, being the result of centuries of careful study. Certainly Henry James, perhaps the greatest epicure in such matters, thought so. But that was a century ago. Now there is a danger that the sense of security, essential to the idyll of the countryside, is being eroded. In turn, this has begun to undermine our sense of ourselves as English.

This can most vividly be seen in attitudes to children. In real life, the children of today are not allowed the free access to the countryside that they would have had thirty years ago. Their parents are less likely to give them sandwiches for lunch and let them roam off for the day, returning only at tea-time. When they go for walks, they are often accompanied by adults. There are fewer people working in the countryside, and in this empty landscape children would be less likely to raise help if they found themselves in difficulty. Dangers have multiplied. Cars are the most obvious threat: they can now accelerate to alarming speeds even on country lanes. With their machinery, blades, ponds and sprays, farms have long been risky places for the unwary, and the dangers have probably got worse. Indeed, for that reason farmers are increasingly reluctant to allow unsupervised children on their land. Every parent has a fear of molesters, whose crimes against children are well publicised in the press. Their numbers appear not to have increased but, thanks to cars and better roads, they are much more mobile. Before, their activities would have been concentrated in their own locality; now there is a feeling that they can strike anywhere. Statistically their attacks are very rare; but public awareness of them still causes parents to restrict the movements of their children. Children are not generally as free to explore woods, streams and fields – or, for example, to camp out by themselves at night – as they used to be. The point is made by television productions that have sought to update some of Enid Blyton's stories. The adventures that her young characters got up to, without the aid of grown-ups, were just about believable in the 1950s: set in the 1990s, adults must play a greater role. It is impossible to imagine that any children would be allowed such freedom on their own.

Equally, the fictional world of the countryside that children are invited to inhabit is, in many cases, quite different from that of Toad and Ratty. Recently, reviewing the contents of my one-year-old son's playpen, I discovered a 'noisy book' called *The Animals of Farthing Wood*, probably bought by someone because it had been reduced to half-price. At first sight, its contents appear unexceptionable. 'Join in the adventures of the Farthing Wood animals and press the buttons to hear the sounds of the woodland come alive!' gushes the blurb on the back. It puzzled me to discover that the sounds of the woodland include a pair of boots and a wheel. Joining in the adventures, as instructed, I found that Farthing Wood was far from the idyllic refuge for the childish imagination that I had assumed. The boots belong to a human who drops a lighted cigarette and burns the wood down. The wheel is that of a tractor rumbling across a field. 'Hurry!' calls Fox. 'It's spraying poison!' William, at an age when he prefers to chew books rather than read them, is unlikely to have his mind clouded by the dismal picture of rural England that this paints; besides, something has gone wrong with the mechanism and it no longer emits any sound. But Heinemann, the publishers of this work, have encouraged a generation of toddlers to see the countryside as a place of threat, with greedy mankind in perpetual conflict with nature. Children may well be forming this impression before having had any direct experience of the countryside for themselves.

The ideology of *The Animals of Farthing Wood* has become the norm in children's publishing. One of the things that distinguishes children's classics, such as the works of Beatrix Potter, is that they combine anthropomorphism with a loving,

detailed knowledge of the natural world. Oddly, anthropomorphism (which one might have thought to be politically
incorrect) does not seem to be 'out', but country lore is. It
has been replaced by a belief in campaigning. No child, it would
seem, is too young to be made aware of man's depredation of
the environment, or whipped into a lather of protest against it.
Take, for example, two books from Bloomsbury in 1996: *Causing
a Stink! The Eco-Warrior's Handbook*, by Caroline Clayton,
published in association with Friends of the Earth, and *Roar!
Animal Rights Handbook for Kids*, by Peter Hoggarth. While
Roar!'s evangelism on behalf of foxes, zoo animals and racehorses
could be largely viewed as an expression of British eccentricity,
any parent who is trying to persuade a twelve-year-old to eat
properly will deplore the chapter extolling vegetarianism and
veganism. Vegetarianism is also on the menu of *Causing a
Stink!*, but its scope is wider, embracing every green issue from
rain-forests to recycling. There is even a chapter on 'Why Some
Countries are Better Off than Others', the reason being unfair
trading practices by the West. Indeed, the wider the range the
worse the bad faith implicit in such books, a tenet of which
is that action by individuals 'can make a difference'. All too
often, though, it cannot. Children may fret themselves sleepless
about the depletion of the rain-forests or pollution in the Third
World, but writing letters to the rulers of China and Brazil will
not stop such things from happening. Children are invited to
worry about global issues before coming to love the world of
nature that exists outside their own back doors.

I would be the first to acknowledge that campaigning has
its place in life. The labours of many generations of people in
creating productive landscapes, which are also lovely to look at,
should not be sacrificed to the blundering late-twentieth century.
But it must be wrong to propagandise the minds of the young,
whatever the cause. The reason why the countryside is worth
defending is precisely because large parts of it are still full of
variety and beauty. Also, there are many people who give up
quantities of their time to nurturing the interests of the wild
things to which children's hearts go out. Surely children should
be encouraged to love and understand wildlife, before being

urged to campaign against imagined ills of which they know little? One would hope that a British child's passion for the global environment would grow from personal observation of the plants and creatures of his or her own countryside, rather than broad theories about the world being used to dictate how something as complex as the country should be treated. Above all, it cannot be right for campaigners to snatch away childhood's image of the countryside as a place of security and replace it by one of anxiety and threat.

What is true for children is true also for the adult world. The countryside has lost some of the old freedom which gave a particular charm to life there; and the change in perception is even worse than the facts that have caused it. For instance, crime in rural areas is rising: this is a weed that must be uprooted before it takes hold. It is noticeable that some of the worst outrages against humanity to have taken place in Britain recently have occurred not in deprived, overcrowded inner cities, but gentle country towns. This is true of the massacres at Hungerford and Dunblane. The phenomenon is not unique to Great Britain; on the other side of the world, a gunman ran amok in, of all places, Tasmania – a sleepy rural paradise which seems to subscribe to the values of the 1950s. The truth is that frustrations are as likely to boil up in small communities as in anonymous towns; perhaps more likely. The horrifying events that result are freakishly rare, but their blanket coverage by the media leaves an impression. So, too, does reporting of individual brutalities such as the murder of a mother and her daughter at Nonington, in Kent. The sister of the slain little girl was attacked. On 11 July 1996, the *Daily Mail* devoted its entire front page to the story, promoting it even above the previous night's decision by Members of Parliament to award themselves a 26 per cent pay rise. The *Daily Express* reported: 'It emerged last night that the family moved to the area just nine months ago – so the two little girls would be safe from crime.' (This seemed less plausible when one read, later in the account, that the family had previously lived in Snowdonia, but it reflects the natural expectation that rural areas should be abodes of peace.)

The fear of attack impoverishes the lives of the elderly and timid, causing them to stay behind locked doors each night. But murders of any kind are still very uncommon, particularly between parties who do not know each other and even more so in the countryside. The crimes that are on the increase are those against property and cars. That is, in its way, bad enough. Time was when it seemed bad manners for country people to lock their houses: it appeared to impugn the honesty of their neighbours. For the same reason, they left the keys in the ignitions of their cars. That era has passed. It is sad, but not surprising. Towns do not hold a monopoly of evil. Besides, the more inner cities – long notorious for their rates of burglary – became defended and policed, the easier the pickings in the countryside seemed for urban criminals. Again, improvements in personal mobility made it easier to reach. Whenever a dual carriageway is built, a crime wave in the locality around it follows. Even so, the scale of loss is not always as great as the publicity given to thefts of Old Masters from country houses might suggest. In the statistics, a tea-urn stolen from a village hall features as an incident, just as much as a Titian from a stately home. What is important, in this context, is the restriction that the fear of crime has imposed on a way of life.

From these observations on child safety and crime, it is evident that perhaps the greatest agent of change in rural areas is the motor-car. Pressure groups such as the Council for the Protection of Rural England tend to concentrate their fire on the amount of land that will have to be taken up by new roads if the government's predictions for car ownership are fulfilled. These roads will divide farms and redefine the boundaries of villages, making their impact even larger than their own physical presence. Here, though, I would rather allude to the effect that cars have on our emotional relationship with the countryside. First, they tend to destroy the sense of locality: a lament that has been made since cars entered life in the Edwardian period. By enabling us to rush from one side of the country to the other, pay a short visit to family or friends, or take part in a sport, then return home the same day, they have inevitably weakened our attachment to place. People do not put the same degree of effort into cultivating the area around home, because they are not there so much. Conversely, they cannot belong to the destination they have reached by car, since they are only there for a few hours. It may be that this is a condition of modern life; it is wrong to blame the car for this social consequence of car ownership. Expectations of mobility are now so high that a world in which it was not possible to set the restrictions of geography at naught would seem very inconvenient – indeed, unimaginable. Still, what has happened, in terms of our losing our sense of place, is worth noting.

It is exacerbated by the other great influence of the car: the tendency for everywhere to look the same, since roads bring the apparatus of suburbia in their wake. With them comes street lighting. Hedges are destroyed and verges mown in case they obscure visibility on bends. Lanes that formerly met at right-angles have their junctions softened into bends to eliminate risk to the car driver. By the very fact of their existence, highways departments in county councils follow an inexorable mission to upgrade the safety standards of country roads, making them look more like all other roads, irrespective of whether safety really needs to be improved. In this, as in everything else, the fear of prosecution, should an accident take place on a stretch of road that had not experienced their ministrations, causes council officers to work on the basis of maximum rather than minimum interference. Also, around new roads spring development. The space between the by-pass and the village it avoids soon comes to be regarded as somehow left over, and is quickly earmarked for new housing. The intersections of major roads are seen as the natural place to put new factories and commercial developments. People arrive in the countryside by car, travel around by car and leave by car, all the time looking out upon roadside paraphernalia that would be interchangeable with any other area of the British Isles. The habits of the towns and other congested places are exported by the car. In Shropshire, a cowman was attacked by a driver impatient to discover that his way was blocked by a herd of cattle: not just an example of road rage, but an illustration of the degree to which car-drivers can regard themselves as superior to other forms of life.

Partly as a result of car ownership, the countryside is now

the place where everyone wants to go – the most popular of all leisure destinations. In the old days, people took their holidays by the seaside, to which they travelled by excursion train. Their impact, both on the journey and once they had arrived, was confined. Cars maximise the impact of visitors to the countryside; they spread the geographical area affected, and each car makes a greater noise and visual intrusion than its occupants would do on foot. The problem for the countryside is made worse by the fact that so many new leisure occupations use machines which, like cars, cover ground quickly and make a noise. Sir John Johnson, a former chairman of the Countryside Commission, has a list of some twenty-five different sports that now take place in the countryside, from ballooning to jet-skiing. Not all these activities are compatible with each other – or with the peace and quiet that other people seek. To the person who owns it, a speedboat may seem a thing of beauty, but this view may not be shared by people who have gone to Lake Windermere to recapture the spirit of Wordsworth.

Then the countryside is also the place where most people in Britain would, given the chance, prefer to live. Again, it is very difficult for everybody to achieve their ideal of a tranquil rural idyll at the same time, for one person's idyll is apt to impinge on somebody else's. We are one of the few European nations where the net rural population is steadily growing, not declining. As a result we are, paradoxically, less studious in finding ways to maintain rural services – shops, schools, health services and the like – than less densely populated countries such as Austria. In Austria, they have to find ways of keeping rural communities alive, or people will leave them. Equally, in remote regions there is often no town nearby. By contrast, English bureaucrats have been content to rationalise services, allowing them to become concentrated in towns, thereby depriving country areas of part of their identity. Pressures on the countryside will increase if more homes are built to meet the Department of the Environment's predictions of housing need. These indicate that 4.4 million new units of accommodation must be built in England over the next quarter-century. The occupants will be shrapnel from the exploding family: young people leaving home earlier, divorcees, old people living longer. Many will be single, so might benefit from living amid the shops, cinemas and public transport of towns. There has been much talk of pressing into service so-called 'brown' sites: derelict land that should be redeveloped. But 'brown' land is not going to provide enough space for everyone. Developers do not like it; they say, rightly, that it is not where people want to live, they can sell houses most easily when they are built on virgin countryside. The 1980s were a dreadful decade for the countryside; the free market ethic was incompatible with the high standards of preservation maintained since the Second World War. The next decade could be even worse.

Already, the traditional image of the countryside as a place of tranquillity is becoming difficult to sustain. Estate agents have recently calculated that even rich house-buyers will be unlikely to find anywhere in southern England that is not affected to some degree by noise. This is said to be true even of the Prince of Wales's Highgrove House, in Gloucestershire. If such developments continue, the countryside will no longer be quite the same place that we turn to in our imagination, and something of our shared sense of Englishness will have been lost.

It used to be thought that the countryside was gloriously free of the constraints of regulation necessary to order life in towns. Rural areas could accommodate more of that eccentricity – sometimes another word for individuality – which is supposed to distinguish the English from other nations. Country people were prepared to put up with the hardships of rural existence because they valued the informal style of living. Now all that is changing. People in the country have been worse affected by the tide of legislation flowing from Brussels than those in towns. Towns always have been regulated. Further, businesses there tend to be larger and better able to absorb the costs of bureaucratic interference.

It is not always the case that rural business cannot adapt to meet the new conditions. Sometimes their proprietors cannot be bothered; they do not think that the fuss is worth it. So small producers shut their doors and we are all reduced to buying a more standardised product from a supermarket. Local distinctiveness suffers.

The incursion of bureaucracy into the countryside is something that would have baffled earlier generations. It cannot all be blamed on the European Union; it is one of the unpleasant conclusions of this survey of national identity that we must now count a propensity to generate pettifogging bureaucracy as a peculiarly British characteristic. One of my colleagues at *Country Life* comes from the Hampshire village of Nether Wallop. There, they have been subject to a rash of road signs, telling the inhabitants that they cannot drive at more than 30mph. There are nineteen signs; the population of the village is only three hundred. Some of the signs have even been placed at the end of farm tracks. Every exit and entrance to the village has one of these wretched signs; then they appear at intervals of 250 yards. No doubt there are rules which dictate where signs should go and at what frequency they must be repeated, but the rules really ought to be applied differently in country areas – where there are not many people – from busy towns. For example, why not just one sign, incorporated into the name-board announcing the village?

The worrying thing is that, in Britain, rules and regulations seem to take on a life of their own. They work by a principle equivalent to that of the selfish gene: they have an in-built desire to propagate. Recently, I stayed at an expensive country-house hotel that was completely renovated, to a very high standard, about fifteen years ago. The owner told me that every year the fire officer arrives and asks her to upgrade the fire precautions. 'Asks' in this context is a manner of speaking: if she does not comply, the fire officer has the power to close the hotel immediately. Often the new requirements, each costing thousands of pounds, are for so-called improvements that could easily have been predicted the year before. It is just that each year the official demands more. When the owner of this hotel visited a country-house hotel with a Michelin-starred restaurant in France, she was amazed that the fire precautions were so primitive. 'Aren't you inspected?' she asked *le patron*. 'Of course, the inspector sometimes comes down from Paris,' came the reply. 'But we give him a nice meal and a good bottle of wine and he goes back very happy.' That may be another extreme, but it is surely closer to how things should be.

In the 1920s Clough Williams-Ellis wrote a book called *England and the Octopus*. The octopus was the suburbia lining the new arterial roads, which had England in its tentacles. These days the octopus is bureaucracy: the application of inappropriate means often to achieve unnecessary ends.

A significant way in which our idea of countryside has begun to alter is in controversy. The whole point of the countryside used to be that, there, people could escape the trouble and turbulence of politics. It was a place to refresh the spirit; it was in the cities that one heard the clash of ideas, it was there that social conflicts were enacted. Already this has begun to change, and it is likely to change more. *The Archers* radio serial used to be a sort of aural duvet, a warm evocation of rural existence which listeners could pull over their heads at five-past seven each evening. Now the village of Ambridge, in which it is set, is presented as a microcosm of every evil afflicting society, including racial attacks, fraud, robbery, family breakdown and domestic violence. If all this happened on one street in New York it would be regarded as either bad luck or rather exciting, but for so much misery to be concentrated in one English village, in a short space of time, suggests that Ambridge is uniquely woebegone. Against this, it could be said that *The Archers* does not reflect real life, or even seek to do so. But it is still a yardstick by which perceptions of the countryside can be measured, and those perceptions are moving away from security towards turmoil.

The trend owes something to politics – which once would not have been a word much used in association with the countryside. Now the strong feelings that rural Britain has always excited are being expressed as political demands, reinforced by attention-seeking demonstrations. Part of the reason for this must be the withering of other protest issues. With the end of the Cold War, a body of people who had been accustomed to demonstrate against nuclear weapons found themselves without a cause. The poll tax presented a diversion. Now, though, it is noticeable that most of the agit-prop issues of the 1990s – tree-felling, road-building, the export of live animals, field sports, access, land use – either belong exclusively to the country or have a strong rural dimension. Perhaps there will be demonstrations against the Department of the Environment's plans to build 4.4 million new homes in England, many of which will have to be located in the countryside. I rather suspect there will be. The people joining them are likely to include disaffected voters who do not believe that their concerns are reflected in party politics at Westminster.

There are signs that even the political mainstream acknowledges the countryside as an issue. The extent to which it has pushed its way up the parliamentary agenda can be measured by the government's publication of a Rural White Paper in the autumn of 1995. Produced in a rare collaboration between Ministries – the Department of the Environment and MAFF – the White Paper presented a shrewd analysis of the different pressures to which rural England and Wales are subject, though short of specific policies or measures to ameliorate them. The remarkable thing about this White Paper was not its content, or what came out of it, but the fact that it was produced at all. It was the first of its kind; there has never been a White Paper on the countryside, from any party, before. Still, country people would be right to remain sceptical about the depth of commitment from a Cabinet distracted by the whirligig of Westminster. Progress was supposed to have been chased by a Cabinet committee, chaired by the Deputy Prime Minister Michael Heseltine: in March 1997 this still had not been met.

Part of the object of the White Paper was to define the different purposes of the countryside, so that its many users could be brought into harmony. There is every prospect that the coming decade will bring more controversy, not less. If Parliament abolishes fox-hunting, those who take part in what they consider to be a necessary, humane and enjoyable activity will not surrender their cause easily. There is too much at stake for them; hunting not only supports part of the rural economy but, during the winter months, forms the centrepiece of many people's lives. It is difficult to predict what the hunting diehards would do; at the least, there would be demonstrations. Country people are not quick to make a fuss, but direct action now attracts unlikely supporters. This has been evident at the protests against road-building and the export of live animals (such exports were stopped, without a murmur from the animal rights lobby, by regulations following the BSE scare, which caused all the male calves that would have been sent abroad to be slaughtered at birth). Such causes attract middle-class matrons as well as young people with matted hair, which perhaps is another reflection of the general disillusionment with party politics.

The protests of the 'tree people' against the Newbury by-pass appal those instincts – deep, certainly, in me – that favour the rule of social order over anarchy. Our planning system is tedious, but it does allow every party to a decision to air its view; decisions reached through the processes of democracy should not be lightly set aside. Still, it is natural that people should do what they can to defend the earthly paradise when they have found it. My spirit stirred when I met some of the protesters, before the battle to protect the trees that lay in the path of the road had been joined. It takes some resource-fulness to live in a tree, throughout an exceptionally long winter, with hardly any money and no sophisticated camping equipment. The people who did this dressed outlandishly, were encrusted with dirt and wore their hair in a style resembling rolls of underfelt, but they spoke lyrically about their experiences of living in direct contact with nature. Waking up in their shelters, high above the ground, they saw deer running through the woods; they went to sleep to the sound of owls. They were living proof of how far the spirit of the English countryside continues to inspire people – in this case, mostly young people. The hardships that they were prepared to undergo for their cause bear witness to the depth of their passion.

More recently, the fortitude shown by the roads protester known as Swampy (aka Daniel Hooper) in his record-breaking, week-long resistance at the bottom of a tunnel at Fairmile, in Devon, won an extraordinary degree of sympathy; his photo-graph, often accompanied by favourable profiles, appeared in every newspaper in early 1997, and he even appeared on *Have I Got News For You*. The lack of general censure that his actions received suggests a surprising degree of public support for the anti-roads lobby, by however extreme and costly means they make their point. Such fanaticism, however, could easily result in someone, either a protester or a bailiffs' man, being killed.

The countryside will not continue to play the same cultural role if it loses its ability to soothe and refresh the spirit. It may be difficult for grown-ups to sustain the innocence of perception about the rural world captured in the children's classics discussed above. But clearly it is important that something of this is retained into adulthood; that is why so many people, even those living in towns, feel passionately about modern farming techniques, afforestation and new building in rural areas. They may know that the rural world is not quite as they were brought up to believe, but they would like to make it so, as far as they can. The countryside is one of the shared ideals of British. Conflict is not part of this ideal; nor are other aspects of life that one would have hoped belonged only in cities. We have become accustomed to the sight of cyclists in urban areas wearing masks. Diesel fumes ... Car exhausts ... Cities ... Our instinct is to escape to the country. Yet the Bracken Advisory Commission now recommends that hill-walkers wear masks against the carcinogenic spores of bracken. Admittedly bracken is on the march, colonising greater areas of hill farm and moorland than one would wish; but must we really venture out on country walks wearing protective clothing? If so, the countryside's meaning for society will have changed. However, I remain to be convinced.

There are reasons for thinking that the present crisis of the countryside, caused by too many competing uses, can only be temporary. In the foreseeable future, agriculture will reassert itself as a national priority, to which all available productive land will be dedicated. The global population is growing at a rate of 3 per cent a year; it is predicted to exceed 10 billion by the middle of the next century, and to reach a theoretical 14 billion by the end of it. At some point, as this curve goes up, Britain's food supplies will be affected. Contrary to past performance, there are signs that scientific agriculture is not capable of producing more and more and more indefinitely. The amount of grain produced per person in the world population is now falling decisively – in the latest growing season, it was the lowest since the mid-1960s. As the populations of China and other developing countries become richer, they will want a better diet. And there will simply be more people to feed. By the year 2030, it is predicted that China alone will be trying to purchase a volume of grain equal to the whole quantity of grain traded in the world at present. Fifty years from now, the deficit in world food may well be severe. Under these circumstances, no government would tolerate putting more of the countryside under bricks and mortar and tarmac because, as in previous ages, it will be needed to feed the home population.

What the countryside will look like by then is, of course, another matter. Part of the answer will lie with the planners. Nowadays, the attitude in many planning departments seems to be that planning should be about where to put the yellow lines at the side of the road. John Gummer, the Secretary of State for the Environment, is eager to stimulate debate about where the 4.4 million new homes that his Department says are needed should be built. But he is understood to be in despair at the absence of planners with vision to lead the debate. However, there are some people with the imagination to lift their eyes above the minutiae. In his plans for London, Lord Rogers demonstrates a feeling for life in cities, though not perhaps English ones (naturally his ideas appeal to Tony Blair, with his fondness for Tuscany; if implemented, they would complete a process of Tuscanisation that started to permeate the planning system with the Prince of Wales's model development at Dorchester). It is odd, however, how few of the internationally acclaimed architects that Britain produces engage themselves with the countryside. Or perhaps not odd, for it is not a subject to which international architects have ever given much thought; that is why they are international.

Failure to protect the countryside during the 1980s is emblematic of the crisis about Englishness. We used to be good at the countryside; it was important to us. We are puzzled that we should have lost our touch, but it is not beyond hope that we should find it again. If we do, we must apply it equally to that element without which Churchill's island race could not have been an island race: the sea.

9

'Bound in With the Triumphant Sea'

We switched on the radio above the chart table for the shipping forecast. No other country hears such a stirring daily litany. It has a loyal following ashore and thousands listen to it as if it were an incantation. These disciples experience a thrilling resonance in the names of the thirty-one watery estates, recited, almost as blank verse, by authoritative BBC voices.

The names speak of history as well as geography. The syllables of Viking, North Utsire, Forties, Cromarty, Forth and Tyne, Dogger, Fisher and German Bight, Humber, Thames and Dover, remind the British of their island state.

Trevor Fishlock, *My Foreign Country*, 1997

'Nowhere does England take on personality so strongly as from the sea,' wrote Hilaire Belloc. This statement resonates at many levels, of which the most humdrum but most demonstrable is that of physical appearance. The English coast – even more so the British – is inexhaustibly varied, yet rarely likely to be mistaken for that of other countries. In parts it is shot through with weirdness and wonder, where the relentless workings of the sea have carved fantastic shapes out of the rocks that project from it. Then comes the drama of precipitous chalk cliffs, and the melancholy of mudflats, and the rustle of surf retreating over pebbly beaches. Little towns nestle into hollows, or string themselves out, like pearls, along the shore. Being a group of islands with a jagged silhouette, Britain has a greater length of coastline than most other European countries. It forms part of our consciousness. For many townspeople, the experience of scrambling over seaweed-covered rocks, while that other sort of ozone – the one without holes in it – fills the nostrils, stays with them in memory, like a favourite bedside book which they leaf through constantly. It is a comfort and an inspiration. They do not live by the sea, but the sea continues to live in them. As a nation, our coast is particularly precious to us, which explains the enormous success of the National Trust's Enterprise Neptune appeal to save the most remarkable parts of it. The Trust now owns over 500 miles.

Not that the coast is just a matter of scenery. Make a journey in imagination around the British Isles and images of industry, or incidents of history, constantly impinge. Herring boats working the Dogger Bank, from the ports of Hull and Grimsby; wherries plying the Norfolk Broads; ocean liners like floating cities leaving Southampton and Liverpool, having perhaps been built in the shipyards of the Tyne or Clyde; colliers bearing coals from Newcastle; crab boats on the beach at Cromer; the Port of London, its grand, implacable warehouses fragrant with spices, tobacco, rum and every other kind of produce from around the world; its less glamorous successor, the container port at Felixstowe; fortifications at Dover; the dockyard at Portsmouth, which once employed 25,000 workers; yachts in the Solent; slave ships in Bristol harbour; the German fleet scuttled at Scapa Flow; coracles bobbing around the coast of Wales . . . such scenes are vivid either in reality or memory. When the latter, an astonishing number of museums abound to perpetuate the myth.

Churchill habitually referred to the British as 'the island race', and it was a shrewd as well as sonorous description. Always an ethnic mixture, priding ourselves on our openness towards refugees, the British can only be defined by geography. We live surrounded by the sea, and it has shaped most events in our history. From Julius Caesar to William the Conqueror, our fortunes turned on the success, or otherwise, in repelling invaders borne by the sea. Later we became the ones to assemble invasion fleets, in pursuit of territorial ambitions on the Continent. In the Elizabethan period, Drake and Frobisher, Hawkins and Raleigh, became national heroes, through their intrepid exploration and thirst for personal enrichment through privateering. Following the defeat of the Armada, England could famously be evoked as:

> This fortress built by Nature for herself
> Against infection and the hand of war,
> This happy breed of men, this little world,
> This precious stone set in a silver sea,
> Which serves it in the office of a wall,
> Or as a moat defensive to a house,
> Against the envy of less happier lands . . .

Security at home, but adventure upon the seas and beyond them. The East India Company inaugurated the era during which Britain was the greatest trading nation upon earth. That could only be achieved by dominance of the seas, and if any schoolboy is not inspired by the feats of Nelson, let him visit the admirable display explaining the Battle of Trafalgar in the National Maritime Museum. It was natural that Britain should also become the biggest nation of shipbuilders in the world, its merchant fleet protected by a policy of fierce protectionism. The sea's inescapable strategic importance reasserted itself during the Second World War. Dunkirk may not have been Britain's finest hour in military terms, but the flotilla of ill-assorted small ships that rescued the stranded expeditionary force personified some of the qualities that the British liked to identify in themselves: courage, tenacity and above all a devotion to almost every form of seafaring that it was possible to undertake. Subsequently, the imagery of the sea-dog was revived in films such as *The Cruel Sea* and *In Which We Serve*. Old memories were revived during the Falklands War, when British honour rested upon the skill and professionalism of the Royal Navy. It was not disappointed.

The sea has been the inspiration for painters, writers and

musicians. In each of the arts there are geniuses for whom the sea had special resonance: Turner, Conrad, Delius, for example. There were also lesser practitioners, such as the marine painters whose work delighted sea captains, or even those humble makers of Victorian seaside views out of coloured sand, bought by tourists. What is remarkable in the context of this book, however, is not so much the work of individual masters as the ubiquity of the sea as a subject and as an image. It permeates British cultural life – it always has, and it continues to do so. One needs only think of Matthew Arnold's *Dover Beach*, Iris Murdoch's *The Sea, the Sea* or the immensely compelling and popular seafaring novels of Patrick O'Brien.

The sea has not lost its power to enthral British imaginations. It is a natural force, still capable of setting some of the most daunting physical and mental challenges known to man. Hardy, daring individuals pit themselves against it to row across the Atlantic or sail single-handed around the world. New records are broken, it seems, almost weekly, but that does not lessen the danger attached to them. Sophisticated technology cannot by itself overcome tempestuous seas, and adventurers can pay with their lives for what is sometimes foolhardiness. In competition, sailing is still a sport at which the British excel. The Royal Yacht Squadron at Cowes, that castellated Valhalla for yachtsmen, continues to serve tea inside a striped tent on an eternal Edwardian lawn. During Cowes Week, the scene of Squadron members moving about the balconies in their white ducks, blue blazers and nautical caps looks just as it did in the 1890s. Here at least is one English institution unruffled by the salty winds of change.

Lucky are the few who dine among the Squadron's silver trophies, surrounded by portraits of past Commodores. Lucky too are those who have been entertained aboard one of Her Majesty's warships. The Navy is still the senior service, beloved of royalty and attentive to the maintenance of tradition. Recently, the diminution that has overtaken it reflects the decline in all aspects of employment, except leisure, connected to the sea. Like a woollen guernsey washed at too high a temperature, the Royal Navy is now a complete little garment fit for a small power, one without world-class ambitions. The complement of surface ships is now only five more than would have escorted a single convoy across the Atlantic in the Second World War. Perhaps this is as it should be, given our more modest world role and changes in strategic military thinking. For our self-respect, what matters is the way this retreat is handled. We withdrew from the responsibilities of Empire, generally with honour. The government has not been so successful in its withdrawal from the military buildings created for an age when the armed forces were larger and more glory-conscious. Often, the level of its imagination seems banal in comparison with the splendour of the buildings and the meticulousness of the tradition which has been preserved in them.

In all areas we are being compelled to revise our emotional attachment to the sea, following material changes that are too substantial to be denied. Seaside resorts, fishing, shipbuilding, the purity of the waters themselves – each has undergone an upheaval. Each threatens to make us adjust our feelings about the sea itself.

Traditionally, the place where the majority of people would be most likely to come into direct contact with the sea that surrounds these islands was the seaside. That statement may sound self-evident, and it is an indication of how far things have changed that it is probably no longer true. More people now see it from the deck of a cross-channel ferry or, glimpsed between the clouds, through the window of an aeroplane than visit coastal resorts. Even when the public does go to Southend, Margate, Cromer, Blackpool, Skegness or other seaside towns, it is less likely to take a dip in the briny. Bathing takes place in specially constructed leisure pools, with elaborate water-chutes or flumes, and palm trees to suggest that swimmers are not somewhere as unromantic as England at all, but in the Caribbean. But what is the point of a seaside resort if it is not the sea? The sea's lack of allure as an object has deprived resorts of their sense of purpose, and it shows. Think of the seaside, and the vision rises of a place sunk in gloom, catering only to the least enterprising class of holidaymaker – those who are unable to find the energy or money (usually the former) to go abroad – and old fossils who have not noticed how much things have changed. The quality of the food, entertainment, modern architecture and civic presentation are all dismal. 'Among the horrors that market themselves as English seaside resorts, Great Yarmouth, which sits like a boil on England's eastern cheek, is perhaps without peer for hideousness and hopelessness,' wrote Michael Thompson-Noel in the *Financial Times* recently. This was hard on Great Yarmouth; there are plenty of other resorts just as bad. It is typical in not having moved on from a halcyon era to which its resemblance becomes dingier by the year. 'It looks as though it has not changed in any respect in half a century, as though its grotesqueness and datedness are protected, for some reason, by a force field.' Those resorts where development has taken place in the last twenty years have managed to avoid any elevation of quality. 'Bugger Bognor' are supposed to have been George V's last words, in response to urging that he should recuperate at his favourite seaside resort. If he were to visit Bognor now, he would think it had indeed suffered the fate he advised.

The role of the seaside in the national consciousness has always been somewhat ambiguous. In the old days, when the public went there in droves, it was where the usually cool, controlled and unconvivial British became disinhibited. They rolled up their trouser-legs, shrieked and acted like clowns. (It is tempting to say that what used to be the seaside way of behaviour has become the norm, at least wherever the English assemble in crowds. Look at Trafalgar Square on New Year's Eve or during a football championship.) The seaside has been a paradox since its invention as a place to take the waters, by drinking as well as bathing, in the seventeenth century. At a time when people at all levels of society muffled themselves up in their clothes, seabathing for a long time customarily took place in the nude. Nakedness aroused comment, but not as much as one would have expected. Men bathed naked, in view of the shore, into the Victorian period. As a curate in the 1870s, Francis Kilvert could not bear the experience of bathing in drawers, and cast them aside. Even when special costumes were introduced, their cotton fabric, clinging to the body when wet, left little to the imagination. It was only when heavier woollens were made the rule for such garments that modesty can be said to have been preserved. But then that is part of the magic of the sea: it liberates us from everyday life.

There were really two seasides. As Marghanita Laski, speaking for the upper middle classes, put it in *Punch* in 1966: 'We want solitude in rural arcadias. They want conviviality in pleasure cities.' 'They', in this context, were the hordes who went to the glittering, noisy resorts, with their mechanical amusements, rather than the self-selecting few whose ideal was an undiscovered cove, which they had to themselves, in Devon. The cheap and cheerful dimension of resorts like Margate developed early. 'Visitors, like mackerel, are valued only by the shoal, and the amusements of the place are consequently chiefly adapted for the Million, who come swarming and steaming, by boat and rail, like the flux and reflux of the tide itself,' sniffed *The Southern Coast of England* in 1849 (its tone of censure being hardly surprising given its subtitle of *A Picturesque, Antiquarian and Topographical Description of the Scenery, Towns and Ancient Remains of That Part of the Coast*). Still, as even *The Southern Coast of England* acknowledged, such places, if cheap, were indeed also cheerful. These days, jollity is in short supply on the coast – or, one is sometimes tempted to think, anywhere else.

Part of the problem is the wave of health puritanism that has swept the country. It is often blamed on Europe, but in reality the people responsible have grown up among us. It is obvious where they come from historically: the joyless puritans of Cromwellian England, who banned the eating of mince pies and Christmas puddings on Christmas Day (offences still on the statue books). Now organised religion has declined, and the cult of health has partially replaced it – certainly it forms the basis of the few moral absolutes in the West. For centuries, these puritans have lain dormant, like wildflower seeds at the bottom of a wood, waiting only for the trees to fall and light to suffuse the woodland floor before springing up as a forgotten but virulent species of nettle. They have contributed towards the demise of the seaside donkey, whose digestive process, working its natural consequence upon the sands, could not be tolerated by the hygiene fundamentalists

195

known as environmental health officers. Donkeys still plod out their lugubrious days at Blackpool, but at precious few other places; and even there they do not cut the figures of charm they once did.

Jet-travel, satisfying the twentieth-century craving to expose flesh beneath the sun, put paid to the British seaside resort. It might be thought its demise was inevitable; on the contrary, it could have learnt the lesson of Disney: that even a mass clientele now want cleanliness, quality and imagination. These principles are embodied in the holiday developments created by Center Parks (none, significantly, by the sea), which succeed despite the British weather. An alternative strategy might have been to accept that nothing will now stop the old 'Million' who flocked to Margate from holidaying on the Costas, and to take the seaside upmarket. It could have been delightful. With bandstands and the best kind of municipal bedding, seaside resorts might have captured something of the atmosphere of prosperous German spas. But it was not to be. As a result, this maritime nation turns inward upon itself, stampeding into an already over-populated countryside, and neglects visiting the sea.

Buried in our emotional response to the sea around Britain is the knowledge that it is often not what it should be. The waters no longer move 'at their priest-like task/Of pure ablution round earth's human shores', as Keats wrote in a sonnet. They are full of sewage for a start. And sewage is among the less harmful ingredients that have been dumped into them. Even the run-off of nitrates from intensively farmed fields is disturbing the natural order of things: brown seaweed around the coast is growing too strongly and vast blooms of algae are appearing, killing the shellfish and baby cod and whiting beneath.

There was a time when the British could pride themselves on better standards of beaches than elsewhere in Europe. It was when people went abroad that they ran risks through sea-bathing. That was the Mediterranean countries for you: being poor, a little backward and generally untrustworthy, they did not get these things right. Just as we did not need to drink mineral water, our tap-water being as good as the stuff foreigners got out of bottles, so we had confidence that the British system would guarantee a decent standard of cleanliness in the seas. If any company or local council was tempted to contravene public expectations in these matters, the authorities would be down on them, compelling them to mend their ways. One of the shocks of joining Europe has been to discover that our partners do not see things in that light: they have sniffed at our sea-water, and found that it stinks. In November 1995, the Department of the Environment made much of the 'marked improvement in UK bathing water quality', since 89 per cent of identified waters were found to meet EU standards. This was certainly better than the year before, when only 82 per cent achieved that level. Nevertheless, a pass rate of 89 per cent still leaves a failure rate of 11 per cent. The revelation that the sea of over one in ten beaches around Britain is not good enough for the European Union is hard for the British public to stomach.

So awful does it seem that some people go into a state of denial. It cannot be like this; at the least, the Continentals must be cheating when they claim that their sea-water is cleaner. Unfortunately, the official results are supported by other studies. In April 1996 the Marine Conservation Society published a report in which the quality of sea-water in the north-west of England made the resorts of Blackpool and Morecambe 'little better than a cesspit'. Their conclusions are supported anecdotally by the surfing fraternity, who claim that they regularly share the waves that they ride to the shore with a disgusting scum of faeces and other foul matter. The European standards, to which 89 per cent of our beaches conform, were laid down in 1976, and many scientists now believe that these minimum requirements are not enough to guarantee a healthy swim in the sea. Nor does one have to go into the water to encounter the detritus deposited there. Walk along the beach itself and, according to a survey published in 1993, you are likely to stumble upon an average 28 plastic bottles, 27 cans and 38 pieces of sewage in the course of a mile.

Huge efforts are being made by local authorities and others to rectify the main problem for beaches, namely sewage disposal.

Southern Water, for example, has embarked on a project at Brighton which is likely to cost £40 million. It is expensive but eventually, given the revenue that could be lost from tourism if nothing is done, no doubt city fathers everywhere will take action. In the meantime, the happy innocence of our bucket-and-spade days, in which the sea was to be feared principally on account of its goose-pimpling temperature, has been lost. There remains the fear that what we have discovered about the water into which we may think of inserting our bodies is nothing to what we do not know about the seas elsewhere. If the health of the seas can be diagnosed from the health of the fish in it, the prognosis is grim.

For a growing number of people, their most intimate experience of the sea comes through consuming its harvest. As the public distaste for red meat increases, so does the desire to eat fish, which possibly illustrates how little most people know about what happens at sea. Urban man understands little enough about animal husbandry, but forms an imaginative bond with the cattle and sheep being raised, sufficient to suffuse him with horror at the thought of their being killed for the table. For the time fish are alive, they live a more natural existence than farm animals – natural in so far as man's depredations of their environment permit, that is. When it comes to their death, however, that can seem far more cruel than any meted out in the slaughter-house. Sole, plaice and some other white fish, for example, can be served white only because they have their guts ripped out as soon as they are landed, often while still alive. Many fish drown in the nets before they are ever hauled up on to deck. The waste of the whole exercise, particularly under the rules of the Common Fisheries Policy, is grotesque. If fish were not wet, scaly and evidently different from humankind they would not be so acceptable as an alternative to meat. If it could be demonstrated that they experienced pain like us, their fate would provoke horror. But then they would not be fish.

Be that as it may, the paradox is in danger of resolving itself through the virtual elimination of some fish species from our seas. For a nation whose national dish is fish and chips, a recent report from the EU Advisory Committee on Fisheries Management makes portentous reading; the stock of cod in the North Sea, it tells us, is down to one-third of the lowest desirable biological level (the minimum required to secure the future of the stock), and there is 'serious concern that the stock is no longer able to replenish itself'. It recommends that for the stock to recover, there should be a fishing moratorium. As the environmental economist David Fleming wrote in *Country Life* recently: 'The cod fishery is not simply in danger of collapse; it is collapsing.' While the state of cod stocks is desperate, those of haddock, whiting and plaice are little better. According to the International Council for the Exploration of the Sea, 92 per cent of all commercial fish stocks around the world are being overfished. At home, even the usually complacent Ministry of Agriculture, Fisheries and Food acknowledges in a report that 'most fish stocks in the North Atlantic are overfished by any rational criteria'.

There was a time when kippers flopped off the side of the plate; now it is impossible to find them in any but miserable sizes, with hardly any flesh between the bones. The opening of Britain's immemorial fishing grounds to other European fleets has decimated stocks. This is also true of other forms of sea life. Sand eels are not eaten by man, but they provide the food for larger fish, as well as seabirds such as puffins. (They are the little fish a line of which is often pictured in the puffin's beak.) They are being fished industrially on so large a scale that a Danish concern has received permission to build a factory at Grangemouth, on the Firth of Forth, to turn them into animal feed. They received a grant from the Scottish Office to do so; the plant created twenty new jobs in a depressed area. But fishing on the scale necessary to service this factory could be disastrous for both the local fishing fleet and the seabirds. The sand-eel fishery in the Shetlands caused the collapse of the Arctic tern population, as well as other local birds. They bred successfully, but could not then find little fish, which could be carried in their beaks, to feed their young. As larger fish decline, so the organisms that they would feast on flourish too abundantly. There have been strange blooms of plankton, some turning the sea red, partly as a result of the enrichment of the waters from the run-off of fertilisers from farmland.

The contamination of sea-waters, not only with fertiliser but other chemicals, oil, nuclear waste and the sewage referred to above, has also taken its toll on the fish population. This is well known to fishermen, though its effects are difficult to quantify and have not yet been very much studied. Anyone who goes out on a fishing vessel can observe the surprisingly high number of mutant fish being hauled in with any catch. These are fish whose heads are too big, or bodies malformed; fish who are misshapen and sick. The fishermen believe that their numbers have greatly increased over the years, the obvious cause being the filth with which the oceans have now been filled. The sickly character of some fish exacerbates the havoc wrought upon stocks by overfishing.

The decline of haddock, cod, herring and other traditional delicacies – if that word does not aggrandise what used to be everyday fare – has been disastrous for the fishermen who depended on them. It is brutal to realise that the hardy, tight-knit communities of our fishing ports are having the reason for their existence snatched away from them. Fishermen want to continue to fish. People who have no economic connection with the activity like to believe that they will do so. Many little towns, such as Padstow in Cornwall, depend for their survival on fishing and tourism. Now they are in prospect of having only tourism. Yet the reason why the tourists came was because of the character of the fishing port. When fishing is over, no doubt tourists will still come. But both sides of the equation will be the poorer.

What has caused the decline in fish stocks? Fishing. So fishermen are to blame; they forfeit pubic sympathy. Once, most people extended the same sort of awed fellow-feeling to fishermen that they did to coal-miners. It was a tough, dangerous job, and they were only too pleased that someone else chose to do it. British fishermen, in their small boats, still deserve that goodwill. They have contributed to the depletion of fish stocks – of course they have – but on the whole they have been slow to modernise and invest. The scale of the catch that an average

British boat can take is dwarfed by that of the much larger vessels from Spain and Eastern Europe. Fishing is an industry which should preserve its inefficiencies. One of the arguments in favour of the continued over-exploitation of the seas is the importance of fishing to coastal communities. But technology has been developed at the expense of people. Big modern boats – our fleet does not have many of them – haul in enormous quantities of fish but employ no more crew members than the ancient craft seen bobbing by the quaysides of our little ports. The last thing our fishing grounds need is more efficient fishing. By a disastrous paradox, it is the skippers of the older boats who find it attractive to take the government's inducements to leave the industry.

Technology has been pushed to the limit in one direction: catching fish. But the seas present another challenge – preventing the grotesque levels of waste now pertaining. Here, technology has done little to help because it has not been asked to do so. It has always been accepted among fishermen that, in most areas of the sea, it is not possible to fish for only one species. If you target cod, for example, you cannot avoid dragging up in your nets a quantity of other fish swimming with it. This unintended haul, known as the by-catch, will contain some fish that have a market value, though not as high as the target species; some fish that nobody wants; and also fish of different ages. When boats were small and fish stocks were plentiful, the by-catch, though wasteful, hardly seemed a problem. The unwanted fish were thrown back into the water; most of them died but, as the expression goes, there were plenty more in the sea. Now, though, industrial fishing practices mean that the by-catch is vast. Attempts to restrict overfishing by imposing quotas mean that even more of it than before cannot be sold. Species for which the quota ceiling has been reached, or 'juveniles' that are regarded as too young to be caught, must be thrown back. Many of these fish are dead before they are returned to the sea, and the survival rate of the others is low. Studies show that four-fifths of fish returned to the sea die.

For a time this caused an explosion in sea-bird populations. All this fish floating on top of the sea: they had never had it so good! Last year, however, they showed the first evidence of decline since the 1980s. Since sea-bird numbers are an accurate index of what is happening at sea, in this case it would seem that the size of the by-catch has fallen. This probably means that the numbers of quota species and juveniles are in trouble, and it confirms what scientists had already told us: that we are entering the last stages of a sort of ethnic cleansing of the seas.

We in Britain know this. Our instincts rebel against waste: we have always rather prided ourselves on our aptitude not to squander resources, unlike the Americans. We regard ourselves as having a special respect and affection for the natural world. Yet here, in the waters of such a maritime nation as Britain, is waste on a catastrophic scale, which is leading to the destruction of an industry and an ecology. When we see this horror before us, we are even more amazed that we cannot do anything about it. Thanks to the Common Fisheries Policy of the EU, we can only stand on the beach and wring our hands. British boats have, in the past, played their part in the depletion of fish stocks, but now the worst offenders are from overseas, legitimately taking advantage of rights over our waters that we signed away. The seas used to be the symbol of our proud independence as a nation. They are now an emblem of our angst.

*   *   *

Oh, where are you going to, all you Big Steamers,
With England's own coal, up and down the salt seas?
We are going to fetch you your bread and your butter,
Your beef, pork, and mutton, eggs, apples and cheese.
Rudyard Kipling, 'Big Steamers'

Membership of Europe has downgraded our island status. We used to pride ourselves on our separateness from the Continent, whose armies have sometimes only been frustrated from invading us by the sea. Now we are part of the European Union, and we can reach the Continental mainland through a tunnel. Conversely, we no longer have an Empire serviced by an immense, efficient, smart and at times romantic merchant fleet. The proportion of our trade with the world beyond Europe has declined. The number of merchant vessels registered in Britain has dropped from over 2,300 in 1961 to under 500 in 1991. Those that we still have are, on average, older than those of other fleets, and they are replaced less often. Our shipbuilding industry, once the biggest in the world, now takes just 1 per cent of the world market. The decline can be traced from 1919, but became a vertiginous descent after the oil crisis of 1973. For a time, work held up while old orders were being fulfilled, then collapsed as Japan, South Korea and now China took the business.

What seems strange, given our maritime history, is the degree to which shipping matters escape the eye of government. The Department of Transport, for so long effectively the Department of Roads, turns its back on the seas and waterways. Far more energy has been spent on rail privatisation than on the arguably more serious issue of our merchant fleet. The majority of British goods is now carried in ships of other countries. Moreover, the decline in shipping has started to have an economic consequence beyond that of the trade itself. Because of our maritime supremacy, the City of London used to have an unrivalled reputation for insurance, broking and the law. These industries are now being challenged by those of countries more directly involved in the day-to-day activities of shipping than Britain. Cyprus has its own register of shipping, attended by specialist lawyers and insurance companies. There are now other insurance markets than the troubled Lloyd's of London. Bermuda, Singapore and other places in the Far East, for example, are developing strong broking houses.

This is an odd state of affairs for a nation which, with a history patterned by the sea, loves ships. As Ian Jack has observed: 'We preserve them, collect prints of them, eulogise them as doughty British artifacts in the Falklands War.' Increasingly we visit them and preserve them, the latest tributes to this veneration of the ship being the *Mary Rose*, the SS *Great Britain* and Captain Scott of the Antarctic's HMS *Discovery*. It is too late now to talk about a crisis in Britain's shipping and shipbuilding industries; there can be no crisis after death. But there remains a crisis of the British soul as we compare the glories of the past with the ignominies of the present.

The sea represents the outward limit of these islands. Their inner workings, in the form of Parliament and the democratic process, are no less troubled.

10

Mother of Democracy

*Who are the English? They are Saxons, who love
the land, who love their liberty, and whose sole
claim to genius is their common-sense.*
      Price Collier, *England and the English*, 1909

The crisis of British self-esteem which, as we saw in the last
chapter, penetrates even the waters amid which the British Isles
are set, is reflected in the low opinion that the public has of the
institutions that govern it. At my prep school, an otherwise iras-
cible English master – who had suffered atrocities in a Japanese
prisoner-of-war camp during the Second World War – would
be moved to tears every time he recounted the history of the
'Winslow Boy', made famous by Terence Rattigan's play of that
name. The child, unjustly accused of cheating, had been expelled
from school; but his father, believing him to have suffered an
injustice, beggared himself by pursuing the case through every
court in the land up to the House of Lords itself, where he
eventually succeeded in clearing the boy's name. This was held
up to us as an example of the Olympian fairness of the British
legal system: open to everyone, whatever the pretext.

From today's perspective, the salient point of the tale might
seem to be that the father was reduced to penury by his
obsessive quest. Justice, in some aspects, has come to seem

accessible only to three sections of society: the very rich, who have the money; the very poor, who qualify for legal aid; and those who employ lawyers on a no-win-no-fee basis. The no-win-no-fee system, permissible from 1995, has an obvious attraction for litigants; but by encouraging lawyers to pursue claims that, to the public, appear to run contrary to common sense, it threatens to undermine the standing of the law. Other developments have already begun to chip away at the apparent immutability of the legal monolith. The system has proved unequal to the task of disentangling complex City frauds. A series of spectacular miscarriages of justice, dating from the 1970s, has brought both the legal system and the police into disrepute. In all trials, evidence gathered by the police – once held to be above suspicion – is now regarded with scepticism. The fault rests partly with the police themselves, not just because of the genuine misdemeanours that have been perpetrated, but also arising from their abandonment of their old homely persona in favour of a more macho, violent image derived from American television programmes.

There is hardly any institution in Britain in which it would be possible to say that public confidence runs high. The one that most visibly portrays the mood of anxiety is Parliament itself: a victim in part of the public's obsessive though perverted interest in it. We live increasingly in a culture of blame. Whatever the tragedy or mischance to afflict humanity, someone can always be held responsible. This may contribute towards the general cry of 'blame the government', whenever life's shoe begins to rub. It can be exaggerated, but the readiness with which people blame the government for common ills reflects their relationship with authority. In the early years of this century, the only regular contact that most people had with government was through the buying of stamps at the post office. Now almost every human activity, from starting a business to building a loft extension, is subject to regulation, whether by local or central government. The more people are aware of being governed, the more they turn their eyes upon the emblem of the British system, the House of Commons.

The way in which Parliament operates is an extreme manifestation of the British character, which is scarcely an accident.
The form taken by the Palace of Westminster was hotly debated
when it was constructed in the nineteenth century. Its Gothic
pinnacles, elaborate symbolism and reverence for traditions of
the building it replaced were all formulated as a conscious
expression of national character. Even within living memory,
its peculiarities were generally regarded as a source of comfort.
No, for heaven's sake, the emotion was more than comfort: it
was pride. The adversarial structure gave rise to moments of great
theatre, as classically educated parliamentarians rolled orotund
phrases at each other across the chamber. The robustness and
the pageantry all seemed pleasingly British. After all, we told
ourselves, we more or less invented modern democracy, and if
certain procedures of the House of Commons seemed arcane,
that was only a function of their antiquity. The ermine-clad
hereditary element of the House of Lords may have been
recognised as an anomaly, but at least its existence demonstrated
the supreme tolerance of the British public, which could never be
bothered to remove it. The two major parties took their turns at
the crease with the decorum of cricketers on the village green.
It seemed to satisfy most people. It worked, or we thought it
did. Now the oddities of the system do not seem quite so cosy,
for we have the uneasy sense that we have come to look like
the buffoons of Europe. Not that we care what our Continental
partners think, of course; but there is a nagging feeling that they
have a point.

The knowledge that, since television has been allowed to
film proceedings, Prime Minister's Questions has become a
cult comedy programme in Europe and America is unsettling.
These knock-about occasions are the activity of Parliament
that appears most frequently on the television news. There is
a certain affection for it: it is admirable that the head of the
government should be sufficiently in command of the broad
sweep of policy that he can be expected to answer questions on
any aspect of it, without notice. Such is the theory. But nobody
expects the answers to illuminate very much, and neither side
sees this as its objective. The Opposition appears not to seek

genuine information so much as an opportunity to catch the Prime Minister out; while stooges on the Prime Minister's side feed lines that enable him to sing his own praises. It is a fatuous exercise, conducted in conditions of rowdiness that have no parallel in advanced societies. Naturally, television excerpts feature the moments of greatest drama when the level of behaviour is at its lowest. At other times, the proceedings of the House seem simply incomprehensible to those outside it . . . perhaps even to those inside it. Certainly, few enough Members bother to turn up for all but the most rousing debates, generally when there is a Cabinet minister at the dispatch box.

To most of the public, such conspicuous absenteeism may just be taken as a sign of laziness. The accusation may not be fair, given the extent to which the MP's duties, whether to his constituents or on committees, have grown in recent years. What should concern them more might be the obvious loss of authority by the House of Commons as a place of debate, which reflects the haemorrhage of power from Westminster that has taken place since the European institutions grew in might. It is with a kind of horror that the British people have come to realise the extent to which the European Commission and the European Court of Human Rights can control domestic policy, from exporting beef to Africa to the administering of a parental slap to a disobedient child. When they see acres of unoccupied leather upholstery on the benches of their own elected chamber, their impression that the Commons is not a place worth bothering with, even for MPs, is reinforced. But that is not the sole reason for the decline, which lies in a loss of interest by the public itself as far as its tastes and wishes are interpreted by the media.

Under the editorship of Simon Jenkins, *The Times* abandoned its parliamentary page on the grounds that he 'couldn't find anyone who read it except MPs'. This was a symbolic act, marking a shift in journalist priorities across what used to be termed Fleet Street. Before 1988 *The Times* devoted between 400 and 800 lines to parliamentary reports, and the *Guardian* between 300 and 700 lines; by 1992 this figure had fallen to fewer than 100 lines in each newspaper. The gallery tradition has perished at the hands of the lobby correspondent and the sketch-writer; the public is now deemed to be more interested in what happens behind the scenes than on the floor of the House. Indeed there is an assumption that actual debates in the Commons are merely window-dressing for a political process whose real substance lies in the machinations and fixes that take place out of sight. There is something in that view, of course, but like everything it can be taken too far. It is not uncommon for newspapers now to report extensively the leaks, surmises and lobbying pressure that supposedly indicate what may happen to a piece of legislation, but then to consign the outcome of the debate, which leads to legislation, to a couple of obscure paragraphs on an inside page. They are so anxious to be ahead of the news that they miss the news itself.

Old gallery hands reported what actually happened in Parliament; lobby correspondents necessarily set their own agenda, by guessing what is most likely to be regarded as newsworthy by their readers – or, more accurately, by their editors. Top of the menu comes the appetising dish of sleaze. Almost one in ten so-called parliamentary stories now feature scandal and misconduct. These issues enjoy far greater prominence than such important policy areas as education, health and law and order. To make way for all the sleaze, something had to give – and this was the serious consideration of less titillating issues. By 1994 the major newspapers' coverage of education and local government plummeted to a quarter, or less than the level of 1990. Given the direction taken by press interest, back-benchers should perhaps be relieved that their names feature so infrequently: in less than a tenth of the stories (and even then back-bench representation is dominated by a few vociferous and sometimes maverick individuals, such as the Tory Euro-sceptics). The House of Lords is also rarely mentioned. By far the lion's share of attention is taken by senior figures from the Labour and Conservative parties (the Liberal Democrats barely get a look in); and even a member of the Cabinet or shadow Cabinet might feel jealous of the column inches devoted to the Prime Minister and Leader of the Opposition upon whom, it would seem, all journalists' eyes are fixed.

The introduction of television cameras in 1989 should, in

theory, have raised the authority of Parliament by making debates accessible to every viewer. However, it has not worked quite like that. Viewers have shown themselves, perhaps not surprisingly, to be just as uninterested in the longueurs of debate, when MPs harangue an empty chamber, as MPs themselves. Television has probably caused some deterioration in the level of debate by inspiring the more media-aware parliamentarians to encapsulate their thoughts in what would previously have been considered rather unparliamentary expressions – as when Teresa Gorman spoke of the need for repeated rapists to have their goolies chopped off. Such vibrant language is guaranteed saturation coverage across the media. But generally the appearance of television cameras has provoked a paradox: the more opportunity programme-makers have to show MPs in debate, the more they choose to film them outside the Palace of Westminster. Interesting politicians are, some say, more likely to be found in the new television studios created at Millbank than in the chamber. Informative conversations take place while waiting for make-up. Equally, the now traditional site for more spontaneous television interviews – College Green, opposite the Palace of Westminster – may be thronged with more MPs than are to be seen on the floor of the House of Commons. This has been a boon to politicians of all kinds, anxious to impress themselves upon their electorates, but particularly to those whom their parties would regard as troublemakers: colourful figures who make good television. Party managers, however, can hardly complain. They have increasingly tailored announcements to media demands at the expense of the House of Commons. The extensive use of 'leaks' to gauge public opinion and soften opposition has removed the element of drama from most Commons statements. Unpredictability is reserved for resignations – and how rare they have become!

When even MPs begin to feel that the Commons is not the place of importance it used to be, a shadow passes across the national landscape. What had seemed unique and unassailable now looks vulnerable. 'One of the greatest weaknesses at the heart of Britain's government is the waning power of the Commons,' wrote *The Economist* in November 1995. 'It is an institution in crisis.' The vulnerability has been exploited by those who wish to represent it as enmired in sleaze. The reporting of sleaze has been out of proportion to the extent of the sleaze actually discovered. Along the way, however, light has been shone on to the corridors of power, revealing them not to be the resplendent spaces, hung with Pugin wallpaper, that had perhaps been imagined; instead they are dank and mildewed. The Ordtech court case, over arms to Iraq, and the 'cash for questions' affair uncovered a culture of self-interest that the public now believes to be endemic. There is a feeling that politicians are on the make. Of course they are; so is most of humanity. But it used not to be quite so blatant. People used to believe in Jeremy Thorpe, though subsequent revelations showed their faith to have been unjustified. These days, all politicians are assumed to be Thorpes.

It is disturbing for the public to discover that, through companies such as Ian Greer Associates, influence can effectively be bought. But almost as worrying is the influence achieved by small groups who do not pay for it so overtly. Parliament, still organised largely on the amateur model established in the nineteenth century, has become susceptible to single-issue pressure groups who are motivated, informed and sometimes generously funded. They know much more about their specialist areas of interest than the average overworked MP. It is tempting for MPs who wish to make an instant contribution to a topical issue to buy the pressure group's agenda, perhaps representing it as his own considered opinion. The talents of some of the better established pressure groups are even employed in the drafting of legislation; their influence reflects the support they attract from the public. The growing disenchantment with politics, seen in the decline in support for political parties, has been mirrored in a boom in the membership of such institutions as the Royal Society for the Protection of Birds, the Royal Society for the Protection of Animals, the National Trust, the Council for the Protection of Rural England, Greenpeace and so on. (According to a recent edition of *Social Trends*, about 10 per cent of the adult population now belongs to an environmental charity but only 4 per cent to a political party.) It could be argued that the political presence of these environmental organisations reflects the public will, expressed through their membership. But there is a suspicion that the powers of individual MPs to exercise their judgement on behalf of all their constituents is being subverted. This suspicion is strengthened by the knowledge that the International League for Animal Welfare, a radical group based in North America, has funded the Labour Party to the tune of £1 million. Its object in doing so is to stiffen the Party's resolve to ban hunting.

The low reputation of Parliament has generated a feeling that 'something must be done'. This has caused the Labour Party to propose not one but a whole basket of somethings – new parliaments for Scotland and Wales, reform of regional government, a new authority for London, a Bill of Rights, a reduced role for the monarchy, adoption of the Social Chapter from Europe, new arrangements in Northern Ireland. The character of Westminster would be changed by the abolition of the voting rights of the hereditary peers in the House of Lords. Most people, even the peers themselves, recognise that accident of birth is not a defensible principle for selecting a second chamber in the late twentieth century. But the trouble with Labour's 'something must be done-ism' is that it has obscured the consequence of the reform: namely, that depriving the Lords of its hereditary element would turn it into nothing but a super-quango, entirely appointed by the Prime Minister.

It could be argued that the hereditary peers, operating by random selection, introduce the most representative note into the Lords. Certainly the life peers are singularly unrepresentative of the nation as a whole, containing a disproportionately high number of lawyers and former Cabinet ministers, with hardly any representation from the arts. Banishing the hereditary peers from the Lords, says Tony Blair, would be only the first step towards a more radical reform of the whole system, leading to an elected second chamber. That policy might not be as axiomatically popular as Labour supposes. The new second chamber, or Senate as it would probably be called, would attract the kind of people who at present become MPs – but not the brightest or most ambitious of them, who would naturally prefer a seat in the Commons or the European Parliament. Careerist MPs are precisely the people whom the public believes to be sleazy. To abolish the Lords and replace it with a chamber composed of dud would-be MPs would be bizarre, and certainly it would hardly rectify the public's disillusion with Westminster. Popular criticism focuses on the Commons, not the Lords.

To recapture public confidence in Parliament, the system must be brought up to date. The excessive levels of secrecy tolerated until now have become unacceptable. Parliament's working practices should be reviewed, to encourage a greater range of personality types to stand as MPs. The workload at Westminster might be redistributed. At present, the Lords are a rather under-utilised resource, whereas the Commons are overburdened. While the Commons should remain responsible for initiating legislation and patrolling the executive, the Lords might occupy themselves not just with revising legislation sent on to them from the Commons, but supervising the vast apparatus of government, much of which is now roaming free in the wilderness where quangos live.

Unhappily for democracy, the sex lives of MPs are easier to convert into spicy news stories than the decay of local government. But the way in which the powers of the lower tiers of government have been progressively stripped from them in recent years is far worse than any apparent seediness in the personal behaviour of politicians. The British system, with which there was a wide measure of content just thirty years ago, has been dismantled. For example, the reason why privatised parking wardens have become so assiduous in central London is that the revenue from parking fines constitutes the largest source of income over which Westminster City Council has unfettered control; this is the one area not subject to government restrictions. Not that local authorities have been alone in their emasculation. As the Labour MP Derek Foster commented to a conference on 'Management in Government' in 1995:

It can be argued that throughout the 1980s many of the checks and balances within the unwritten British constitution were systematically dismantled. Every source of resistance to central government was squashed or brow-beaten into submission. First the trade unions, and the nation applauded because we were not all trade unionists ... Then the Church, and the nation walked by on the other side because the Church was run by effete liberals. Then the BBC, and the nation bit its tongue because there was a dangerous hotbed of lefties in the BBC. Then every professional association was denigrated as a vested interest, and the nation held its tongue because the government was on the side of the consumer against these self-serving producers.

Now unelected quangos control the astonishing total of £55bn, which is a fifth of all public expenditure.

This leaves British democracy in an enfeebled condition, from which it will be hard to recover quickly. It is hardly surprising that it should have become difficult to find councillors of distinction to contest seats on local authorities; because freedom of action has been so reduced that council work is now tedious and frustrating. The kind of people who enjoy this unrewarding drudgery are not on the whole those whom one would choose as representatives. The crisis can be seen most vividly perhaps at the lowest echelon of all: the parish council. Here, it is estimated that as many as 45 per cent of seats are not contested at all, and that 30 per cent of councils are unable to fill all the available seats.

This level of apathy raises the question of why we still suffer parish councils to exist. According to Tony Travers, a leading expert in local government at the London School of Economics, quoted recently in *Country Life*, they are a sort of bauble dangling from the governmental Christmas tree:

We keep them on because they are part of the English cultural fantasy: you know, country cottages, village greens, pubs – and parish councils. It is a Miss Marple kind of world, with warm beer and old ladies riding down the high street on upright bicycles. We English are very strong on this. Walter Bagehot said that the monarchy was part of the 'dignified', rather than the 'effective' part of the British constitution; at the other end of the political spectrum, the same is true of parish councils.

This is a harsh judgement. The success of parish councils – town councils, in the case of small towns – depends upon the enthusiasm and commitment of the councillors, and some have both in abundance. Further, the English cultural fantasy is not lightly to be dismissed; in fact it should be cherished. But generally parish councils cannot be said to bring a sense of vibrant, participative democracy to every front door in rural England. A good place to begin the reinvigoration of democracy in Britain would be the parish council, which should be the tier which has the most intimate relationship with the electorate and could, using modern communications technology, provide a point of intercession between the British subject and government.

In Bagehot's terms, the parish council has unassailable dignity but needs more effectiveness. That other dignified element of the constitution, the monarchy, is unquestionably effective in fulfilling its constitutional role: the head of state is head of state to perfection. Dignity is not a quality that the late twentieth century has much time for, and it has done what it can to strip it from the institution that most personifies Britain.

11

Royalty and Loathing

The slow decline of our Island Race
Alien prophets have long foreseen,
But still, to symbolise English grace,
We go to London to see the Queen.

Our far-flung Empire imposed new rules
And lasted a century or so
Until, engrossed with our football pools
We shrugged our shoulders and let it go.

But old traditions are hard to kill
However battered about they've been.
And it's still, for some, an authentic thrill
To go to London to see the Queen.
                    Noël Coward, 'Not Yet the Dodo'

The Englishman hates to reveal himself; in fact it is
considered bad manners to talk about oneself.
             Kurt von Stutterheim, *Those English*, 1937

There is a strange parallel between the disaster of BSE and the present state of the royal family. Like agriculture, royalty used to be something most people did not think much about, but assumed to be a British success. Now even the royal family are victims of the uncertainty and lack of direction that characterise modern Britain. For a decade and a half, the monarchy was a rock upon which the waves of ordure produced by the British media were allowed to break without response. Not surprisingly the experience engendered a sense of pessimism within the institution, which again reflects the mood of the nation as a whole. Having withstood the tempest for so long, the Queen now appears to have signalled a retreat by establishing a committee, chaired by Prince Charles, to consider the monarchy's role and scale. It has hardly set itself an urgent timetable: it will meet only once every six months. Nevertheless, that it is meeting at all is a public acknowledgement of the doubt by which the royal family is beset. Had the committee been formed ten years ago, it would have been able to lead events. All the questions it will now address might have been asked then. It would seem that the monarchy – previously so skilful in knowing when to give a little, when to retreat with dignity – has lost its touch.

Most people agree that the rules by which the monarchy operates need revision. It is absurd that the monarch should be barred from marrying a Roman Catholic, while free to unite with a Hindu, Bhuddist, Shintoist or pagan (though the prospect of the monarch's eldest child being brought up a Catholic and in due course ascending the throne would still not be acceptable in some parts of the country). At present the heir to the throne, Prince Charles, has only male children; but if the elder one had been a girl, most people would think it unfair that the accident of sex should prevent her from succeeding to the throne. Nevertheless, a slimmed-down, rationalised, corporate, bicycle-riding monarchy would not answer the British people's expectations of the institution. In terms of national identity, the significance of the monarchy lies in being extraordinary. Its panoply, mystique and archaism are a remarkable thing about Britain. They may not be to everybody's taste, but they distinguish Britain even from those other countries which still have royalty. Their royals seem less 'royal' than ours. Divest the monarchy of its trappings, and the nation itself will feel naked. Look at it with the cold eye of rationality, as the formation of a committee invites us to do, and the whole shooting match will not withstand scrutiny. The glory of the monarchy is that it is not a rational construct of the late twentieth century. It is *there*.

In preserving their extraordinariness, the royal family has been astonishingly successful – perhaps more successful, even, than they know or intend. In 1993 the Queen volunteered to pay tax. It was an astute public-relations gesture, though only an accountant could say how much more than a gesture since very rich people can usually arrange their affairs to exclude much depredation from the Inland Revenue. The decision was made after three-quarters of a century of not paying tax – that period of history which saw the decimation of the fortunes of the aristocracy among whom the royal family lived on terms of equality. In the last century, Queen Victoria was not as rich as some of her subjects: Buckingham Palace was outshone by the Duchess of Sutherland's town house; Sandringham, Balmoral and even Windsor could not compete with the glories of Hamilton Palace. Her son, Edward VII, moved in a set who made his own financial circumstances look positively humble. Certainly the friends of the royal family would not have thought their way of life remote or strange. They had footmen, cooks, carriages, fine furniture, private palaces, dozens of gardeners, stables of horses, grouse moors, mistresses . . . but then so did everyone else at that level of society. In other words, there was a background against which the royal family seemed normal; if anything, dull. Against an aristocracy ripe with eccentrics, they have remained, by and large, sober and stolid.

In the twentieth century, the taxation necessary to finance two World Wars was borne more heavily by the aristocracy than anyone else. Inflation took its toll with particular severity on a way of life that depended upon employing large numbers of people. So they went into retreat. If they managed to retain their country houses, they did not inhabit them in the same way; they became businesses. Owners developed an interest in the arts that would have seemed positively suspect at the beginning of the century, but is easily explained when one realises that works of art were now a valuable asset. The royal family became marooned on an atoll of superwealth, with only the Duke of Westminster for company. For people who sometimes appear to yearn for normality, it was a tragedy. But a tragedy of their own making: even the Duke of Westminster has created a family life with which the rest of the world could identify. When King George VI died in 1952 the young Queen Elizabeth decided against change.

By the 1980s the royal family had come to seem survivals from an earlier life-form, since they alone had escaped the demise of the deference culture. There was a time when dukes and other grandees were accorded semi-mythic status by their compatriots, their appearance in a public meeting or restaurant being regarded as a kind of avatar of the godhead. A few still exude the glamour conferred by the ownership of fabulous possessions. But their currency has so far fallen that most people would not know the correct form of addressing them, according to the etiquette books, even if they were minded to show deference to that degree. If they did, the dukes and grandees would be embarrassed by it. The respect they wish to command is that which would be naturally accorded to the head of any successful enterprise, for these days managing great estates requires business acumen. They are aware – how could they not be? – of the glee shown by tabloid newspapers when their progeny take to drugs or otherwise fail to set an example. Nobody really expects them to set an example anyway, because nobody much cares. But with the royal family it is different. Even in the 1990s, they expect deference. In Shakespeare's word, they continue to monarchise.

In the closed corridors of the royal household, the rules still make perfect sense; everyone knows the steps of the minuet, and it pleases them to dance it. When these courtly motions are exposed to the gaze of a world more attuned to reggae and rap music, they look rather sad. Most people, when meeting the Queen or another member of the royal family, wish to please, and so themselves attempt to perform what is usually a slightly rustic version of the polished courtier's dance. There are members of the royal entourage on hand to explain how to move their feet; the system is perpetuated. But the gap between the illusion (what the royal family expects) and the reality (the amount of deference that the public actually feels) has grown dangerously wide. It continually tempts comedians and newspaper editors to burst the balloon. One of the most damaging revelations – if true – was that, as a bachelor, Prince Charles insisted that his many girl-friends should – whatever their state of intimacy – call him 'Sir'. This suggested a man of so alien a set of assumptions that he might have arrived in a meteorite from Mars.

Courtiers buzz around in their own sealed atmosphere, like flies in a bottle. In their attempts to protect the royal family, they believe that it should operate in a way of its own, quite different from that of the rest of the world. So do the royal family themselves, but they take their knowledge of the world from the people around them. Nobody told them that the difficulty they experienced in finding a bride for the Prince of Wales indicated that their values had fossilised. Their expectations of girlhood were Edwardian: in the post-lapsarian age that followed the 1960s, women often did have relationships before they were married. When the nation's eye lighted upon Lady Diana Spencer as a possible future bride, they saw a girl who, albeit an aristocrat, lived in almost exactly the same way as thousands of other people. She was not an aristocrat of the Edwardian stamp; she shared a flat in Earls Court with some girl-friends, and drove a Mini Metro. She was an example of the Sloane Ranger, and they were only modestly privileged. Their privileges were mostly of the kind that only they themselves would have regarded as such (background, way of speaking, tastes in clothes and food): they did not help them make money. Lady Diana, as she then was, worked in a nursery. Her marriage was portrayed as a fairy-tale wedding, but it demonstrated how far the royal family had become separated from the class into which it once fitted that the Cinderella in the story was an Earl's daughter.

The royal wedding bells should have rung the alarm in the office of every courtier in the Palace. For by its sheer dazzling brilliance the occasion demonstrated how far the image that had served royalty well for half a century had become empty. Everything about the wedding was designed to show how supremely different royalty are from ordinary people. Yet for half a century the royal family had been cultivated on the myth of their being fundamentally the same: a family like other families, only more so.

In the 1930s, George VI and his inspired Queen Elizabeth, now the Queen Mother, rescued the monarchy from disaster by reinventing the myth. After the abdication, when a selfish, weak and vain King threw over his responsibilities in pursuit of a fast-living divorcee, the new monarch rallied beneath the banner of family. The King was not, by nature, a rackety individual; he liked domestic stability. So keeping up an appearance of contented home life was not difficult: indeed, the appearance matched the reality. It became natural to speak not just of the King or Queen, but of the royal family. The royal family, with tastes that could be mocked as rather suburban, became the iconic family of the nation. In them the nation recognised – or so it thought – people who felt as they did. The Queen Mother's most famous remark is the one made after the bombing of Buckingham Palace during the Blitz: that now she could look the East End in the eye.

When the present Queen ascended the throne, the image seemed to suit her very well. Her husband may have had the misfortune, as some people saw it, to be Greek; if a recent biography is to be believed, her marriage operated with different assumptions from that of her parents. But when, famously, she first allowed television cameras to observe royal lives at close quarters, it was the domestic trivia that seemed most compelling. It seemed hardly possible that the Queen could herself do the washing-up, or Prince Philip marshal a barbecue. The illusion of ordinariness was only, of course, an illusion. The reason why the Queen rather liked washing-up was that she could only do it very rarely. Whatever her private tastes and yearnings – which some suppose to be personified in the overblown suburban villa which she built for the Duke and Duchess of York – the circumstances of her daily existence were different. But the illusion, for a time, worked.

However, the illusion could only be sustained when everyone knew the rules and was prepared to play by them. That was possible in the case of the immediate family; but when the family came to expand by marriage, the illusion was shattered. Not even army officers, the daughters of the aristocracy and those of gadfly polo managers were prepared to play the royal game any more. The royal divorces make that plain, but it should have been evident at the time of Prince Charles's wedding.

For decades the Queen radiated an image which, like it or loathe it, most people could agree to be typically British. She was most at home in the country, her passions are her horses and her dogs. She has an exceptional knowledge of racing form. Except on her racehorses, she does not spend money with extravagance. She carries large handbags, wears sensible clothes made by British designers and even uses a British scent, Bluebell by Penhaligon. Preserved and stoical, she brings upon herself tasks, such as visiting magazine offices, that she cannot regard as anything other than drudgery. On such occasions, no one would suppose that she was enjoying herself. But she gets on with it, and people admire her for it. She is possessed of such natural authority that to dream of meeting the Queen, in a situation embarrassing to oneself, is apparently one of the commonest nightmares to haunt the sleep of Britons.

Until recently, Philip won respect for performing a difficult role with fortitude. He was known to be both peppery and salty, but people on the whole liked his outspokenness – they sympathised with him for having to put a curb on his opinions. Recognising that it was infuriating for a man of that generation always to have to play second fiddle to his wife, they admired the fact that he got on with it. They both got on with it. The most common conclusion to any conversation about them was 'it must be a ghastly job'. They embody the ideal of public service, which has somewhat fallen from fashion. Sense of duty, stiff upper lip: these were qualities that even republicans could admire, and recognise as stereotypically English.

After the Prince of Wales's wedding, the royal family ceased to be monolithic in the values it projected to the world. Princess Diana consciously formed her own style. As her difficulties within the marriage and the family grew, her own style appeared increasingly to be set in opposition to that of her husband and in-laws. It was not just a matter of self-expression – of choosing a perfume or deciding upon a length of hem. This was style wars. Diana sought to represent an alternative image of Englishness which, to her husband's bewilderment, enjoyed (at least for a time) far greater popularity than his own.

Prince Charles inherited his mother's instinctive conservatism. As a boy and young man, he accepted that other people – the directors, so to speak, of the family firm – would decide his future. It is a striking aspect of Jonathan Dimbleby's biography of him that he appears not to have made any major decision over his career for himself before the age of thirty. He believes that it is his destiny to sacrifice himself to his inherited role.

This extends to his personification of Englishness. It would not occur to him to question certain assumptions: for example, that he should buy British. So it is inconceivable that he would ever own a foreign make of car, whatever the fury he may have felt when his £140,000 Aston Martin Volante broke down in the Cromwell Road the day after its delivery. In his own person, he expresses a version of that identity. His taste for the country, for field sports, for gardening, for individuality, landscape and classical architecture – all are those of an English gentleman. The way he dresses encapsulates the same qualities. Like many of his family, notably his great-uncle Edward VIII, he pays considerable attention to his clothes. His manner of wearing Anderson & Sheppard suits may win the accolade from fashion pundits of 'effortless', but there is nothing accidental about the look he achieves. He is a closet dandy. A slave to convention would not wear boldly striped shirts and starched white collars with his morning dress, nor a flamboyant watch-chain across the waistcoat (despite the fact that he already wears a wrist-watch). At the same time, his tastes seem stubbornly unchanging. Only Prince Charles wears enormous belted, double-breasted over-coats that come half-way down his calf. It says all the more for his Englishness that he should claim to be a fashion disaster: 'I come into fashion about once every twenty-five years,' he said once. But the classic English style which he espouses is not subject to the vagaries of fashion.

In his Hamlet-like manner, Prince Charles consciously seeks a way of representing national values. His forays into subjects such as the teaching of English in schools cause consternation among educationalists, but are intended to contribute to the debate about national identity. Who could be more invincibly English than Camilla Parker-Bowles?

Unlike Prince Charles, his former wife strives never to be out of fashion. It is difficult to think when a previous member of the royal family attracted so much attention for her clothes – even Edward VII's beautiful Queen Alexandra created less of a stir. The Princess's obsession with appearance is unusual in an Englishwoman of her background. Judged by the highest standards she does not dress well – 'she has very pretty legs,' was all Hubert de Givenchy felt he could say on the subject. She shops compulsively and carries clothes well, but she has not – despite enormous expenditure – developed her own style. That is partly because she neurotically oscillates between one designer and other, and partly because she lacks the austerity of eye that would raise her taste above the ordinary.

The one thing that can be said is that Diana's style is not that of her inlaws. She patronises British designers, to their considerable benefit, but there are hardly enough of them to satisfy the needs of her wardrobe; so from 1995 she has also been dressed by Versace and other foreign designers. For swimsuits she summons the American firm Jantzen to Kensington Palace (the bikinis are given free). Her favourite scent is said to be First by Van Cleef and Arpels, though this vies with the light fragrances of her youth (Diorissimo, Miss Dior, L'Air du Temps by Nina Ricci, and Chanel 19) and the headier ones of her divorced state (Mitsouko and Shalimar from Guerlain, L'Eau d'Hadrien from Annick Goutal of Paris). She has a penchant for baseball caps (favoured also, as *The Times* noted, by Nick Leeson, Michael Barrymore and Robert Maxwell). In case the message conveyed by this emblem of Americanised popular culture was missed, she reinforced it by wearing, on three consecutive days at the Chelsea Harbour Club, a sweatshirt emblazoned with the stars and stripes. The *Evening Standard* revealed that this was a souvenir of the American Superbowl. It was one in the eye for her husband's family, stuffily English to the last.

The Princess has no time for immemorial royal rituals such as August at Balmoral. Like most other Britons of her generation, she would rather go to the Caribbean than to Scotland. When she cannot take her children to Disney, she goes to its nearest English equivalent, Thorpe Park. By doing so, she demonstrates her identification with popular taste, and it goes down a storm in the tabloids. Her obsession with exercise and therapy fits less naturally into the culture of England than that of New York or Los Angeles. She has a taste for fast cars, which British manufacturers were only too happy to support; but despite their generosity she has succumbed to the allure of foreign marques. In 1991 it was a Mercedes. This caused such a commotion that a year later she sent it back and was seen, instead, at the wheel of the new Ford Mondeo and Rover 620GSi. That episode did not last long; after a few months she was back with an Audi convertible.

The Prince is a fogey, so the Princess becomes a modern. When Jonathan Dimbleby's portrait of the Prince was shown on television, the Princess went to a party. In a new designer dress she knew she would upstage her husband. Who gave the party? None other than Lord Palumbo, a dedicated modernist and developer who once promoted the Mies van der Rohe tower by the Mansion House which the Prince damned as a glass stump. Planning permission for the tower was refused. The party might be seen as Lord Palumbo's revenge. It will be interesting to see if, in the future, the Princess is persuaded to articulate more fully the alternative cultural vision to the Prince. She is in danger of being used. Besides, her actions show that she is already expressing it in the best way she knows how: through her life.

Diana is the post-modern princess. Post-modern because her fame and position around the world rely little upon her now semi-detached relationship to the old structure of the royal family, but almost entirely upon her genius for working the media, particularly television. Her devotion to charitable work, whatever the motive, cannot be questioned. She must be applauded for raising large sums of money; she is, so to speak, the geyser through which the bubbling subterranean pool of public sentiment is able to spout. Sometimes this sentiment is unfocused: so be it. However, another legacy of the post-modern princess will be the effect her example wreaks on thousands of ordinary lives. When she connived – perhaps through extremely closely briefed friends – with Andrew Morton in the writing of *Diana: Her True Story*, she broke a taboo that most people held sacrosanct, not just in the royal family or the upper classes but at all levels of society. The taboo was against revealing the secrets of a marriage. (In the case of the Andrew Morton book one should write 'the supposed secrets': her account was contradicted by Prince Charles in his television interview with Jonathan Dimbleby 'Charles: The Public Man, the Private Role'.) In the United States, people are habituated to talking about intimate subjects – cancer, divorce, money – with an apparent frankness that the British find uncomfortable: it has not traditionally been the British way of doing things. The areas of existence least open to general scrutiny were the intimate relations between husband and wife. Diana's decision to throw open the innermost recesses of her marriage to public debate will have consequences for everyone. What used to be held sacred by most people has been profaned by a woman at the very head of our society. Now one profanity can be expected to follow another.

The success of the royal family has been based on the acceptance that its leading members lead a life of self-sacrifice. 'I would not want to do that job for all the tea in China,' used to be a frequently aired comment whenever the subject of royalty came up. With the benefit of what we know now, the extent of the self-sacrifice may have been overplayed: the male members of the royal family are not generally saints. But equally they shouldered burdens which quite obviously could not have given them any joy. The greatest of these was the abnegation of any ability to choose their own way of life – an old-fashioned notion that seems scarcely imaginable today. Prince Edward succeeded in rebelling against it, by leaving the Marines. For his sisters-in-law – the Princess of Wales and the

Duchess of York – the principle was one to which they refused to subscribe. Nothing could better demonstrate the extent to which they belonged to a different world from that of the royal family: a world of children born after the era of wartime rationing. It would be difficult to imagine two individuals for whom the concept of self-sacrifice meant so little.

For a time it seemed that Diana did express more of the instincts of the people of Britain than the family in to which she had married. She has great powers of empathy, and a lot of what might ungenerously be called animal cunning. But she overreached herself. The *Panorama* interview may have seemed at first a triumph, but as time passed, and viewers came to reflect more on its content than on a performance laced with psycho-babble and self-pity, they doubted their first response. It was in every sense disloyal to imply that her then husband would not become King. It might have suited her cause for the crown to pass directly to her son William, but nobody can be certain that William would make a better monarch than his father; given the sustained acrimony of his parents' divorce, even the well-disposed must be inclined to wonder. Then came her alleged relationship with Will Carling; her inappropriate appearance in an operating theatre, wearing a surgical mask; and her resignation as patron of a hundred charities, apparently in pique at the loss of her status as HRH. In political terms, she lacked a party; she had no means of translating her ambitions into reality. She relies for her position on popular support, expressed through her relationship with the media. But the media are as fickle as Fortune herself. They had a reason for idolising her when she was still a member of the royal family – it was a means of needling royals – but they do not need her quite so much now. So her popularity is likely to have peaks and troughs, as with any media celebrity. The higher the peak, the deeper the trough. It is natural, inevitable, the way of the world. But it will come hard to a woman as eager for adulation as Diana.

The way in which Diana, a vulnerable woman, is treated by the press will be a test of our humanity as a nation. Clearly she has a high expectation of it, having refused the police bodyguards who could keep some of the paparazzi at bay. One wishes one could be sanguine. The tragedy is that the royal train – on which, for this purpose, the Princess still finds herself – has run out of control. Signalmen from the upper reaches of the Establishment are trying to divert it, even some members of the media would like to slow it down; the rest of the population simply watch in horror as what seems like an inevitable calamity, which nobody wants, approaches. Most of the nation are voyeurs at this impending accident, a little guilty that they find the spectacle rather enthralling. If the train leaves the rails in a mess of twisted metal, they will feel ashamed of themselves for having watched.

Already the treatment meted out to the royal family provokes feelings of self-disgust. For *Spitting Image* to portray the Queen surrounded by sex aids, or for *Beadle's About* to place impersonators of royalty in the audience of strip shows, shows how far programme-makers have lost their sense of decorum. They would reply that they have an audience for this crass filth. There can scarcely have been an adult in Britain who failed to read the transcripts of Princess Diana's immature outpourings to her beau, James Gilbey (the famous 'Squidgy tapes'): some people heard them verbatim by dialling a telephone number. The sensation was relived when an equally intimate conversation between Prince Charles and Camilla Parker-Bowles was published. The contents of both were endlessly debated, analysed and joked about. Yet most people had the uncomfortable feeling that they were participating in an outrage against decency. There are some taboos that no sensible person wishes to see broken, since eventually everyone will suffer, but now some of society's shared standards of decency have perished. Ostensibly, the public knows more about the protagonists of the royal divorce than it is proper to know about any stranger, or even friend – except that the public really knows nothing. All that has been achieved is for us all to feel that we have become peeping Toms.

There are some who say that the royal family get the press they deserve. Plainly, the royal family do not know why the rest of the world has come to find them so irritating. Part of the answer lies in Shakespeare. He understood about courts, and that which surrounds the present royal family has a complete cast of flatterers, manipulative uncles, placemen, toadies, Poloniuses. In its dynamics it is identical to the Shakespearean model. Power, in the eyes of the courtier, still depends upon access to the monarch or the prince. The people who surround the royals make it their business to control that access. It is thus for a reason: namely, that the principals like it that way. When the Queen sought to discover what the public truly felt about the institution she represents, she asked the Lords Lieutenants to report. The Lords Lieutenant are no doubt a splendid body of people, but one does not see them on the Clapham omnibus.

But the journalists responsible for the bad press are the last group in the country who would want to see the monarchy abolished, since they make too much from it. They see their attacks as 'having a go' at royalty, but do not really expect them to be taken seriously. That is not quite how their articles are seen outside Fleet Street. In the Establishment, they are a test of public opinion – the only one, other than opinion polls, that exists. The present tone of the press reminds some people of the tide of ribaldry and sexual allegation that surrounded Louis XVI and Marie Antoinette before the Revolution. Their lives are being trivialised, and matters which in any civilised community would be regarded as private have been made the stuff of general titillation and guffaws. It is as though the tide of excrement were sweeping them inexorably towards the guillotine.

The consequence of such relentless debasement could be measured after the fire which destroyed part of Windsor Castle in November 1992. When that night the Queen returned to Buckingham Palace, described as 'covered with smuts and clutching under her arm a box containing the few precious things she had managed to salvage', she was the image of grief. The Heritage Secretary at the time was Peter Brooke, one of the dwindling number of MPs who see their position at Westminster as a matter of public service, in his case following a family tradition that dates back centuries. His response was what everyone in the country would once have expected: he announced that the public purse would meet the bill for repairs to this great national landmark, open to the public and used for state entertaining. There followed an immediate outcry from the media, the public and Brooke's parliamentary colleagues. The royal family were pictured as cheapskate, Brooke as a buffoon. Polls showed nearly all those people questioned to be against the government shouldering the whole cost. This reaction was said to leave the Queen and her court in a state of shock; as one courtier was reported as saying: 'All of us had relied on the fact that, in such a tragedy, there would be nothing but sympathy. We must all have got it wrong. At the moment of her desolation, this woman who had done nothing but give service to her country, didn't even have the solace of her people's sympathy. It just blew up in her face.'

It would be understandable if the public behaved in this uncharitable way because the existence of the monarchy obstructed the installation of some alternative, more popular regime. But that is not the case. There is no significant body of opinion routing for a presidency or other method of providing a head of state. It is undeniable that the British have lately come to think of themselves more as citizens than as subjects, though they are not very sure what citizenship means. But there is little serious agitation, with a concrete agenda, for Britain to be turned into a republic. That is the nature of the present malaise: the British have become discontented with what they have, without any positive ideas about replacing it. The monarchy is not being challenged by a different system, yet it could wither at the roots through the outpouring of poison towards it.

If the monarchy were to fall, the nation would not feel it had won a great triumph. Most people would feel shorn of something that, in a corner of their being, was important to them. Even in its present state of crisis, the royal family is the symbol by which the nation expects moments of great shared emotion to be represented, as shown in 1995 by the commemorations to mark VE Day and VJ Day. The passing of the monarchy would cause the British to go into mourning. Even people who dislike members of the present royal family would feel their identity to have been diminished.

This says as much as anything about the present state of

Britain. We have become too cynical, too universally disparaging, for our own good. Once, it was a function of the monarchy implicitly to celebrate British excellence through the goods they bought, the tastes they displayed and the warrants and awards they presented. Now its own prestige is not high enough for it effectively to fulfil that role. The media must take much of the responsibility for this. Consequently, the media should try to fill the vacuum it has created. To do this it will have to fuel the debate about what it means to be British, what British values are, and what we still have to be proud of.

12

Anyone for England?

'When there is no vision the people perish.'
Keir Hardie

We were all born in a world made in England and the world in which our great-grandchildren will mellow into venerable old age will be as English as the Hellenistic world was Greek, or better, Athenian.
Claudio Veliz, 'A World Made in England',
Quadrant, March 1983

The object of this book has been to examine how far some of the absolutes of my childhood ideas about Britain have survived into the 1990s, or have disappeared. It could be said that life was never like the stereotypes I have evoked – and that would be true. It could be said that the character of a nation is always changing – and that would also be true. Change of itself is not my concern. My worry is that change should not break the threads of continuity with the past. Whatever we change to become must be something with which we feel comfortable, and about which we feel good. Anyone who has read this far will realise that this does not, in my view, seem to be the case.

We are living through an age not just of rapid change, but of experiment. Science is making the world – and the human species in particular – its laboratory. It has its fingers on the key that unlocks the mysteries through which life is created. It has the persistence of a toddler in a kitchen; it will go on until it has opened the cupboard, even though that cupboard may be full of dangers it cannot know or understand. The efficiency of farming is being improved through techniques of genetic engineering. The scientists responsible tell us that the release on to the planet of organisms that have been genetically modified by man is, like the irradiation of food, perfectly safe. They cannot, however, know this for sure since no one has been able to observe the effect these organisms will have on the natural environment over decades. Previous generations of scientists assured the public about the safety of asbestos, pesticides and cattle-cake enriched with the ground-up carcasses of animals. According to the information available at the time, these assurances were plausible. Unfortunately, the passage of time proved them to be wrong. Rhododendrons are attractive in gardens, but in some places they have escaped to run riot over the countryside as weeds. The grey squirrel must have seemed an appealing novelty when it was first imported from America, but it now threatens to eliminate the even more charming native red squirrel from Britain. We can only hope that genetically modified organisms will not inflict their own perhaps far more devastating damage.

These developments transcend national boundaries. Those of us who are grateful that the British government has not licensed the use of the hormone BST for dairy cows are alarmed to realise that it is widely used in the United States, and American dairy products are imported into Britain. The consumer takes part in the experiment without knowing it.

Britain has also become a country of political experiment. Since 1979, the Conservative government has not been much dedicated to conserving things, but has been fearlessly radical in overthrowing the status quo. In some ways we have been made the better for it. It is difficult now to remember how dreary and defeatist the Britain of the late 1970s had become. The Thatcher experiment can be judged by the admiration openly expressed for her by the Leader of the Opposition. It changed Britain, it changed people, it changed attitudes, which was what it set out to do. But parts of the experiment ended in a bad smell and puff of smoke, and the poll tax caused an explosion. The poll tax was an experiment too far. But it has not discouraged the taste for experiment, which is the aspect of Thatcherism to which Tony Blair seems most attached. 'New Labour' has a laboratory full of experiments it wants to try out.

Then there are the experiments that are being conducted at home. The notion of family has been reinterpreted so that an essential constituent element is no longer two parents, with one of each sex. In 1996, a mother conceived octuplets while receiving fertility treatment through the National Health Service. Not only had she previously conceived perfectly easily, by natural means, but the father was living with another woman. Born prematurely, each of the eight little babies perished.

The thought that we are living through an age of experiment is disconcerting. It reinforces the need for that sense of belonging to the nation to which I have referred throughout this book. I have dwelt on the ways in which some assumptions about Englishness and Britishness no longer seem valid. These breakages in the national store cupboard have not always been replaced; we have been left with hardly enough common property to lay the table, which contributes to the air of glumness that has settled upon Britain. We do not need to be so long in the mouth, for we are doing better than we are prepared to admit. Even economically our decline relative to other Western countries has been halted, and some economists claim that it has not just been halted: that we have actually started to do better than them. The last point is contentious, but one hardly needs to be convinced of an economic miracle to see that Britain has plenty to shout about, if only it would clear its throat.

There is, to begin with, the incontrovertible historical fact that British influences now dominate world culture. This point was argued persuasively by Claudio Veliz, Professor of Sociology at La Trobe University, in the paper quoted at the opening of this chapter. His case could only be sustained by expanding the English orbit to include the English-speaking peoples: the cinema, the television, the motor-car and the telephone were all given their characteristic shape in the United States. Nevertheless, anyone who plays football, joins a club, takes part in athletics, posts a letter, takes out an insurance policy or reads a detective story – and throughout the world an increasing number of people participate in these activities every year – will have enjoyed part of a cultural legacy that is British. Obviously this will also be the case for anyone who learns the English language. That other great lingua franca, pop music, has been, and perhaps still is, disproportionately influenced by British bands. On the death of John Lennon in 1980, a leader in *The Times* positively gushed – insofar as a *Times* leader is capable of gushing – about the achievement of The Beatles. They 'created an indigenous and unmistakably British sound, which became, within a very short time, the dominant mood of pop . . . The Beatles made English patois the language of the new music, and the Liverpool sound became a staple not just of Britain and the United States, but of the Soviet Union as well, and virtually every country in the world.' Since then there have been Punk and Britpop: perhaps not, in the case of Britpop, so world-conquering, but still commanding a significant global following.

How can Britain's overpowering cultural influence be explained? The strength of the Empire is only part of the answer. Spain also had an empire: 'The richest, largest and most formidable since that of the Romans,' as Professor Veliz observes:

> It was ruled by monarchs not renowned for diffidence and who, in common with their subjects, seldom entertained doubts about the worth of their religion, manners, language, morals or domestic habits. It was also an empire remarkably well served by the creative talents of a people who from the sixteenth century onwards, almost without pause, even in the darkest periods of decline and despondency, astonished the civilised world with the originality and excellence of their literary and artistic productions. There was an abundance, in that extended Castilian ambit, of will and of ability, and yet, apart from a couple of glorious archetypes (Don Juan and Don Quijote), the

common canary, the world *liberalismo*, the guitar, Merino sheep, and the Society of Jesus, the significances generated under the Castilian hegemony failed to win widespread national acceptance; bull-fighting and castanets travelled badly, while Figaro, Carmen, and Escamillo cannot be included as they, and much else popularly associated with Spain, were the creatures of enthusiastic foreigners some of whom never set foot on Spanish soil.

It is difficult to explain the ubiquity with which British ways of doing things have been accepted, and the fact that they have been makes Britain's present identity crisis seem all the less necessary.

The positive character of some recent developments also contrasts oddly with the prevailing angst. For instance, London now has a Globe Theatre, built after decades of struggle to raise money: a wooden replica of the theatre upon which Shakespeare himself acted. Suddenly London Fashion Week, having been on the point of collapse three years before, has become generally acknowledged, at least by the British fashion press, as perhaps livelier than Paris or Milan. The television news programmes celebrated by rerunning old footage of Carnaby Street in the 1960s. People are seriously talking about London as having better restaurants than Paris. One still has to pinch oneself to believe it. British universities may be woefully funded in comparison with those across the Atlantic, yet often scientists manage to overcome their scant resources and carry out brilliantly original research. For example, we still lead the world in astronomy, despite the government's refusal to put money into the enormous ground-based telescopes which have become the latest tool with which to search the heavens. It is no longer an axiom that English cricket is superior to all others; but we still produce many more successful Formula One racing drivers than the size of the country should dictate. We also design and build most of the cars. The only Formula One vehicles not to be designed and built here are those of the French team and Ferrari – and even the Ferraris are designed in Britain, by John Barnard of Guildford.

The success of our specialist craftsmen, both in the manufacture of racing cars and luxury marques such as Rolls-Royce and Aston Martin, contrasts with the poor condition of the motor industry as a whole. Craftsmanship in many areas is a strength that the British economy should exploit. In common with other European countries, we still possess an extraordinary number of people who practise specialist skills. The restoration of the National Trust's Uppark, in Sussex, showed that this age is capable of producing workmanship to equal that of the high point of invention in the eighteenth century. But it is not just the traditionalism of British culture that can be admired these days, but another enduring characteristic: its eccentricity. Foreigners envy our innovation, irreverence, non-conformism and willingness to break taboos. What might be described as the present British renaissance has been more celebrated abroad than at home. Recently the Italian version of *Vogue* devoted a whole issue to British pop bands, models and actresses, while the straitlaced *Le Monde* published a special style supplement on the *energie* and *dynamisme* of British design.

Surely then, we British ought to feel more self-confident. One of the reasons that we do not is that we have developed the habit of continually running ourselves down. As a nation, we have never been very comfortable with success, but now we seem unable to diagnose success as anything other than failure. Take the National Lottery, for example. It is not, as it has been represented, a tax. The people who buy tickets do so willingly. They have generated enormous quantities of money for sport, the arts, charities and some grand millennium projects. Instead of having been welcomed as a wonder-working contribution to national life, it was greeted with nothing but moans. With all this money, the well-chosen, distinguished group of people responsible for distributing it have been able to solve some long-standing problems. It would have been a national disgrace, for example, if Sir Winston Churchill's papers had been sold at auction and gone overseas. Negotiations over them had been going on for years, but there was no general jubilation when the Lottery made it possible for them to be saved for Britain. Quite the reverse. The press see only controversy, if not scandal, in the way Lottery money is allocated. It is just the same with examination results. As I observed earlier, there are good reasons why children should be achieving better grades; one might say, given how the middle classes have expanded and girls now expect more of themselves, it would be surprising if they did not. But the press assume that the better grades must be explained by the standards of marking in examinations having become more lenient.

This habit of self-excoriation is an unattractive aspect of what might be called the new British identity. Equally unpleasant is the taste for small-minded bureaucracy that has overtaken us. We used to laugh at it in the Ealing comedy era, but now life has come to be dominated by a parking warden mentality in which over-regulation has been allowed to infect every aspect of existence. Londoners, for example, love the noble trees that line so many of the capital's streets. But increasingly these are being felled on the orders of busybodies from the local council. Our environmental health officers personify a kind of lunacy that has come to afflict the British mind. We used to think of ourselves as a nation of robust common sense. All too often common sense is now thrown out of the windows as petty-minded people in authority enforce the letter of the law. This exacerbates the feeling, which has become a paranoia of the 1990s, that the small man is being pushed around.

These symptoms are not life-threatening, but they should be watched. They may have no obvious cure. After all, what can you do to convince people that life is not gloomy when they are determined to think that it is? But being aware of the condition may bring its own correction. We have slipped into this way of thinking without intending to or realising it. If we did think about it a bit more, we might realise we did not intend it, and then we might avoid it.

Fortunately, modern Britain is not made up only of whingers; nor have all the things that used to bind us together been rubbed away. An inventory of modern-day Englishness records a good tally. We are still a nation of gardeners – perhaps more than ever. In London, the balconies of the flats opposite my house overflow with a forest of greenery, while the Friday of Chelsea Flower

Show week shows what appears to be Burnham Wood moving to Dunsinane as the public carry home plants they have acquired. It is a reflection of the levelling utilitarianism under which we now labour that spending on the royal parks – a unique attribute of this country that should be a source of pride – has been cut back, with unfortunate consequences. That has become all too typical of Britain's public face. Behind a million privet hedges, however, Englishmen are still stirred by that most primitive of male urges: the need to mow lawns and prune roses.

Equally, we are a nation of music-lovers and music-makers, not only with an astonishing range of professional performances to choose from every night of the week (and a superb radio channel devoted to almost nothing except serious music) but also a vibrant amateur tradition. We remain, as we always shall, a nation besotted with animals. As more people live in cities and more women work, we own more low-maintenance cats than walk-demanding dogs. But we also display our affection for rural activities by keeping more horses than ever before. If we have become less successful at breeding competition horses than the Germans and other Continentals, that is partly because we cling to the old-fashioned, gentlemanly approach of the First World War era. Some things never change, though it might be better if they did.

We still have the armed forces, a source of prestige around the world. The spectacle of our military ceremonial remains second to none. Military bands continue to play in the bandstands of parks and at agricultural shows. As a nation, we have kept our fondness for the soft colours that look well under a watery sky. Perhaps, as Britain becomes more like the Mediterranean in climate, this palette will come to seem out of place, but for the time being, it suits us and our complexions. We continue to enjoy a different taste in furniture and decoration from the Continentals and Americans. Antique dealers call it 'distressed', the rest of us 'beaten up'. We nurture a taste for absurdity: as soon as the bust of our founder appeared in our offices at *Country Life*, someone put a hat on it. The English have always liked these things. We make ourselves incomprehensible to Americans through a use of irony which defeats them (they take everything literally).

Our genius for circumlocution remains undimmed, with trains stopping at 'calling places' rather than stations.

The velvet darkness of a night sky is now a luxury more likely to be enjoyed in Africa than in East Anglia. So is silence – meaning the absence of man-made noise. But the limitless green of British fields seen from the air still triggers an emotion in me every time I take a flight home from abroad. From the aeroplane, the countryside seems more intact than one sometimes believes it to be from terrestrial observation. Even from the ground, the play of light – the inspiration for all those painters of the English School – continues to surprise and delight the eye, as it transforms commonplace scenes into poetry. A rainbow over cornfields following a thunderstorm; the setting sun like an immense blood orange above the Fens; the ridge and furrow of medieval fields preserved in old pastureland – these and a million more ordinary occurrences are impressions stored somehow in the collective memory bank of the English soul. Odd that they should be so moving, but they are.

Then there are those people who, like hedgerow trees, grow into shapes peculiar to our own landscape. One has only to listen to Alan Bennett reading *The House at Pooh Corner* on Radio 4 to realise that British individuality has not perished. It is hardly necessary even to hear, say, John Mortimer or Lord Rees-Mogg: a glance is enough. We must be proud of the national physiognomy. People in British public life look as though they have experienced things in the course of their years. Sir Cliff Richard is a phenomenon who remains, in this country, rare. The British male ages, and does so gracelessly. Not for him the smoothness of feature so much cherished in the United States, where men of retirement age look as though they have been as little buffeted by life as babies. The Houses of Parliament are a showcase of creased, battered, jowly, grizzled and high-coloured visages – not always faces of distinction, but faces of character.

This all symbolises an individuality that should be celebrated. Britain is a country of variety, expressed in the ever-changing character of its topography. A journey of fifty miles can take one through many quite different landscapes; it is almost bewildering.

Contrast this with, say, the lakes, mountains and trees of the Adirondack National Park in New York State – so beautiful, but after eight hours' driving they still seem to be the same lakes, mountains and trees. Few regions in Continental Europe can equal Britain's diversity. There are also – or used to be – as many local cultural differences as variations in the landscape. Britain's individuality must be preserved from the Magimix of modern life, with its tendency to liquidise everything into the same smoothness of pap. There has been much outcry against the enormous salaries of some boardroom fat cats; what is really depressing, though, is the lack of vibrancy of these people upon whom such incomes are conferred. In receipt of such sums, the least they could do is to provide diversion and amusement for the rest of us, through the colour of their lives. Unfortunately that colour is universally grey. In this they personify the corporate tendency, which in Britain is reinforced by the mania for red tape (in terms of safety, hygiene, disabled access and so on) that has overtaken a government supposedly dedicated to deregulation. As I mentioned in Chapter One, we used to be considered the tolerant nation: tolerant not only of foreigners seeking refuge in this country, but of each other's habits of life. Tolerance is the first victim of doctrines such as political correctness, which seek to impose uniformity of thought and behaviour.

Preserving the traditions that are dear to us is not simply a matter for government. It is a symptom of Britain's present condition that everything is blamed on government, and everything (it is assumed) can be rectified by it. That is partly because central government has taken more powers to itself. But as Chapter Ten showed, government has not thereby become stronger. Some aspects of life are slipping out of its grip, and that may not be altogether a bad thing. Besides, people used to take greater responsibility for their own lives. The blame culture, in which every accident to befall humanity is not simply a misfortune but must be somebody's fault, has helped to change that. But there are still moments when individuals are successful in taking command of their own circumstances, which can be seen happening at a local level all the time. It is heartening that the spontaneous strength of feeling of many individuals occasionally still comes together to make a collective statement of intention about how we all wish our society to be. A recent example was the outcry of emotion following the Dunblane massacre. Throughout Britain, people let it be known that they would not allow this country blindly to follow the United States into the morass associated with the free availability of handguns.

On this issue, the government brought forward legislation to embody what was clearly the popular will. There are other ways in which one branch or other of government could contribute towards the sustenance of national identity. For example, the national curriculum determines the core of subjects now taught in state schools, so through this curriculum there is the opportunity to shape children's understanding of what is important in their country's tradition. Already efforts are being made to ensure that pupils acquire some knowledge of the span of British history. The warmth with which Sir Roy Strong's *The Story of Britain*, the first narrative history of Britain for a generation, was received on its publication in 1996 shows how widely the loss of a common sense of the unfolding sequence of British history was mourned. But history is a selective process. As a nation, we must choose the events, personalities and values from our past which we most want to transmit to the future. Perhaps these should be drawn less from the worlds of politics, the monarchy and soldiering, than the great humanitarian tradition of William Wilberforce, Florence Nightingale and others, in which Britain's distinction is second to none. In the last century Britain led the world in its campaigns against slavery, child labour, noxious prisons, slum housing, cruelty to animals and other evils, and the ideals of the reformers associated with those movements are in tune with the present age.

Nonconformism has always been strong in Britain. We should celebrate the arts, scientific research and those areas in which Britain's effort has been outstanding, yet which receive little kudos or representation in public life. Engineering particularly comes to mind. Other countries are more generous in their appreciation of this profession than ourselves; in Singapore, two thirds of the Cabinet are engineers.

The government cannot do everything, but it could promote

a greater sense of social cohesion if it appeared to value more highly those things that are common to all. The public face of Britain is besmirched. We must wipe the dirty nose of our cities. We must put the quality of life for the people who live in them and use them above the apparent expediency of car-owners. We must encourage greater respect for the streets, by showing that the appropriate authorities do themselves respect them. There is no reason why London could not be cleaned as well as Paris. The pavements do not have to be encumbered with the abysmally designed tat of modern pay-phone booths. Chapter Eight suggested some of the things that could be done to enhance the countryside. A small but symbolic step towards preserving the diversity of our seas would be to establish more marine nature reserves.

It has become fashionable in some political circles to talk about Great Britain plc, as though it were a company, the implication being that everything can be expressed through the balance sheet. But if Britain really were a company, its board of directors would certainly have called in the marketing people to define its core values. They would then seek to test every activity and new initiative of the company by the degree to which it conformed to those values. The core values of Britain are its identity. Much could be achieved if the government were to examine whether all the activities in which it has an interest express that Britishness.

Finally, we need to find ways in which the nation can come together in self-recognition. The anniversaries of the Second World War in 1995 showed how much the desire for such moments exists throughout Britain. We have an advantage over other countries in the millennium obsession that has developed here. (Elsewhere 1 January 2000 seems to be regarded as a date like any other; perhaps few other countries are so anxious to slough off the end of this century as Britain.) A fountain of wealth gushes out of the Lottery for the purposes of celebration. Yet so far, with their miserable requirement that Lottery funds should be matched by business, the Millennium Commission's plans have failed to set alight the public imagination. How much better that this national jubilee should be made a real Festival of

Britain. In 1951 the original Festival of Britain lifted the spirits of the nation after the gloom of war and rationing. It took place not just on the South Bank of the Thames but in towns and cities around Britain, and even a converted aircraft carrier plied its way around the coast bringing the exhibition to major ports. In the year 2000, the Millennium Festival should provide an occasion for each person in the country to say: 'I know who I am; I am British; I am proud of it.'